Journal of a Mountain Man

Also by Win Blevins

Journal of a Mountain Man

Classics of the Fur Trade

Book 6

Win Blevins

WOLFPACK
PUBLISHING
— EST 2013 —

Journal of a Mountain Man
Paperback Edition
Copyright © 2024 (As Revised) Win Blevins

Wolfpack Publishing
1707 E. Diana Street
Tampa, FL 33610

wolfpackpublishing.com

Paperback ISBN 978-1-63977-558-3
eBook ISBN 978-1-63977-557-6

Contents

Foreword

You can generally count on a mountain man not to tell a story small. After all, yarning was an art among the trappers of the Rocky Mountains, and scaring pilgrims was one of their favorite sports.

So these journals of James Clyman, mountain man, are especially valuable. Among the first-hand recollections of the beaver hunters, often gaudy, these journals are a conspicuously sober and meticulous record. Though Joe Meek certainly caught the spirit of the mountains in his book, *The River of the West,* we can't rely on Meek's details. Clyman, by contrast, has the details right; if he says he crossed a river or found a spring at a certain spot, we can be sure it was so. Where Meek waxes colorful about a happening, Clyman shows the mental bent of a surveyor: he scrupulously takes measurements and notes down facts. Likely that's because, before he went to the mountains, Clyman held a job surveying land. Alongside the vivid but exaggerated sketches some mountain men have left us, we are lucky to have the record of one man who was a keen, thorough, and precise observer.

Not that his narrative doesn't have plenty of exciting tales, and hairbreadth escapes against heavy odds—Clyman was a mountain man. But he stubbornly understates them. In the most desperate situation his style remains cool and almost detached. Sometimes he's ironic, or humorous, but he doesn't draw a line under his own hardships. Likewise he does not judge his companions much. Instead of praising or criticizing, he records; he lets the record speak for itself.

Clyman was an unusual man even among the mountain men, the physical and mental elite of their time. When he went to the mountains with the second expedition of William H. Ashley and Andrew Henry in 1823, he helped recruit his fellow enlistees from, as he put it, "grog Shops and other sinks of degredation"; the battalion of scalawags and ruffians who followed Shakespeare's Falstaff "was genteel in comparison." Many of his companions were crude, illiterate frontiersmen, sometimes on the run from the law, the church, their families, or anything else that inhibited their impulses, wild and hairy as Huck Finn's Pap.

Dressed in what LeRoy Hafen called "perhaps the only original American costume—the fringed buckskin suit," with powder horn, shot pouch, tomahawk, knife, maybe a pistol and certainly a muzzle-loader, the mountain man was self-supporting, independent, and downright dangerous. He didn't really need anything he couldn't get with that equipment, and he often survived after he'd lost everything but his life. Clyman clubbed a badger to death with bones he found on the prairie when he was hungry enough.

A mountain man had to be tough and savage to survive. Francis Parkman wrote, "I defy the annals of chivalry to furnish the record of a life more wild and perilous than those of a Rocky Mountain trapper." The average trapper knew all about peril, and probably very little about chivalry.

Not so James Clyman. Born into a family of respectable tenant farmers, he grew up on the lands of George Washington. He was educated, even literary—he read Shakespeare and wrote verse himself. He had bearing and dignity. And while some of his fellow adventurers were runaway boys, Clyman was a matured and experienced man— thirty-one years old, blooded as an Indian fighter and militiaman.

General Ashley appointed him clerk. In his first year, Clyman would sew Jedediah Smith's ear back on after a grizzly attack, save William Sublette's life in a blizzard, help discover (or rediscover, if you prefer) South Pass, and walk across most of Wyoming and Nebraska alone and starving. Thus he earned the title mountain man.

If we are lucky to have Clyman's record of those trapping years, he was a lucky diarist. He seems to have had a knack for being in historic places at historic times to record what he saw.

Consider: Clyman was a trapper during the key years of 1823-27, when the Rocky Mountain and Inter-Mountain West were being opened.

Ending his trapping career four years later, he didn't just disappear, as so many mountain men did. He became a businessman and solid citizen of the frontier, and again served in the military in his nation's defense—along with a private named Abraham Lincoln.

Seventeen years later—at the peak of covered wagon emigration—he saddled his horse and headed for Oregon, taking his diaries along. Once he got there, he didn't just settle down—he surveyed the area, and sent his observations back to others who were considering trekking to the Pacific Coast.

Then Clyman re-crossed the deserts and mountains and plains, toward the east. On the way he met some emigrants later known to history as the Donner party and gave them advice they should have taken—to follow a route that would have saved them from a snowbound, starving winter in the Sierra Nevada. Unfortunately, the Donners and fellow travelers preferred the fantasies of a publicist named Lansford Hastings to the hard realities of surveyor James Clyman.

Clyman crossed the country again, westward, settled in California, and set down in his notebooks something of the processes of farming and family and community life that turned California into settled country. He also turned more to writing his rough-hewn sort of verse, some of which is reproduced here.

And there his luck ran out: he married and had children, and all but one of them died young. The surviving daughter was too busy to copy in detail the life story Clyman began to record on his slate.

Surprisingly, considering all he did, we hardly know him. He was an accomplished mountain man, a leader from the day he was hired, a man certified as a skilled veteran by the experiences he relates here. The men he worked and fought with we know—the Sublettes, Ashley, Jedediah Smith, Tom Fitzpatrick. They have come down to us in frontier history and folklore. Beside their campfires, in the early years, sat Jim Clyman, balancing a notebook on his knee, scribbling; yet somehow he has remained obscure.

And what we've missed! The diaries reveal a man who upheld fundamental qualities we call good, as a nation: intelligence, integrity, honesty, patriotism, a sense of humor, self-confidence, courage tempered with common sense. Perhaps he was also a little remote, stingy with words, wary, not easy to know, proud, and the better for it. But if there was a job to be done, Clyman was there. He was a man to have at your back, a man equal to the occasion. And the occasion was the exploration and settlement of the American West.

———

The Journals: Publishing History

These diaries have appeared previously, but earlier editions were not prepared with the general reader in mind. After running them in its *Quarterly* from 1925 through 1927, the California Historical Society published the journals in book form in 1928, edited by Charles L. Camp. Only 330 copies were printed, and fewer than 300 offered for sale.

Because the demand so far exceeded the supply, Camp put together a new edition in 1960, now also out of print. In both editions he carefully considered most historical details and documented what he considered; the scholar is advised to find a copy of Camp for the smaller details and references to repositories of original Clyman material.

———

The Text

All of Clyman's journals, much of his correspondence, and a little of his verse are reprinted here; the text, with the single exception of the "Memorandum and Diary, 1840" from the 1960 edition, is based on the 1928 California Historical Society edition.

Clyman was an educated reader, but his spelling and punctuation left something to be desired by those who consider such matters important. We have reproduced Camp's original version of the journals exactly, with a few elucidations added by Camp and the editor. Clyman's idiosyncratic spellings may slow an occasional reader, but should defeat none. Besides, we agree with the historian who said, "I have no respect for a man who can only spell a word one way."

Journal of a Mountain Man

Chapter 1
The Youth of a Pioneer

When James Clyman was born on Feb. 1, 1792, his parents and grandparents were farmers, holding a life-tenancy on a farm in the foothills of the Blue Ridge Mountains of Virginia. The land, in the northeast corner of Fauquier County, belonged to President George Washington.

Here, in post-revolutionary Virginia, Clyman grew up, obtaining a "smattering of education," which no doubt included glimpses of the nation's first President as well as the hard work of a farm, and the experience in hunting which put meat on the table. He received, in short, the practical training that fitted him for the active life he led—a life that took him into the Rockies with the Ashley fur brigade, through the Black Hawk War, and twice across the continent before the Gold Rush. He was often well ahead of the advancing frontier.

Though Clyman's formal education was probably sketchy, he learned to read, write and "cipher"—and made the most of his abilities later when he kept journals of his travels across the continent. Some of his journals demonstrate that he read rather widely for a man of his era, and for the places where he spent his time. His literary tastes included Shakespeare, Byron and—of course—the Bible. Toward the end of his life he wrote poetry typical of the time, on philosophical and religious subjects, in complex and florid phrases.

But his primary education was doubtless in the hills and valleys around his home, where he learned early to handle a rifle, hunting squirrels, turkeys, deer and coons to supplement the family larder, and to work at clearing the land and planting it to crops. He was part of a pioneering family, and shared in the hardships and abilities that the time demanded. From that early training he developed a body that matched his mind, adapted to living under whatever conditions required.

West from Virginia

When James Clyman was about fifteen, after the death of his grandfather and of General Washington, the family moved on again, to another frontier. Clyman's parents and a family consisting of at least three brothers wintered in Pennsylvania, then bought a quarter section in Stark County, Ohio. They settled in just after the Battle of Tippecanoe in 1811. Before long raiders were striking everywhere in the neighborhood, killing settlers and burning farms; in self-defense, the settlers organized committees of safety. James was one of the area's young men appointed as rangers to scout the countryside on horseback and ward off Indians. Thus, at a young age, he experienced military service and Indian-fighting in the War of 1812.

During 1814 Clyman reportedly served as a substitute for a neighbor, and was stationed in Greenville. After service of only a month he returned; historians have found no reason for this short service, but he later served in the militia for two months at Jeromesville.

After four years on his father's farm, James drifted into Jennings County, Indiana, in 1818; there he cleared twenty acres, planted corn with a hoe, and then traded the crop to Indians for ponies and rode on out to Illinois. About 1820 he got a job furnishing provisions for a surveyor;

he had apparently decided, at the age of twenty-four, that farming wasn't for him. When the surveyor became too sick to finish the job, James was proficient enough to finish surveying half a township subdivision.

Surveying in Illinois

In the summer of 1821 he went to Terre Haute, Indiana, where he worked harvesting crops. Later he worked as a wood chopper with Treat and Blackman, at a small salt factory fifty or sixty miles north of the settlement on the Vermillion River in Illinois. Col. William S. Hamilton was in the area on a surveying tour, hired Clyman, and in the summer of 1822 left him to complete the work. The next autumn Clyman did another surveying job on the Sangamon River. During all this time, Clyman was gaining the experience that would fit him for a part in the next chapter of America's history: the fur trade, and the westward exploration.

The Fur Trade

The brief history of the fur trade is one of the most colorful our nation ever experienced. At first, fur traders simply visited the Indians, and swapped trade goods for furs the Indians already had on hand. Eventually, this practice dissatisfied the traders; the Indians were unpredictable, and it was hard to calculate the profit and loss margin. So the idea of sending white men into the mountains to trap beaver was born, and the era of the mountain men began.

In 1822, William H. Ashley, a Missouri politician, and Andrew Henry, a former fur trader, entered a fur-trading partnership. At first Henry led men to the mouth of the Yellowstone River and began construction of a fort. Supplies worth $10,000 being sent up river later were lost in a boat wreck, and Ashley had to outfit another boat, and bring another expedition to the fort.

While Ashley returned to St. Louis that winter, Henry remained at Fort Henry to direct trapping and trading operations. In the spring of 1823, Henry sent Jedediah Smith downriver to meet Ashley with the list of supplies needed for the coming year. Ashley assembled the necessary supplies and set out for the Yellowstone with a mixed crew, a crew that included a clerk by the name of Clyman. The supply boats were attacked by the Arikaras, and Ashley lost 15 men and a great deal of supplies. By the time reinforcements arrived, much time had been lost.

In spite of these problems, the partners sent out two main trapping expeditions that year. One group, under Henry, returned to the post on the Yellowstone, and moved from there to the Big Horn River where another Fort Henry was built. From the new location, Henry sent trappers southwest.

Ashley's group, led by Jedediah Smith, left Fort Kiowa on the Missouri in September of 1823 and headed west to meet Henry's men, camped with the Crows. James Clyman was along, and his abilities with a needle were a big help to Smith, who was attacked by a grizzly bear which tore his ear off and lacerated his scalp.

Jedediah Smith's party wintered in the mountains, then traveled west into the Green River country in the spring, where they found a beaver paradise. When the spring hunt was over, Thomas Fitzpatrick and James Clyman took the furs back to St. Louis while the others continued to trap.

The report of these trappers on the abundance of beaver available changed the course of fur trade history. Ashley decided to take needed supplies to the mountains each year, to save the trouble of sending men back and forth with supplies and furs. He organized a supply train to the Rockies in 1824, and the distribution of these supplies in 1825 was the official beginning of the fur trade's best-known legacy, the rendezvous.

Rendezvous

At rendezvous, which became an annual event, mountain men met after a year of freezing, suffering, being shot at, and chased by Indians, as they trapped mostly alone or in small groups. At rendezvous, the mountain men were free to trade their furs, to obtain supplies for the next year's trading, to visit with friends they hadn't seen for months, and to find out who had gone under during the winter. Indians of many tribes camped near the trappers to trade, visit, and swap stories and challenges. At rendezvous, a wilderness valley became the site of a colorful, raucous fair. The first rendezvous lasted only one day, and Ashley supplied no liquor. He soon remedied *that* situation, and later rendezvous lasted weeks.

By 1840, the demand for beaver for the fashionable hats had died, swept away in some other fashion, and the period of rendezvous—and the fur trade, for all practical purposes—was over. The trappers scattered: some few back to civilization; others to new frontiers or jobs guiding emigrants. Some retreated to the mountains with the Indians and lived their wild way of life to the end.

Chapter 2
Narrative of 1823–24

In the spring of 1823, at the age of thirty-one, still unmarried, still not "settled down," Clyman went to St. Louis, perhaps to draw his pay for the surveying work. There he met William H. Ashley, then Lieutenant-Governor, and already renowned as a fur trader. Ashley hired him at once to enlist men for the second expedition up the Missouri. Clyman helped to hire a crew—his journal says they would have made Falstaff's friends look genteel; many of the expedition members were drawn from the grog shops and other sinks of degradation in St. Louis. Clyman took the berth of clerk on one of the boats at $1 a day.

When he joined Ashley's men, Clyman was no raw recruit; he'd been providing meat for his family since at least the age of fourteen. He'd fought Indians, and worked at jobs that honed him fine in the wilderness university, where survival was the diploma. He was at his peak, and ready for the great adventure of fur trapping. He became one of the best.

The party of trappers wasn't moving during all of the long winter covered by Clyman's journals; part of the time they were necessarily snowed into camp, and the newer hands in the mountains probably took the opportunity to learn from the tales of those who had been here before. Clyman was among the oldest and most experienced in general woodcraft, if not in this part of the country. Bill Sublette and Tom Fitzpatrick were twenty-four, Jedediah Smith twenty-five. Jim Bridger—who was elsewhere this winter—was not yet twenty. Around the campfire, eating ribs if the day's hunt had been successful, repairing moccasins, making bullets or cleaning rifles, they must have talked about the methods for trapping beaver.

The first trick was to find them—first the stream, then the dams that they built. Traps had to be placed at strategic locations along the beaver's daily route: at the base of his slides into the water, or near the path along which he dragged his wood for dam building. Most of the trappers picked another method: making the animal "come to medicine." Castoreum, the beaver's own secretion, was mixed in with other ingredients in various exotic combinations and carried by the trapper in a box or stoppered bottle, often carved of horn. Once the trap was set, a twig was dipped in the musky mixture and placed in such a way that the beaver would have to step in the trap to sniff the twig. Often traps were set in shallow water, then anchored with a stake driven into the stream bed, so that once the beaver was caught, his instincts to head for deep water would drown him.

Meriwether Lewis, the explorer, recorded a beaver recipe which included castor, half a nutmeg, a dozen grains of cloves and thirty grains of cinnamon, ground together and mixed with "spirits." The mixture could be used immediately, but was better if allowed to ripen for a few days or months. When cloves were unavailable, Lewis suggested the use of allspice, which accounts for its appearance among the supplies brought to the mountains for rendezvous. The mixture was understandably on the strong side; the trappers probably got used to it, but the smell was one of the reasons they weren't acceptable in civilized society.

Naturally, if some of this mixture spilled on their hands, they wiped it on their buckskins; they didn't stop there, but wiped their greasy hands on their skins after eating, and wiped off the blood when skinning. The resulting color and flavor of the skin was not the clean gold of fresh-tanned deer hides, but, as Berry says (in *A Majority of*

Scoundrels), "...black. Dirty black, greasy black, shiny black, bloody black, stinky black. Black."

Besides buckskin pants and shirt, the trappers wore blanket capotes, an overcoat made from a blanket, usually Hudson's Bay blankets. Since buckskin garments had no pockets, the trapper's tools were tied to the strap of the powder horn slung over one shoulder, or carried in a bag that came to be known as the "possible sack," since it contained everything he could possibly need in the mountains.

At night, the trappers may have bedded down in rough shelters if they were staying in one camp for awhile—that is, if there was enough forage nearby for the horses, and meat for the hunters' rifles. Or they may have simply rolled up in their blankets. Ruxton speaks of suffering constantly in his winter travel, in spite of sleeping close to the fire. His bedding consisted of two blankets, all he had between his body and the snow. Once the blankets got wet and froze hard, they were little protection from the cold. Killbuck, Ruxton's fictionalized trapper, spread his buffalo robe on the ground and used a stone under it for a pillow, tucking his pouch, powder horn and rifle inside the scanty shelter to keep them dry.

During the winter, too, there was time for reading whatever books had found their way into the baggage. Meek later spoke of the "Rocky Mountain College," the winter camps where some of the men learned to read. Clyman, since his "smattering of education" included reading, might have supplied some of the textbooks for the others.

Picture Clyman, seasoned by life on the eastern frontier, as he heads toward the West for the first time. Of his appearance at this time, he later said, "I think I was something of a fop in those days and sometimes have a good laugh to think how I must have looked in my fringed suit of buckskin with ruffled shirt to match."

Friends who described Clyman in later years agreed that he was tall —six feet or more—and thin, with brown hair and "clear greyish blue" or blue eyes. His face was described as "rather long and sharp." He had a sandy complexion, a roman nose and high forehead. His mouth was a little twisted, as if he had lost many teeth on one side.

So, here we have James Clyman, dressed in his buckskins, outfitted with his customary rifle, knife, tomahawk, embarking with Ashley's men on the Missouri River to begin his march into history. Following is Clyman's own story of this first year in the mountains, 1823-1824. Clyman wrote this part of the narrative in 1871; since so much time had passed, his memory failed him on some dates, so correct dates have been inserted.

———

Narrative of 1823-24

Nappa—April 17, 1871

"According to promis I will now attempt to give you a short detail of life and incidents of my trip in & through the Rockey Mountains in the years [1823] 1824-25, 26, 27, 28 and a portion of 1829

"Haveing been imployed in Public Surveys in the state of Illinois through the winter of 1823 [1822] and the early part of 24 [23] I came to St Louis about the first of February to ricieve pay for past services and rimaining there Some days I heard a report that general William H Ashly was engageing men for a Trip to the mouth of the Yellow Stone river I made enquiry as to what was the object but found no person who seemed to possess the desired information finding whare Ashleys dwelling was I called on him the same evening Several Gentlemen being present he invited me to call again on a certain evening which I did he then gave a lenthy acount of game found in that Region Deer, elk, Bear and Buffalo but to crown all immence Quantities of Beaver whose skins ware verry valuable selling from $5 to 8$ per pound at that time in St Louis and the men he wished to engage ware to [be] huters trappers and traders for furs and peltrees my curiosity now being satisfied St Louis being a fine place for Spending money I did not leave immediately not having spent all my finds I loitered about without (without) employment

"Haveing fomed a Slight acquaintance with Mr Ashley we occasionly passed each other on the streets at length one day Meeting him he told me he had been looking for me a few days back and enquired

as to my employment I informed him that I was entirely unemployed
he said he wished then that I would assist him ingageing men for his
Rockey mountain epedition and he wished me to call at his house in
the evening which I accordingly did getting instrutions as to whare I
would most probably find men willing to engage which [were to be]
found in grog Shops and other sinks of degredation he rented a house
& furnished it with provisions Bread from to Bakers – pork plenty,
which the men had to cook for themselves

"On the 8th [10th] of March 1824 [1823] all things ready we shoved
off from the shore fired a swivel which was answered by a Shout from
the shore which we returned with a will and porceed up stream
under sail

"A discription of our crew I cannt give but Fallstafs Battallion was
genteel in comparison I think we had about (70) seventy all told Two
Keel Boats with crews of French some St Louis gumboes as they were
called

"We proceeded slowly up the Misouri River under sail wen winds
ware favourable and towline when not Towing or what was then calld
cordell is a slow and tedious method of assending swift waters It is
done by the men walking on the shore and hawling the Boat by a long
cord Nothing of importance came under wiew for some months except
loosing men who left us from time to time & engaging a few new men
of a much better appearance than those we lost The Missourie is a
monotinous crooked stream with large cottonwood forest trees on one
side and small young groth on the other with a bare Sand Barr inter-
vening I will state one circumstance only which will show something
of the character of Missourie Boats men

"The winds are occasionally very strong and when head winds
prevail we ware forced to lay by this circumstanc happend once before
we left the Settlements the men went out gunning and that night came
in with plenty of game Eggs Fowls Turkeys and what not Haveing a
fire on shore they dressed cooked and eat untill midnight being care
full to burn all the fragments the wind still Blowing in the morning
several Neighbours came in hunting for poultry liberty was given to
search the boats but they found nothing and left the wind abateing

somewhat the cord was got out amd pulling around a bend the wind became a farir sailing breeze and [the sails] wa[r]e ordred unfurled when out droped pigs and poultry in abundance

"A man was ordred to Jump in the skiff and pick up the pigs and poultry

"Ariveing at Council Bluffs we m[a]de several exchanges (8) eight or Ten of our men enlisting and 2 or 3 of the Soldier whose [terms of enlistment] was nearly expired engageing with us The officers [at Fort Atkinson] being verry liberal furnished us with a Quantity of vegetables here we leave the last appearance of civilization and [enter] fully Indian country game becomeing more plenty we furnished ourselvs with meat daily.

The Arikara Fight

"But I pass on to the arickaree villages whare we met with our defeat on ariveing in sight of the villages the barr in front was lined with squaws packing up water thinking to have to stand a siege

"For a better understanding it is necessay that I state tha[t] the Missourie furr company have established a small trading house [perhaps one of the Teton River posts] some (60) or (80) miles below the arrickree villages the winter previous to our assent and the arrickarees haveing taken some Sioux squaws prisoners previously one of these Squaws got away from them and made for this trading post and they persuing come near overtaking her in sight of the post the men in the house ran out and fired on the Pesueing arrickarees killing (2) others so that Rees considered war was fully declared betwen them and the whites But genl. Asley thought he could make them understand that his [company] was not resposable for Injuries done by the Missourie fur company But the Rees could not make the distiction they however agreed to recieve pay for thier loss but the geeneral would make them a present but would not pay the Misourie fur companies damages

"After one days talk they agreed to open trade on the sand bar in front of the village but the onley article of Trade they wantd was ammunition For feare of a difficulty, the boats ware kept at anchor in the streame, and the skiffs were used for communications Betteen the boats and the shore. we obtained twenty horses in three d[a]ys trading, but in doing this we gave them a fine supply of Powder and ball which on [the] fourth day wee found out to [our] Sorrow

"In the night of the third day Several of our men without permition went and remained in the village amongst them our Interperter Mr [Edward] Rose about midnight he came runing into camp & informed us that one of our men [Aaron Stephens] was killed in the village and war was declared in earnest We had no Military organization diciplin or Subordination Several advised to cross over the river at once but thought best to wait untill day light But Gnl. Ashley our imployer Thought best to wait till morning and go into the village and demand the body of our comrade and his Murderer Ashley being the most interested his advice prevailed We laid on our arms e[x]pecting an attact as their was a continual Hubbub in the village.

————

Escape from the Indians

"At length morning appeared every thing still undecided finally one shot was fired into our camp the distance being however to great for certain aim Shortly firing became Quite general we seeing nothing to fire at Here let me give a Short discription of an Indian City or village as it is usually cald Picture to your self (50) or (100) large potatoe holes as they are usuly caled in the west (10) to (15) feet in diameter and 8 to 10 feet high in the center covered on the outside with small willow brush then a (a) layer of coarse grass a coat of earth over all a hole in one side for a door and another in the top to let out the smoke a small fire in the center *all Told* The continual wars between them and Sioux had caused them to picket in their place You will easely prceive that we had little else to do than to Stand on a bear sand barr and be shot at, at long range Their being seven or Eigh hundred guns in village and we having the day previously furnished them with abundance of Powder and Ball [There were] many calls for the boats to come ashore and take us on board but no prayers or threats had the [slightest effect] the Boats men being completely Parylized Several men being wounded a skiff was brought ashore all rushed for the Skiff and came near sinking it but it went the boat full of men and water the shot still coming thicker and the aim better we making a brest work of our horses (most) they nerly all being killed the skiffs having taken sevarl loads on Board the boats at length the shot coming thicker and faster one of the skiffs (was turned) was let go the men clambering on Boad let the skiff float off in their great eaganess to conceal themselves from the rapid fire of the enemy I seeing no hopes of Skiffs or boats comeing ashore left my hiding place behind a dead hors, ran up stream a short distance to get the advantage of the current and concieving myself to be a tolerable strong swimer stuck the muzzle of my rifle in [my] belt the lock ove my head with all my clothes on but not having made sufficien calculation for the strong current was carried passed the boat within a few feet of the same one Mr Thomas Eddie [saw me] but the shot coming thick he did not venture from behin the cargo Box and so could not reach me with a setting pole which [he] held in his hands K[n]owing now or at [least] thinking that I had the river to swim my first aim was to rid myself of all my encumbraces and my Rifle was the greatest in my attempt to draw it over my head it sliped down the lock ketching in my belt comeing to the surface to breathe I found it hindred worse that it did at first making one more effort I turned the lock side ways and it sliped through which gave me some relief but still finding myself to much encumbred I next unbucled my belt and let go my Pistols still continueing to disengage my self I next let go my Ball Pouch and finally one Sleeve of my Hunting shirt which was buckskin and held an immence weight of water when rising to the surface I heard the voice of encoragemnt saying hold on Clyman I will soon relieve you This [from] Reed Gibson who had swam in and caught the skiff the men had let go afloat and was but a few rods from me I was so much exausted that he had to haul me into the skiff wh[ere] I lay for a moment to cacth breath when I arose to take the only remaining ore when Gibson caled oh, god I am shot and fell forward in the skiff I encouraged him and [said] Perhaps not fatally give a few pulls more and we will be out of reach he raised and gave sevreral more strokes with the oar using it as a paddle when [he] co[m]plained of feeling faint when he fell forward again and I took his plac in the sterm and shoved it across to the East shore whare we landed I hauled the skiff up on the shore and told Gibson to remain in the Skiff and I would go upon the high land whare I could see if any danger beset us thair. After getting up on the river bank and looking around I Discovered sevral Indian in the water swimming over [some] of whoom ware nearly across the stream I spoke to Gibson telling him of the circumstance he mearly said (said) save yourself Clyman and pay no attention to me as I am a dead man and they can get nothing of me but my Scalp My first Idea was to get in the skiff and meet them in the water and brain them with the oar But on second look I conconcluded there ware to many of them and they ware too near the shore then I looked for some place to hide But there being onley a scant row of brush along the shore I concluded to take to the open Pararie and run for life by this time Gibson had scrambled up the bank and stood by my side and said run Clyman but if you escape write to my friends in Virginia and tell them what has become of me I [ran] for the open Prarie and Gibson for the brush to hide at first I started a little distance down the river but fearing that I might be headed in some bend I steered directly for the open Prarie and looking Back I saw three Inians mount the bank being intirely divested of garments excepting a belt around the waist containing a Knife and Tomahawk and Bows and arrows in their [hands] they made but little halt and started after me one to the right the other to the left while the third took direct after me I took direct for the rising ground I think about three miles of[f] there being no chanc for dodging the ground being smooth and level but haveing the start of some 20 or 30 rods we had appearantle an even race for about one hour when I began to have the palpitation of the heart and I found my man was gaining on me I had now arived at a moderately roling ground and for the first time turned a hill out of sight I turned to the right and found a hole was[h]ed in the earth some 3 feet long 1½ feet wide and

Pehaps 2 feet deep with weeds and grass perhaps one foot high surrounding it into this hole I droped and persuer immediatle hove in sight and passed me about fifty yards distant both my right an left hand persuers haveing fallen cosiderably in the rear and particularly the one on my right here fortune favoured me for my direct persuer soon passed over some uneven ground got out of sight when I arose and taking to the right struck into a low ground which covered me and following it soon came into a moderately steep ravine in all this time I gained breath and I did not see my persuers until I gained the top of the ridge over a Quarter of a mile from my friend when I gained this elevation I turned around [and saw] the three standing near together I made them a low bow with both my hand and thanked god for my present Safety and diliveranc

"But I did not remain long here wishing to put the gratest possible distance between me and the Arrickarees I still continued Southward over a smoothe roling ground But what ware my reflection being at least Three Hundred miles [an overestimate] from any assistanc unarmed and u[n]provided with any sort of means of precureing a subsistance not even a pocket Knife I began to feel after passing So many dangers that my pro[s]pects ware still verry slim, mounting some high land I saw ahed of me the river and Quite a grove of timber and being verry thirsty I made for the water intending to take a good rest in the timber I took one drink of water and setting down on a drift log a few minuits I chanced to look [at] the [river] and here came the boats floating down the stream the [men] watcing along the shores saw me about as soon as I saw them the boat was laid in and I got aboard

"I spoke of my friend Gibson whe[n] I was informed he was on board I immediately wen[t] to the cabin where he lay but he did not recognize me being in the agonies of Death the shot having passed through his bowels I could not refrain from weeping over him who lost his lifee but saved mine he did not live but an hour or so and we buried him that evening the onley one of (12) [13] that ware killed at the arrickarees Eleven being left on the sand bar and their Scalps taken for the squaws to sing and dance over.

"Before meeting with this defeat I think few men had Stronger

Ideas of their bravery and disregard of fear than I had but standing on
a bear and open sand barr to be shot at from behind a picketed Indian
village was more than I had contacted for and some what cooled my
courage before leaving the grave of my friend Gibson that [day and]
before I had an oppertunity of writeing to his friends I forgot his post
office and so never have writen We fell down a few miles and lay by
several day to wait and [see] if any more men had escaped the
but[c]hery when on the third or fourth day Jack Larisson came to us
naked as when he was born and the skin peeling off of him from the
effects of the sun he was wounded a ball passing through the fleshy
part of one thigh and ldging in the other the ball was easily exticated
and in a few (a few) days he was hobbling around Larrisson had lain
between two dead horses untill the boats left and he saw no other
chance of escape but to swim the river then divesting himself of all his
clothing he took the water the Indians came running and firing at his
head but [he] escaped without further injury the wound Before
mentioned he had recieved in the early part of the battle if it can be
called Battle supposing no more men had survived the slaughte[r] we
again droped down the river and landed under the side of an Isle
[Ashley Island] and two men [Jedediah Smith and a French Canadian]
ware sent up to [Ashley's post at] the mouth of the yellowstone and
one boat containing the wounded and discouraged was sent down to
Council bluffs with orders to continue to St Louis This being the fore
part of June here we lay for Six weeks or two months living on scant
and frquentle no rations allthough game was plenty on the main Shore
perhaps it was my fault in greate measure for several of us being
allowed to go on Shore we ware luckey enough to get Several Elk each
one packing meat to his utmost capacity there came on a brisk shower
of rain Just before we reached the main shore and a brisk wind arising
the men on the (men on the) boat would not bring the skiff and take us
on board the bank being bear and no timber neare we ware suffering
with wet and cold I went off to the nearest timber made a fire dried
and warmed myself laid down and went to sleep in the morning
looking around I saw a fine Buck in easy gun shot and I suceeded in
Killing him then I was in town plenty of wood plenty of water and

plenty of nice fat venison nothing to do but cook and eat here I remained untill next morning then taking a good back load to the landing whare I met several men who had Just landed for the purpose of hunting for me after this I was scarcely ever allowed to go ashore for I might never return

"In proceess of time news came that Col. Livenworth [Leavenworth] with Seven or eight hundred Sioux Indians ware on the rout to Punnish the Arrickarees and (18) or (20) men came down from [Ashley's post on] the Yellow Stone who had gone up [under Andrew Henry] the year prevous these men came in Canoes (came in canoes) and passed the Arrickarees in the night we ware now landed on the main Shore and allowed more liberty than hertofore (at) Col. Levenworth [with] about (150) mem the remnant of the (6) Regiment came and Shortly after Major Pilcher with the Sioux Indians (Indians) amounting to 5 or 600 warriers and (18) or 20 engagies of the Missourie furr Company and a grand feast was held and speeches made by whites and Indians

"After 2 days talk a feast and an Indian dance we proceded up stream Some time toward the last [the eighth] of August we came near the arrickaree villages again a halt was made arms examined amunition distributed and badges given to our friends the Sioux which consisted of a strip of white muslin bound around the head to distinguish friends from foes

"The third day in the afternoon being 2 or three miles from the villages the Sioux made a breake being generally mounted they out went us although we ware put to the double Quick and when we arived the plain was covered with Indians which looked more like a swarm [of] bees than a battle field they going in all possible directions the Rees having mounted and met the Sioux a half mile from their pickets But as soon as we came in sight the Rees retreated into their village the boats came up and landed a short half mile below the village but little efort was mad that afternoon except to surround the Rees and keep them from leaveing the Sioux coming around one side and the whites around the other Quite a number of dead Indians streued over the plain I must here notice the Bravery of one Sioux a

Ree ventured out some distance from the pickets and held some tantalizeing conversation with the Sioux, one Siox on a fast horse
approached him slowly Still bantering each other to approach nearer at
length the Sioux put whip to his horse taking directly for the Ree and
run him right up to the [village] then firing at full speed wheeled to
retreat the Rees inside of the pickets firing some 40 or 50 of them
covered him completely in smoke but Sioux and his horse came out
safe and the Rees horse went in through the gate without a rider the
Rees friends came out and carried in the man Several Rees lay dead
and one in long shot (shot) of the pickets the old Sioux chief Brought
one of his wives up with a war club who struck the corps a number of
blow with [the] club he tantalizeing the Rees all the time for their
cowardice in [not] comeing out to defend thair dead comrad and
allowing his Squaws to strike their braves in gunshot of their village a
common habit of the Indians in war is the first man that comes to the
body of a dead enemy is to take his Scalp the second will take off his
right hand the third his left the fourth his right foot the fifth his Left
foot and hang thes trophies around their necks to shew how near they
ware to the death of their enemy on the field of Battle and in this case
a member of our Sioux shewed Trophies one more circumstance and I
am done one large middle aged Sioux blonged to the grizzle Bear medicine came on hand [and] feet to the body of a dead Ree in the attitude
of a grzzly Bear snorting and mimican the bear in all his most vicious
attitudes and with his teeth tore out mouth fulls of flesh from the
breast of the dead body of the Ree

"But I will not tire you with details of the savage habits of Indians
to their enimies but I will merely state that it is easy to make a savage
of a civilised man but impossible to make a civilised man of a savage in
one Generation

"The third day in the afternoon one of the Ree chiefs came out
alone offering terms of peace a Schedule was drawn up to be
confirmed on the morrow in a half hour after this was undestood our
Sioux packed up and ware out of sight also the most of the Missourie
companies men

"The night was Quiet but the two previous we had a lively picture of pandimonium the wa[il]ing of squaws and children the Screams and yelling of men the fireing of guns the awful howling of dogs the neighing and braying of hosses and mules with the hooting of owls of which thy [were] a number all intermingled with the stench of dead men and horses made the place the most (most) disagreeable that immaginnation could fix Short of the bottomless pit In the morning however our Quiet night was easily accounted for the Rees having dserted thair village early in the night previous a few men with an Interpeter ware sent forward to hunt them up and bring them back they returned about noon not being able to overtake them one circumstanc I must not omit to mention Captain [Bennett] Riley since General Riley who gave California her constitu[ti]on was present and in command of company of Company A. .6.th Regiment and requested pemition to lead a forlorn hope into the villag but was denied that honour he then became allmost furious and swore that he demande the prviledge stating that they had been laying at garison at Council Bluffs for 8 or 10 years doeing nothing but eating pumpkins and now a small chance for promotion occured and it was denied him and might not occurr again for the next 10 yeares (again)

"We Remained one night more in our stinking disageeable camp when we loosed cable and droped down stream 4 men of our mountanier corps was left behind and in an hour after we left a great smoke arose and the acursd village was known to be on fire three Squaw 2 verry old and feeb[l]e and one sick and unab[l]e to move ware found to have been left as not worth caring for these ware removed into a lodge which was preserved Col. Levenworth had given special orders that the village be left unmolested & ordered the boats landed and role called to assertain who if any ware missing the sargent called over the roles rapidly and reported all present then [the inference was that] it must be Souix.

"We having to hunt for our living we soon fell behind the Col. and his corps droping down to a place called fort Keawa [Kiowa] a trading establishment blonging to Missourie furr Company

"Here a small company of I think (13) men [under Andrew Henry] ware furnished a few horses onley enough to pack their baggage they going back to the mouth of the yellow Stone on their way up they ware actacted in the night by a small party of Rees killing two of thier men and they killing one Ree amongst this party was a Mr Hugh Glass who could not be rstrand and kept under Subordination he went off of the line of march one afternoon and met with a large grissly Bear which he shot at and wounded the bear as is usual attacted Glass he attemptd to climb a tree but the bear caught him and hauled to the ground tearing and lacerating his body in feareful rate by this time several men ware in close gun shot but could not shoot for fear of hitting Glass at length the beare appea[r]ed to be satisfied and turned to leave when 2 or 3 men fired the bear turned immediately on glass and give him a second mutilation on turning again several more men shot him when for the third time he pouncd on Glass and fell dead over his body this I have from information not being present here I leave Glass for the presen we having bought a few horses and borrowed a few more left about the last of September [1823] and proceded westward over a dry roling highland a Elleven in number I must now mention honorable excep-tions to the character of the men engaged at St Louis being now thined down to onley nine of those who lfet [left] in March and first Jeded-diah Smith who was our Captain Thomas Fitzpatrick William L. Sublett and Thomas Eddie all of which will figure more or less in the future in [the] evening we camped on White clay Creek [White River] a small stream running thick with a white sediment and resembling cream in appearance but of a sweetish pu[n]gent taste our guide warned us from using this water too freely as [it] caused excessive costiveness [constipation] which we soon found out

"We prceeded up this stream one day [Trees] not in sight since we left the Missourie part of the nxt day same when our guide infomed us to take what water we could as we would not reach water untill about noon the next day our means of taking water being verry small we trailed on untill dark and camped on a ridge whare the cactus was so thick that we could scarcely find room to spred our Blankets Starting early about 11 oclock we arived at our expected water But behold it was entirely dry not even dam[p] mud to be found but here we found a few Shrubby oaks to protect us from the scorching sun We rested perhaps half an hour 15 miles to the water yet and being all on foot and a pack horse to leade can we if we hold out reach it before dark we urged and hauled our stubron horses along as fast as posible our guide getting a long way ahead and finely out of sight my pack horse being more tractab[l]e than most others I soon got ahead of my companions and we got strung out a mile in (tingth) [length] the country some what roling and one steering off to the right or left in search of water we ware not onley long but wide and it appeared like we might never all collect togather again I followd as near as possible the last appeance of our guide but deveating slightly to the right struck on a hole [of] water about an hour before sunset I fired my gun immedeately and then ran into the pool arm deep my horse foloing me

"Comeing out I fired my gun again one man and horse made their appearance the horse out ran the man plunging into the water first each man as he came fired his gun and Shouted as soon as he could moisten his mouth and throat Sufficienty to mak a noise about dark we all got collected except two who had given out and ware left buried in the sand all but their heads Capt Smith Being the last who was able to walk and he took Some water and rode about 2 miles back bringing up the exhausted men which he had buried in the sand and this two days of thirst and Starvation was made to cross a large bend of the white clay River in the morning we found it yet 4 or 5 miles to the [Teton or Bad?] river whare our guide [was] waiting for us I have been thus particular in describing the means and trobles of traveling in a barren and unknown region here our River is a beautiful Clare stream running over a gravely bottom with some timber along its course having [emerged] from its bed of mud and ashes for the sediment spoken of is nearer it mouth Continued up the vally of this stream [Teton or Bad River] to Sioux encampment of the Bois Brulie [Burnt Wood] tribe whare we remained several days trading for Horses and finely obtained 27 or 28 which gave us 2 horses to each man and two or three spare animals so far the country is dry not fit for cultivation (Tere may) However there may be and pro[b]a[b]ly is better soil and better gr[a]ising higher up amongst the hills as it certainly grew better (was) the farther we proceeded up the stream and there was an incr[e]as of

Shrubery and soil Likewise here our guide left us to return with the Horses we had borrowed of the Miourie Furr compy.

"We packed up and crossed the White Clay [Teton] river and proceeded north westernly over a dry roling Country for several days meting with a Buffaloe now and then which furnished us with provision for at least one meal each day our luck was to fall in with the Oglela tiribe of Sioux whare [we] traded a few more horses and swaped of[f] some of our more ordina[r]y.

"Country nearly the same short grass and plenty of cactus untill we crossed the [South Fork of?] Chienne River a few miles below whare it leaves the Black Hill range of Mountains here some aluvial lands look like they might bear cultivation we did not keep near enough to the hills for a rout to travel on and again fell into a tract of county whare no vegetation of any kind existed beeing worn into knobs and gullies and extremely uneven a loose grayish coloured soil verry soluble in water running thick as it could move of a pale whitish coular and remarkably adhesive there [came] on a misty rain while we were in this pile of ashes [bad-lands west of the South Fork of the Cheyenne River] and it loded down our horses feet (feet) in great lumps it looked a little remarkable that not a foot of level land could be found the narrow revines going in all manner of directions and the cobble mound[s] of a regular taper from top to bottom all of them of the percise same angle and the tops share the whole of this region is moveing to the Misourie River as fast as rain and thawing of Snow can carry it by enclining a little to the west in a few hours we got on to smoothe ground and soon cleared ourselves of mud at length we arived at the foot of the black Hills which rises in verry slight elevation about the common plain we entered a pleasant undulating pine Region cool and refreshing so different from the hot dusty planes we have been so long passing over and here we found hazlenuts and ripe plumbs a luxury not expected We had one [or] two day travel over undulating Pine with here and there an open glade of rich soill and fine grass but assinding the Ridges un[t]ill we arived near the summet our rout became brushy mainly Scruby pine and Juniper the last covered in purple beries comencing our desent the ravines became steep and rugged an rockey the waters flowing westward we suposed we ware on the waters of Powder river one evening late gowing d[o]wn a small stream we came into a Kenyon and pushed ouselves down so far that (that) our horses had no room to turn while looking for a way out it became dark by unpacking and leading our animals down over Slipery rocks three of us got down to a n[i]ce open glade whare we killed a Buffaloe and fared Sumpiously that night while the rest of the Company remained in the Kenyon without room to lie down we now found it would not do to follow down any stream in these moutains as we ware shure to meet with rocky inaccessible places So with great exertion we again assended to the top of a ridge and ware Quite lucky in gitting a main devide which led us a considerable distance before [we] had to desend again but this portion of the mountain furnished our horses with no food and they began to be verry poor and weak so we left 3 men and five horses behind to recruit while the rest of us proceded on there being some sighn of Beaver in the vicinity and hoping to soon find more where we Might all Stop for a time The Crow Indians being our place of destination a half Breed by the name of Rose who spoke the crow tongue was dispached ahead to find the Crows and try to induce some of them to come to our assistance we to travel directly west as near as circumstances would permit supposing we ware on the waters of Powder River we ought to be within the bounds of the Crow country continueing five days travel since leaveing our given out horses and likewise Since Rose left us late in the after-noon while passing through a Brushy bottom a large Grssely came down the vally we being in single file men on foot leding pack horses he struck us about the center then turning ran paralel to our line Capt. Smith being in the advanc he ran to the open ground and as he immerged from the thicket he and the bear met face to face Grissly did not hesitate a moment but sprung on the capt taking him by the head first pitc[h]ing sprawling on the earth he gave him a grab by the middle fortunately cat[c]hing by the ball pouch and Butcher K[n]ife which he broke but breaking several of his ribs and cutting his head badly none of us having any sugical Knowledge what was to be done one Said come take hold and he wuld say why not you so it went around I asked

Capt what was best he said one or 2 [go] for water and if you have a
needle and thread git it out and sew up my wounds around my head
which was bleeding freely I got a pair of scissors and cut off his hair
and then began my first Job of d[r]essing wounds upon examination I
[found] the bear had taken nearly all his head in his capcious mouth
close to his left eye on one side and clos to his right ear on the other
and laid the skull bare to near the crown of the head leaving a white
streak whare his teeth passed one of his ears was torn from his head
out to the outer rim after stitching all the other wounds in the best way
I was capabl and according to the captains directions the ear being the
last I told him I could do nothing for his Eare O you must try to stich
up some way or other said he then I put in my needle stiching it
through and through and over and over laying the lacerated parts
togather as nice as I could with my hands water was found in about
ame mille [a mile] when we all moved down and encamped the
captain being able to mount his horse and ride to camp whare we
pitched a tent the onley one we had and made him as comfortable as
circumtances would permit this gave us a lisson on the charcter of the
grissly Baare which we did not forget I now a found time to ride
around and explore the immediate surroundings of our camp and
assertained that we ware still on the waters of [South Fork of] shiann
river which heads almost in the eastern part of the Black hill range
taking a western course for a long distance into an uneven vally whare
a large portion of (of) the waters are sunk or absorbd then turning
short to the east it enters the Black hill rang th[r]ough a narrow
Kenyon in appeareantly the highest and most abrupt part of the mountain enclosed in immence cliffs of the most pure and Beautifull black
smooth and shining [slate] and perhaps five hunded to one thousand
feet high how [far] this slate extends I cannot tell We passe[d] through
this slate Quary about 2 miles and one of the men observed here or at
some such place Mosses [Moses] must have obtaind the plates or tables
on which the declogue was inscirobed some miles farther west I visited
[a] place of a different character containing Quite a grove of Petrifid
timber standing laying and inclining at various angles one stub in
Perticular wa[s] so high that I could barely lay my hand on the top

sitting in the saddle the body and main branches scatered on the ground dismouted and picked up several fragments which ware so hard so to bring fire f[r]om steel A mountaneer named [Moses] Harris being St Louis some yers after undertook to describe some of the strange things seen in the mountains spoke of this petrified grove in a restaurant whare a caterer for one of the dailys was prese[n]t and the next morning his exagerated statement came out saying a petrified forest was lately di[s]covered whare the trees branches leaves and all were perfect and the small birds sitting on them with their mouths open singing at the time of their transformation to stone This is a fine country for game Buffaloe Elk Bare deer antelope &c likewise it produces some Hazel nuts Plumbs white thorn Berries wild currant large and of fine flavour and abundance of nutricious grass and some land that would bear cultivation after remaining here ten days or 2 weeks the capt. Began to ride out a few miles and as winter was rapidly approaching we began to make easy travel west ward and Struck the trail of Shian Indians the next day we came to their village traded and swaped a few horses with them and continued our march across a Ridge [of] mountains not steep & rocky (in general) but smooth and grassy in general with numerous springs and brook of pure water and well stocked with game dsending this ridge we came to the waters of Powder River Running West and north country mountainous and somewhat rockey.

Encounter with the Crows

"Rose with 15 or 16 Crow Indians came to our camp as soon as we raised a fire in the evenin they had been watching for two days passed to assure themselves that no Shians were with us they and the Shians being at war they the Crows brought us several spare Horses which relieved our Broke down animals and gave us a chance to ride but they caused us to travel to fast for our poor horses and so Capt Smith gave them what they could pack sending Rose with them and we followed at our own gait stoping and Traping for beaver occasionly Crossing several steep and high ridges which in any other country would be called mountains Crossed Shell river Quite a stream running into the bighorn as I believe the mountains here do not appear to have any rigular direction but run in all directions are tolerable high but not generall precipitous Before l[e]aving this perticular Region I think it the Best Supp[l]ied with game of any we passe[d] through in all our Travels and therefore do not wonder that the Indian would not give it up and if it is not too cold there some soil that will bear cultivation we ware there through the month of November the nights war frosty but the days ware generally warm and pleasant on Tongue river we struck the trail of the (of the) Crow Indians Passed over another ridge of mountains [Owl Creek Mountains] we came on to Wind River which is merely another name for the Big horn above [south of] the Big horn Mountain the most of this Region is barren and worthless if my recollection is right from the heads of the Shian untill we came on to Wind river we ware Bountifully supplied with game but here we found none at all two causes may be assigned for this first the country not being well supplied naturely an Second the Crows haveing passed recntly through they had killed and drove off all the game in our reach our meals being few and far betwen our only hope being to push a head and overtake the Crow village The weather being cold and blustry and I thought the River was well named slight Snows and Strong north winds prevailed continually our horses and urselves became completely exausted before we reached the main Encampment Still passing up Wind river untill we came immediately north of Freemont peak [later so named] on the Wind River Mountain, whare we halted for the winter. [likely near the modern Dubois, Wyoming] The vally is here narrow and uneven but tolerable well set in grass and Buffalo plenty at the time of our arival several grand hunts taking place which being the first I had witnessed I will attempt to give some description the whole grown male population turning out Early in the morning and taking rank along on eeach side of a narrow vally those on fleetest horses taking a circuit and getting behind a large herd Bufflo drove them pell mell down the vally those Stationed on the sides falling in as they passed they run down the Buffaloe so that [the] old and slow could catch them and even men on foot Killed them with Bow and Arrow the Squaws old men and children following and Buchering and secureing meat and skins as fast as possible the night after this grand hunt not more than half the people came in to camp they remaining out to watch the wolves fom the meat untill they could get it packed in d[r]ying now commenced on a grand scale and wood was in demand

"In a few days we moved a short distance to whare wood was more plenty and had another gran hunt after which individuals ware allowed to hunt at their pleasure all though this vally is in heart of the rocky Mountain range Snow did not fall deep and every Clear day it thawed whare the sun struck fairly In the second grand chase I did not go out on horseback as in the first but took it on foot with the foot men the day being too cold for pleasant riding we proceeded to the lower part of the vally whare the stream that passes through the vally enters a narrow Kenyon it being 6 or 7 miles from whare the race commenced and standing on a cliff nea[r]ly ove[r] the buffaloe we had rare Sport shooting them on enquiry as to how many ware slaughterd that day every one said a thousand or upwards thi[s] I did not dispute thinking it fell near the fact myself and about 20 Indians who stood on the rocks of [the] Kenyon Killed Seventy by my own count It is remarkable the amount of cold these Crows can withstand I have frequently seen them dozens of them runing bufaloe on horseback for hours togather all their bodies naked down to the belt around their waists and dismount with but a slight trimble and many of them take a bath every morning even whn the hoar frost was flying thick in the air and it was necessary to cut holes in the ice to get at the water

"They put their children to all kinds of hardships and the femals in particular pack the littl girls and dogs when on march the whole employment of the males being hunting and war and at the time we ware there at least one third of the warriors ware out in war parties in different directions they being in a state of warfare with all the neighbouring tribes in February [1824] we made an effort to cross the mountains north of the wind River [ra]nge but found the snow too deep and had to return and take a Southern course east of the wind river range which is here the main Rockey mountans and the main dividing ridge betwen the Atlantic and Pacific.

Clyman Saves Sublette from Freezing

"In traveling up the Popo Azia [Green River] a tributary of Wind River we came to an oil springe neare the main Stream whose surface was completely covered over with oil resembling Brittish oil and not far from the same place ware stacks [of] Petrolium of considerable bulk [near present Lander, Wyoming]. Buffaloe being scarce our supply of food was Quite scanty Mr Sublett and my self mounted our horses one morning and put in quest of game we rode on utill near sundown when we came in sight of three male bufalo in a verry open and exposed place our horses being too poor to run we made an effort to aproach them by crawling over the ice and snow but our game saw us and was about to brake when we arose and fired luckeyly we broke ones Shoulder had we had our horses at hand so as to mount and follow we would soon [have] had meat but our horses ware narely a mile Distant so Sublett went back for our horses and I loaded my rifle and followed the wounded buffalo there being an uneven riadge about a mile distant in the direction the game went and (and) my hope was to head him there and git another shot I ran with all my speed and fortunately when I came out of cover was in easy gun shot when all breathless mearly pointing my [gun] in the direction of the game to my surprise I gave him a dead Shot bifore I could reload he fell dead in a steep gutter whare I could not commence butcering untill Sublett came up to assist me night came on before we got our meat buchered we gatherd some dry sage and struck a light by which we got of[f] a small Quantity of meat Shortly after the sun left us the North wind arose and grew stronger and stronger and a cold frosty snow commenced falling before [we] finished our suppers there being no wood and sage being small and scarce and [wind] scattering what little fire we had in all directions we spread down our scanty bed and covered ourselves as close as possbele from the wind and snow which found its way through ever[y] crevice

"Allthough the wind blew and the fine frosty snow crept in and around us this was not-the worst for the cold hard frozen earth on which we lay was still more disagreeabl so that sleep was out of the Que[s]tion by turning every method for rest day light at last apeared when we consulted what we had best do under the circumstances and it was agre[ed] that I should arise and gather some sage brush which was small and scarce and [Sublette] wold remain under the Buffaloe robe and keep his hands warm if posibl to strike fire but all our calculations failed for as soon [as] our hands became exposed to the air they became so numb that we could not hold thee flint and Steel we then [took] re[c]ourse to our guns with no better Success for the wind was So strong and for the want of some fine metireal to catch the fire in we or my comrade raped himslf in his robe and laid down after a great struggle I made out to saddle my hor[s]e and was about to leave the inhospitable [place] not wishing to leave my friend I asked him if he Could ride if I saddled his horse but he thought not and was unwilling to try I then made several unsuccesful efforts to obtain fire Just as I was about to mount and leave I run my hand in the ashes to see if any warmth remained to my Joy found a small cole of fire alive not larger than a grain of Corn throwing it in to [a] hand full of metirial I had gathered it starte[d] a blaze in a minuit and in one minuit more I had a fine fire my friend got out and crawled up to my side drawing our robe around our backs we tried to warm ourselves but the wind being so strong the smoke and fire came into our faces by the back current I sadled the other hors packed up the meat while Sublet gathered sage-brush to keep up a fire which was no little Job for [it was] carried away allmost a[s] fast as he put it on at length we mounted and left I put my friend ahead and followed urging his horse along We had about four miles to timber I found I would be liable to freeze on ho[r]seback so I got of and walked it being a north inclination the snow was about one foot deep I saw my friend was too numb to walk so I took the lead for the last half mile and struck a grove of timber whare there was an old Indian [lodge] but one side of which was still standing I got fire

allmost Immediately then ran back and whoped up my friends horse
assisted him to dismount and get to the fire he seemed to [have] no life
to move as usual he laid down nearly assleep while I went Broiling
meat on a stick after awile I roused him up and gave him his Breakfast
when he (he) came to and was as active as usual

"I have been thus particular in discribing one night near the sumit
of the Rockey mounta[n]s allthough a number simular may and often
do occur

"We [the entire party] now moved over a low ridge and Struck on
Sweet Water Since assertained to be a tributary of the Platte river it was
cold and clear the evening that we encamped on Sweet water many of
[the] South sides of the hills ware bare of Snow Buffalo scarce and
rations limited some time in the night the wind arose to a hericane
direct from the north and we had [to] Keep awake and hold on to our
blankets and robes to keep them from flying away in the morning we
gathered a large pile of dry pine logs and fixed up our blankets against
the wind but the back current brought all the smoke and ashes into our
faces in fifteen or twenty minuets after taking down our Screen ou[r]
fire blew intirely away and left us the wood but no fire we then cleared
away the snow under the lea of a clump of willows fixed ourselves as
comfortable as circumstances would permit laid to sleep the wind still
blowing all day and night without abatement the next morning several
of us wrapt ourselves in our robes and (and) attempted to take some
exercise following down the stream it became confined in a narrow
Kenyon under the points of some rocks we would be partly secure
from the cold blast toward evening my companion Mr Branch Saw a
mountain sheep on the rocks allmost perpedicular over us and fired at
him had the good luck to hit him when he came tumbling down to our
feet we soon prepared him and packed him to camp whare efforts were
made to broil small pieces but soon gave it up the wind still keeping up
such a continual blast as to prevent even a starving mountaneer from
satisfying his hunger we all took to our blankets again it being the only
way to keep from perishing the blast being so strong and cold Late in
the night however the lull came on and being awake I arose and found
it Quite comfortable I struck up a fire and commenced cooking and

eating by broiling thin slices of meat after a short time my comrades began to arise and we talked cooked eat the remainder of the night in the morning we started out in various directions some to look for game and some to look for more comfortable Quarters our prsent camp being close to the East foot of the wind River mountain and on a low divide directly south of the Wind rever vally having a full sweep for the North Wind [which] Caused us such [an] uncomfortab[l]e time Two pa[r]ties proceeded one in Quest of game the other for a camping ground I went down the sweet water some four or five miles to whare the Kenyon opened out into Quite a valley and found plenty of dry aspin wood in a small grove at the Lower end of the Kenyon and likewise plenty of Mountain Sheep on the cliffs which bounded the stream one of which I had the luck to kill and which I Buried in a snowdrift the next morning we packed up and moved down to the Aspin grove whare we remained some two or three weeks Subsisting on Mountain sheep on our way to our new camp we ware overtaken by one of the heaviest falls of snow that I ever witnessed with but verry slight wind the snow came down in one perfect sheet but fortunately it did not las[t] but a short time and we made our camp in good season as I before said we did not leave this camp until the Mountain Sheep began to get scarce and wild and before leaving we here made a cash of Powder Lead and several other articles supposed to be not needed in our Springs hunt and it was here likewise understood that should circumstances at any time seperate us we would meet at this place and at (and) all event we would all met here again or at some navigable point on the stream below at or by the first [of] June acording to our recording on leaving sweet water we struck in a south westerly direction this being some of the last days of February I think in 1825 [1824] our stock of dried meat being verry scant we soon run out entirely—no game to be found It appears this winter was extremely dry and cold one fourth of the g[r]ound on those ridges south of Sweetwater being entirely bare from the effect of strong west winds which carried the snow over to the East and south sides of the ridges about sixth morning out Mr Sublette and myself ware in the advance looking out for game a few antelope had been see[n] the evening previous a slight snow falling we came on the fresh track of a buffalo and supposing he could not be far off we started full speed after him in running about a mile we came in sight of him laying down the animal being thick a[nd] hevy it [was] difficult to hit a vital part when he is laying down we consulted as to the surest way [of] disabling him and came to the concusion that I fire at the rump and if posible breake his coupling while Sublett would fire at his Shoulder and disable him in forward parts so we [a]greed Sublett counting one two three while we both drew aim and both pull trigger at the word fire when both of our rifles went of simutan[eo]u[sly] and both effected what we desired the animal strugling to rise but could not Sublett beat me in reloading and approached and shot him in the head Just as the company came in sight on a hight of land when they all raised a Shout of Delight at [the] sight many not having tasted food for four days & none of us from two to three now you may suppose we had a happy time in butchering.

————

Green River

"Our company coming up we butchered our meat in short order many of the men eating large slices raw we packed up our meat & traveled on untill in the afternoon in hopes of finding water but did not succeed but finding large clumps of sage brush we camped all eaving & part of the night continuing on we found we had crossed the main ridge [South Pass] of the Rocky mountan in the month of January [February] 15 days without water or only such as we got from melting snow our horses eating snow and living fairly when beaver ground was found although we struck Sandy [River] about noon some of the men went immediatly to cutting the ice with thier Tomahauks called out frose to the bottom I walked down they had got down the length of thier arms and was about to give it up I pulled out one of my pistols and fired in to the hole up came the water plentifull for man & horse there being a small growth of willows along the stream we had wood & water plenty but our supply of meat had given out passed down the

stream on[e] day in the eavning a buffalo was killed and we were all
happy for the present this stream and one other we passd and on the
20th of February we reached Green river where I had the luck to kill
two wild geese here Capt Smith with seven men left us he going farther
south we left to trap on the branches of the stream as soon as the ice
gave way in a few day[s] wild geese became plenty on thawy & Springy
places the ice giving way we found beaver plenty and we commenced
trapping We found a small family of diggers or Shoshone Indians on
our trapping ground whom we feed with the overplus of Beaver the
snow disapearing our diggar friends moved off without our knowledge
of when or where and when they had gone our horses runing loose
on[e] night they all disapeared and we were unable to find them or in
what direction they had gone we continued trapping on foot with fair
success for about six weeks when the 10th of June was drawing close
and we had promised all who were alive to meet at our cash on Sweet
Water accordingly we cashed traps & furs hung our saddle & horse
equipments on trees & set out for Sweet water the same day about
noon on turning the point of a ridge we met face to face with five & six
indians mounted on some of our horses preparing to take possesion of
as many horses each on[e] taking hold of a lariet and ordering our
friens to dismount but after a short consultation we decided to go with
them to thier camp about one mile up a steep mountain where we
found six lodges 18 men with a large supply of squaws & children &
our old acquaintences that we had fed with the fat of Beaver while the
earth was thickly covered with snow we made our camp on rising
ground in easy gunshot of thier village all our horses wer given up but
one and we concluded this one was hid in the mountain so we caught
one of the men tied him fast told them we intended to kill him if our
horse was not given back which soon brought him we gave them a few
presents and left for our old camp dug up our cashe cut down our
saddles and again started for Sweet water this brought us to the 15th of
June no sight of Smith or his party remaining here a few days Fitzpatrick & myself mounted & fowling [following] down stream some 15
miles we concluded the stream was unna[vi]gable it beeing generally
broad & Shallow and all our bagga[g]e would have to be packed to

some navigable point below where I would be found waiting my comrades who would not be more than three or four days in the rear I moved slowly down stream three days to the mouth where it enters the North Platt Sweetwater is generally bare of all kind of timber but here near the mouth grew a small thick clump of willoes in this I cut a lodging place and geathered some driftwood for a fire which I was just preparing to strike fire I heard human voices on the stream below carfuly watching I saw a number of Indians advance up along the opisite side of the stream being here about 4 rods wide they come up & all stoped on the other side there being a lot of dry wood they soon raised 4 or 5 fires turned loose or tithered all their horses thier being 22 Indians and 30 horses I did not feel myself perfectly safe with so large number a war party in my rear vacinity recoclecting that for ½ mile back the country was bare & sandy the moon a few days before the full I could be trased as easly as if it had been snow so I walked backward across the sandy reagon out to a narrow rocky ridge & following along the same to where the creek broke through it I crossed over to the east side and climbing a high point of rocks I had a fair vew of my disagreeable neighbors at about 40 rods distance some of them lay down and slept while some others kept up the fire about midnight they all arose collected up thier horses too of the horses crossed over the creek two Indians on horse back folowed after when a shout was raised & eight or ten mounted went to assist hunting the fugitives after an hours ride backward & farword they gave up & all started of north I crawled down from my pearch & caught a few moments of cool feverish sleep. next day I surveyed the canyon [Devil's Gate] through which the river passes fearfuly swift without any perpendicular fall while on one of the high cliffs I discovered about 20 Ind[ians] approach the stream right where I had left a bout halfhour before all on foot they soon mad a small raft of driftwood on which they piled their war equipments & clothes swam the stream and went South I returned to my observatory on Sweetwater I remained in this vacinity eleven days heard nothing of my party began to get lonsome examined my store of amuniton found I had plenty of Powder but only eleven bullets.

"Reconitering all the curcumstances in my mind I thought if I spent a week in trying to find my old companions & should not be lucky enough to meet with them I would not have balls enough to take me to civilisation & not knowing whither I was on platt or the Arkansas on the 12th day in the afternoon I left my look out at the mouth of Sweetwater and proceeded down stream knowing that civil[iz]ation could be reached Eastward the days were quite warm & I had to keep near the water nothing occured for several day worth mentioning at length I found a bull boat lying drifted up on a sand bar and the marks of a large Indian ranch on the main shore I knew by the boat some white men had [been] here for the Indians never made such boats this gave me a fient hope of meeting some white men in this Indian world but continuing down stream several days I saw several persons running Buffalow on the hills on the other side of the river but to far to tell who they were Great herds of Buffalo were drivin across the river right around me I shot one and dried some meat remained here two days in hopes of meeting some human beeing even a friendly Indian would be a relief to my solitude but no person appearing I moved off down stream some two or three days after [this] I came into a grove of large old cottonwoods where a number of village Martins were nesting

"I laied down in the shade and enjoyed their twittering for some hours it reminded me of home & civilisation I saw a number of wild horses on the [prairie?] and I thought I would like to ride there is what hunters call "creasing"; this is done by shooting the animal through the neck close above the main bone this stuns them for a minute or more The next buffalo I killed I made a halter, I was forced to keep near the watter for there were no springs or streams on the plain. A fine black stallion came down to drink and beeing in close gun shot I fired as soon as he had gained the main bank he fell & I ran up & haltered him but he never moved for his neck was broken so I missed my wild ride still continuing my journy at length I came to a large recent lodge trail crossing the stream I thought it would be plesent to communicate with humans even though it were Indians, so I plunged into the stream and crossed over the water was only breast deep any where the villiag was about two miles out in the hills on my approach to them I did not attract thier attention untill within a few rods of thier lodges when a lot of men & boys came running up to me yelling most hidously when one man ran up & snatched my butcher knife and waved it across my breast I thought this a bravado so bared my breast for the fated streike & this perhaps saved my life for he immediatly commensed taking such things as suited him others taking my blankets then all my balls firesteel & flint another untied my powder into a rag when one or two cam rapedly up on horseback then they all left one of the mounted me[n] talking very loud & rapidly then he ordered me to mount behing him which I was glad to do he took me to his lodge and gave me to understand that I must not roam around any for some of them were bad and would kill me I remained in his lodge all night and after the morning meal he had three horses broght he & his son each mounted one and told me to mount the other he rode forward his son in the rear we rode basck over the river & about two miles on the trail where I dismounted and went on a foot again they sitting on their horses watched me untill I had passed over half mile when they returned, my hair had not been cut since I left St Louis I lost my hat at the defeat of the Arickrees and had been bareheaded ever since my hair was quite long my friend had beged for my hair the morning before we left his lodge I had granted his request so he barbered me with a dull butcher knife before leaving me he made me understand he loved me that he had saved my lief and wanted the hair for a memento of me as soon as my friends were fairly out of sight I left the trail fearing some unfriendly Indian the grass was thick and tall which made it hard to brake through so I frequently took ridges which led me from my course the second day in the afternoon I came to a pool of water under an oak tree drank sat down under the shade a short time ate a few grains of parched corn (which my friends had given me) when I heard a growling of some animals near by I advanced a few steps and saw two Badgers fighting I aimed at one but my gun mised fire they started off I geathered some bones (horse brobly) ran after & killed both I struck fire with my gunlock skined & roasted them made a bundle of grass & willow bark. it rained all the later part of the night but I started early in the morning the wet grass beeing more pleasant to travel than the dry it continu[ed] showery for several days the mosquitos be uncommonly bad I could not sleep and it got so damp I could not obtain fire and I had to swim several rivers at last I struck a trail that seamed to lead in the right direction which I determined to follow to its extreeam end on the second day in the afternoon I got so sleepy & nervous that it was with difficulty I kept the trail a number of times I tumbled down asleep but a quick nervous gerk would bring me to my feet again in one of these fits I started up on the trail traveled some 40 rods when I hapened to notise I was going back the way I had come turning right around I went on for some time with my head down when raising my eyes with great surprise I saw the stars & stripe waving over Fort Leavenworth [Atkinson] I swoned emmediatly how long I lay unconcious I do not know I was so overpowered with joy The stars & stripes came so unexpected that I was completly overcome being on decending ground I sat contemplating the scene I made several attemps to raise but as often fell back for the want of strength to stand after some minnites I began to breathe easier but certainly no man ever enjoyed the sight of our flag better than I did I walked on down to the fort there beeing no guard on duty I by axident came to the door of Cap Rileys quarters where a waiter brought out the Cap who conducted me to Generl Leavenworth who assigned me a company & gave me a writen introduction to the settelers where I got credit for a change of clothing some shoes & a soldiers cap I remained here receiving rashions as a soldier for ten days when to my surprise Mr Fitzpatrick Mr Stone & Mr Brench [Branch] arived in a more pitible state if possible than myself. Fitspatrick went back to the cashe after leaving me they opened the cashe found the powder somwhat damp spread it out to dry got all ready to pack up when Smith and party arived the day being quite warm the snow melted on the mountains and raised the water & they came to the conclusion to build a boat there & Fitspatrick Stone & Branch to get the furs down the best way the could Cap Smith to take charge of all the hunting & traping and to remain in the country the season so acordingly they made a skin boat & Cap coming down on horsback to bring me back again, (but I was off surveying the canyon) he saw where the Indians had

been where I had cut my lodge in the willows and not finding me came
to the conclusion the Indians had killed me so made that report the
three men hauld the boat down stream untill it was nearly worn out
and the water still falling so they cashed the furs on Indipendence rock
and ran down into the Canyon thier boat filled & they lost two of thier
guns & all of thier balls they broke the Brass mounting of the gun with
rocks bent it into balls with which they killed a few buffalo, the Skin
boat I saw on the sand bar was made by four men [Hugh Glass' party]
who crossed over from the mouth of the Bighorn thier winter camp
and landing on the shore walked up into the valliage which proved to
be Arickaree two of them escaped but the other two were killed this
[tribe] afterward proved to be the same people I saw runing buffalo by
axident I escaped from them the camp I waided the river to meet were
Pownees and here too I bearly saved my scalp but lost my hair."

Mourn not dear friends to anguish deriven
Thy children now unite in Heaven
Mourn not for them who early blest
Have found in Heaven eternal rest.
So ends this part of the record.

Notes on Chapter Two

This narrative, written late in life, reveals much about Clyman. We can appreciate the humor with which he refers to his companions, the story of stolen pigs and poultry told without comment. After the group is ambushed on a sand bar following some amazingly inept maneuvers under orders, Clyman calmly comments on how courage can desert one under fire. He displays the sensible attitudes of a mountain man when, hunting for the hungry company after days of short rations, he shoots a fat buck—and stays on the spot eating all he can hold. It was the smart thing to do; with his strength restored, he was more likely to be able to carry the meat back to camp. But the leaders didn't trust him after that, thinking him a potential deserter, and wouldn't let him hunt on shore for some time.

The Army's battle with the Arikaras following the Indians' skirmish with the trappers has been called "the worst disaster in the history of the Western fur trade." It plugged the river to travel for some time. Boats could no longer move on the river, and relief of Henry's men on the Yellowstone was delayed. Most of the 700 Ree warriors escaped the Army's ineffectual attempts at punishment, and survived to make later attacks on other trapping parties.

Major Henry's dilemma was this: if he couldn't take his trappers up river on the keelboats, he'd have to buy or trade for horses and outfit an expedition to go overland. In addition, many of their supplies had been sent back down river after the initial skirmish, and if the trappers reached their fort overland, they'd still be short of supplies for the fall hunt and winter camp. When the Army failed to discourage the Rees sufficiently, Jedediah Smith's party, of which Clyman was a member, did have to be outfitted and sent toward the mountains through country still comparatively unexplored; this probably accounts for some of the misery Clyman later reported as they searched for the Crows and a good pass across the mountains.

Clyman's notes make it clear that he was not part of the group with Hugh Glass when that notorious trapper was attacked by the grizzly. In fact it was only when Clyman staggered into Fort Atkinson after his casual stroll across the plains that he heard the story of Hugh's battle with the grizzly, and his later search for Fitzgerald, one of the men who abandoned him. The bull boat Clyman had found near the Indian village was Hugh's, a nice bit of corroboration for Glass' incredible tale.

When Clyman notes the "remarkably adhesive" soil, which "loded down our horses feet in great lumps," he'd just been introduced to the soil called "gumbo" and cursed by residents of the area ever since. Clyman's cool narration of the group's search for water across the alkali plains obscures some of the drama of the event. Many of the other men had apparently given up, and it was Clyman, pushing ahead, who found the water hole slightly off the line of march. Before he drank, he fired his gun to let the others know relief had been found. Jedediah Smith's heroism showed itself in this incident as well, since it was Smith who drank, then took water back to the two exhausted men he had buried in sand.

Despite his familiarity with wilderness travel, Clyman was in new country, and he made some errors. When he referred to White Clay Creek, Clyman was actually on White River; other sources show Smith's route of 1823 along the north side of White River for about 160 miles, bringing the party to the point where they left the river and turned northwest toward the Black Hills, which they probably entered at Buffalo Gap, still a landmark. The narrow canyon where the group remained all night "without room to lie down" was probably Hell Canyon, southwest of Pringle, South Dakota.

―――――――

Grizzly Bear Attack

Clyman apparently had no surgical experience when he sewed Jedediah Smith's face together, but he'd skinned a lot of animals, and he had the courage to go ahead, a quality ably demonstrated by Smith as well, especially considering that he probably also had broken ribs. Those who are amazed that the wound didn't become infected should remember Jim Bridger's words when Whitman removed the arrow-point so long embedded in his back—"meat jest don't spoil in the mountains."

The petrified "grove" Clyman located is probably the one located about eleven miles east of the present Buffalo, Wyoming. Though Black Harris wasn't along on this trip, some of the stories told by this group of trappers might have been added to his later tales of the "putrified" forest.

―――――――

Edward Rose

Edward Rose, who accompanied the Crows to the trappers' camp, is one of the stranger characters in the fur trade drama. He was one of the earliest trappers, having been associated with Manuel Lisa and the Astorians. He played a brave part in the Arikara disaster, and acted as interpreter in Crow country—though Clyman indicates that the party still had trouble getting good information about the country westward. Rose's reputation, even this early in the fur trade, was one of trickery, cheating the fur companies of goods, says Camp, in order to glorify himself in the eyes of the Indians. His employers found it wiser not to trust him, and he was full of fight and dangerous when angry. Yet since he lived among the various tribes of Indians, he was often useful when fighting broke out, and few authorities have questioned his bravery, which approached idiocy at times.

Of mixed blood, part Negro, Cherokee and white, he looked like an Indian; his face was made more fierce by a brand on his forehead, and the piece missing from the end of his nose, bitten off, Rose said, in a fight. His fearlessness gained him great respect among the Crows, and often he seemed to act as a war leader for them. His history is murky, with much disagreement among the authorities, but Andrew Henry did pick him up at the Arikara village and took him along to the mountains. Here Rose again joined the Crows, adopted their dress and costume, and traded his favorite rifle for a wife. As far as Clyman's account is concerned, he disappears after he joins the Crows in the mountains. Camp has more information on him, though much of his history after that point must be pure speculation.

Clyman seems to indicate that the trappers had already attempted to cross the Wind River mountains at Union Pass when they met Rose, but were blocked by deep snow.

When Clyman spoke with Montgomery in 1871 about this part of the trip, he mentioned that, in spite of Edward Rose, it seemed impossible to obtain information about the country west of the Big Horn. "I spread out a buffalo robe and covered it with sand, and made it in heaps to represent the different mountains, (we were then encamped at the lower point of the Wind River Mountains) and from our sand map with the help of the Crows, finally got the idea that we could go to Green River, called by them Seeds-ka-day...Fourteen days, from the Sweetwater to Green River we had not a drop of water, using snow as a substitute."

————

South Pass

With the help of Clyman's map, the trappers circled the south end of the Wind River Range and crossed the more open South Pass to the

Green River. The crossing was harder than Clyman indicates at that season, since the Pass is over eight thouand feet in elevation, and the weather was bitter cold.

Historians have argued, in their genteel (and sometimes not so genteel) manner about who crossed South Pass first, and who brought it into general use as a route across the mountains. Clyman's journal, with its casual mention of the route taken by the party he accompanied, at least makes this early crossing clear. It seems likely to assume that Clyman crossed the pass with his party in that first season, since he—a seasoned surveyor—says he did. Once the report of this crossing was carried to Ashley, the Pass came into general use by trapping parties, which led to its later use by pioneering parties. Clyman's journal entry for August 20, 1846, when he was on his way to Oregon, seems to indicate his knowledge that the party under Jedediah Smith brought the pass to the attention of the fur trade, even though other trappers may well have crossed the pass even earlier. As Berry remarks, "The pass is not a hidden crevice in a mountain chain, but a depression that ranges from twenty to thirty miles wide, which makes a good deal of the discussion about routes seem a bit beside the point."

Most of the mountain men took the Crows' designation of the Green River, calling it the Seedskeedee Agie, (Sage Hen River) variously spelled as Seeds-kee-dee, SeetKadu, Seetskeeder, Seeds-ka-day, Siskadee, and so on. Both names were used until about 1840, when Green River won out, for reasons that are probably obvious.

Clyman is modest in his narration of his hunt with Sublette, and passes casually over the fact that Sublette would probably had frozen to death had Clyman not found a live coal in their fire, warmed his companion, and then literally driven Sublette's horse ahead of him to safety. The story of Sublette, later one of the men who controlled the fur trade, might have ended right there without James Clyman.

———

Clyman's Long Walk

When Clyman began his lonely walk across 600 miles of wilderness to Fort Atkinson, at Council Bluffs, he couldn't know that Smith was nearby, and Fitzpatrick was only one day behind him in a bullboat loaded with the season's catch of beaver fur, a boat that would capsize in the boiling rapids at Devils Gate. Fitzpatrick and two other trappers walked into Fort Atkinson ten days after Clyman, after having made almost entirely the same journey. Jedediah Smith had ridden ahead searching for Clyman, seen his abandoned camp and Indian sign everywhere, and concluded that Clyman had gone under.

Camp says, "poor Clyman, confused and distracted, determined to walk to civilization, not knowing for sure whether he was on the Platte or the Arkansas, and seriously misjudging the immense distance to the Missouri."

But Clyman's notes on this period, though of course they were written decades later, give no indication that he was "confused and distracted," and he was an honest writer, who showed no hesitation in confessing that his courage was tested severely by being pinned down on a sandbar to be shot at by Indians. Much as Camp is to be respected, it is the editor's belief that Clyman assessed the situation, and that his decision to risk the walk was based on logic. As he mentions in his notes, if he turned back to find Smith or Fitzpatrick, he might find them; but he might run out of bullets first, and be in a worse fix. Or the rest of the party might have been wiped out by Indians. If he started walking toward the fort, some of the party might catch up with him, or he might find game, but he would certainly be no worse off. Whatever his thoughts, he walked and starved and struggled across part of present Wyoming and all of Nebraska; his mind was clear enough to keep him going.

John Hustis, a Wisconsin friend, later wrote of an experience from Clyman's long walk to the Fort:

He was cut off from his party & he was obliged to turn his face eastward. Avoiding rivers as dangerous he with his rifle and eleven bullets began his dangerous journey. Shooting such buffalo as was necessary for his subsistence he occasionally would rest & dry his meat. Once he killed a badger for his skin to cover his feet as his mocasins had given [out] & it cost him one bullet now becoming precious. At last after killing in succession three buffaloes with one bullet which he successfully cut from the animals & rounded again with his teeth & after eighty days wandering having three remaining bullets & a small amount of powder wearily plodding his way, at once he saw the American flag flying at Council bluffs & some men making hay near or at the present site of Omaha & he fainted away.

Since Clyman does not dwell on this almost unbelievable feat of survival in the story he later told Montgomery, the reader must imagine just how taxing it must have been, especially after the Pawnees relieved him of the tools of survival, and cut his hair. ("I bearly saved my scalp," Clyman later said, "but I lost my hair." Perhaps that's why he was so reluctant to cut it in later years.)

If your imagination needs help visualizing the hardships, read Win Blevins' description in *Give Your Heart to the Hawks*. But, just as he did not give up in the search for water, or quit during the long freezing night with Sublette—and on numerous other occasions when other men had—Clyman did not give up just because it was hopeless to think of walking 600 miles of prairie, much of it with no gun, no knife, no food. Still, it takes a tough man, not merely a desperate one, to club a badger to death with a bone, and eat him raw.

Clyman's reference to Fitzpatrick's cache of furs on Independence Rock before running down the river was no doubt as he heard the report, but was inaccurate. In August of 1842, John Charles Fremont attempted to float down the North Platte from the mouth of the Sweetwater in a rubber boat, with Fitzpatrick as one of the crew. Fremont's craft swamped in the second canyon. Apparently after they'd crawled out of the river—at least sometime after the swamping—Fitzpatrick mentioned that he'd lost a complete load of furs in the same river 18 years before. Fremont was no doubt a bit annoyed that he hadn't mentioned that fact earlier. (J. C. Fremont. *Report of the Exploring*

Expedition to the Rocky Mountains...1842, and to Oregon and North Caliornia...1843, Washington, 1845, p. 73.)

William M. Anderson, in his Diary of 1834, says Fitzpatrick's cache was near the mouth of present Alkali Creek, 60 miles west of Independence Rock.

The dangers of the fur profession can be seen in a memorandum written by Smith, Sublette and Jackson to John H. Eaton, Secretary of War, in 1829. The partners said that though they employed only about 80 to 180 men, 94 had been killed by Indians in a six-year period. Of course, Jedediah Smith lost 25 of those himself to the Mojave and Umpqua tribes during the disastrous explorations and travels through the Southwest in 1827–28. (Morgan, *Jedediah Smith,* pp. 344–5).

Chapter 3
Trapping in the Rockies, 1823–27

Clyman went to the mountains in 1823 and didn't return to St. Louis until the fall of 1827. His narrative of 1823–24, done in 1871, covers only his first year as a mountain man. Frustrating as it is not to have as much detail as we'd like about this year, it is far more regrettable that we have almost nothing at all from Clyman about the next three years. But by examining some of the other books written by men who won fame in this period, we can make some educated guesses about what Clyman was doing from 1824, when he crawled into Fort Atkinson after walking 600 miles in 80 days, until 1827, when he sold a pack of high-grade beaver in St. Louis and headed back to a life in Illinois that should have been a bit more quiet.

Fitzpatrick caught up with Clyman at Fort Atkinson, coming in ten days later after a journey almost as hard. He wrote at once to Ashley, giving him news of the wealth of furs found beyond South Pass, and the ease of the route. Once the word spread, the route became the great highway: first for trappers, then for missionaries, settlers, the whole cast of characters for civilizing the West.

Then, with an outfit furnished by Lucien Fontenelle, tough Fitz, who was also exhausted by his journey to the fort, turned around and went back to the cache near Independence Rock. He recovered the furs

(Berry says he had to dive for them, a miserable job), packed them on mules, and was back at Fort Atkinson October 26, 1824. Clyman may or may not have gone with him. We have no clear evidence either way, except what we may feel about Clyman's character and sense of duty.

By the time Fitz got back to Fort Atkinson, Ashley had arrived. Fitz had already sold his furs to Fontenelle, a promise probably made when Lucien outfitted him. According to Camp, "Ashley dealt with these men as independent free trappers and had no hold on them unless he could be first on the ground with supplies to trade for their furs." This information doesn't match the later descriptions of free trappers by Bonneville and Joe Meek. At this time, Fitzpatrick and some of the other trappers were trapping for Ashley at a set wage, so it is possible that Camp was misled, and that Fitz turned the money over to Ashley.

Ashley had other disappointments. He'd been campaigning all spring and summer for governor of the state, but lost. At about the same time, Major Henry had appeared in St. Louis with unwelcome news: he was quitting the fur trade. On September 24, Ashley received a license to "trade with the Snake Indians," but with Henry's resignation, he was without a field captain to handle the mountain end of the trade. So Ashley gathered up his supplies and headed for Fort Atkinson with his new license.

For two years now, white trappers were actually going to hunt furs themselves, not simply trade for them with the resident Indians. This was a new beginning for the fur trade—and was at least partly surreptitious. Some government authorities may have known the whites were trapping rather than trading, but ignored it. Camp said in his 1960 edition that this is why Fitzpatrick's letter to Ashley has never been revealed. Camp also indicated that, even at the time he completed his 1960 edition of Clyman's journals, it was difficult to get information from government files on these important times, the actual foundations of the expansion beyond the Rockies.

At least one writer on the period, Don Berry, suggests that the hostility of the Indians at the Arikara villages, and later, was in part because they would lose part of their market for furs with white trappers sent into the mountains. It's sound reasoning.

Back to the Mountains

The trappers under Jed Smith, including Clyman, had been west of the mountains all spring and summer, but they had no respite. Ashley apparently waited a week at the fort, hoping Henry would change his mind. But he left Fort Atkinson early in November, 1824, with a party of twenty-five men, fifty horses, and a wagon. The wagon, the first wheeled vehicle to travel the plains north of the Santa Fe trail, probably didn't last long in the snow. Clyman didn't comment on it, and neither did Ashley, in his narrative, so no one knows with certainty what happened to it.

Clyman was along on this trip, with Fitz, Zacharias Ham, and the half-breed James Pierson Beckwourth. Beckwourth wrote at some length about this period, but he wasn't content to stretch just a few stories; he stretched them all. Ashley's notes give more reliable information about Clyman's activities.

The trip must have been a nightmare. According to Ashley, quoted by Camp, the trail was knee-deep in snow, and no doubt the wind made the men even colder, even though they were fortunate in living before the invention of "wind chill factors." Riding a horse in a plains blizzard is risky; the rider may feel warm even while legs freeze from lack of movement. It's necessary to get off and walk to keep warm, but then clothing gets wet in the snow, and freezes solid upon remounting. In addition to these problems, Ashley expected to find food and fodder at the Loup Pawnee villages, but the Indians had moved on. Rations went down to a half-pint of flour a day cooked into gruel, with meat from horses that had died on the trail thrown in for flavoring. Plenty of horses must have died, since there was almost nothing for them to eat but cottonwood bark.

Crossing the Rockies

At the Forks of the Platte, they finally caught up with the Loup Pawnees and got horses and buffalo robes. Apparently the Pawnees also suggested that Ashley, who up to now had been following the route taken by Tom Fitzpatrick the previous summer, should move up the South Platte to find wood and better horse feed. For whatever reason they chose this route, they were now moving into country untraveled by any of the party before, and the route is an incredible one. The trappers came in sight of Long's Peak, and followed the Cache la Poudre northwest into the Rockies, by this time bound in snow and ice. Horses and men must have suffered terribly in crossing, as the route is high and rough. Ashley later wrote "The snow was now so deep that had it not been for the numerous herds of buffalo moving down the river, we could not possibly have succeeded."

They crossed the mountains somehow, and found grass and herds of buffalo, antelope, and mountain sheep in the Laramie Plains. Once the men had enough food they could begin to trap—but the going was slow because of the poor condition of the horses.

Late in March, 1825, they passed Medicine Butte (Camp's 1960 edition says this was Elk Mountain, about twenty miles southeast of present-day Rawlins, Wyoming). They crossed the North Platte, and went west by the Great Divide Basin, the Sand Hills and Steamboat Mountain (about forty miles northeast of Rock Springs, Wyoming). In that area the Crows stole 17 horses, reducing the party to a "dreadful condition." The men put their gear on their shoulders and walked on, picking up a few skinny horses the Crows had probably left behind as not worth the bother. The snow began to melt a bit, and a little grass showed. Then two more horses were recovered, and finally they found their own trail of the previous spring on the west side of the Continental Divide near South Pass.

Clyman and Fitzpatrick, now in familiar territory, were probably in a group sent to the Sweetwater to catch the horse thieves, but they returned with no horses, having missed the Crows.

Trapping the Green River

The party went on to the Green, where Ashley decided to explore. The men became a little restless while he was making plans, since they hadn't eaten for two days, but one of them killed a buffalo. On April 22, 1825, Ashley split his trappers into four divisions. Clyman, with six men, and Zacharias Ham, with seven, were chosen as leaders of parties to trap the headwaters of the Green to the north and west. Fitzpatrick's party, with six men, went south toward the Uinta Mountains, and Ashley took seven men to explore the river itself. He wanted to know whether the Green (Seeds-ka-dee) was a branch of the Colorado or whether it headed westward. His party took buffalo-hide boats down the river, finally dropping into the canyons where the Green slashes into what is now Dinosaur National Monument.

In choosing Clyman as a leader, Ashley called him one of his "most intelligent and efficient" men. His orders were to go to the sources of the Green and to try to find parties headed by Jedediah Smith and John H. Weber, supposed to be west of the mountains. Reading Jim Beckwourth's stories makes it clear that he was with Clyman, whom he calls "Clements." (Beckwourth, *Life and Adventures*, New York: 1856; pp. 62–67.)

Ashley agreed to take goods and baggage down the river to "some conspicuous point not less than 40 or 50 miles from this place." If the river didn't run that way, he'd choose "the Entrance of some River that may Enter on the West side of the Shetskedee [Green] for a desposite.... The place of deposite as aforesaid will be The place of randevoze for all our parties on or before the 10th July next & that the place may be known—Trees will be pealed standing the most conspicuous near the Junction of the rivers...or above the mountain as the case may be—." If there was no timber at the site, Ashley would pile a mound of earth five feet high, or set up rocks and paint the tops with vermillion. At a nearby point, a foot deep, he'd put a letter telling the parties any news they'd need before coming into camp. (Morgan,

"Diary of William H. Ashley," *Bulletin Missouri Historical Society,* 1954, vol. 11, No. 1, p. 34–5.)

So were plans made for the first rendezvous, that most famous legacy of the mountain men.

Clyman's group found beaver at once, which they trapped and shot. Game was easily found. But on a creek later called La Barge Creek, Indians who had been friendly a few days before attacked the camp at night. Clyman told the story to Montgomery in 1871.

After the parties separated, my party were doing well trapping beaver—when one day 17 Indians came to us and stayed for 3 or 4 days. At last, one night the Indians crept up and killed the man on guard [La Barge] with an ax, and charged on us with two guns a ball passed through my *capot* that answered for a pillow but did not touch me. We all sprang up. The Indians flew into the brush, we crawled out into open ground and made a little beastwork or fort of stone, just about daylight. They tried to get us out from behind it but didn't succeed. We fired at them and I think I killed one. We were very much discouraged—being only 3 [5] men in a country full of Indians, and concluded to take Fitzpatrick's trail and join him." (Montgomery, "Biographical Sketch of James Clyman," Bancroft Library, Calif MS; quoted in full in Appendix B of Camp's 1960 edition.)

Clyman's Fork of Green River was probably named, at least unofficially, at this time, as was La Barge Creek. Creeks were named for most of the original leaders of trapping expeditions, with the exception of Fitzpatrick. However, Clyman's name remained on the creek just slightly over ten years; eventually it became known as Fontenelle Creek, as it is known today.

———

The First Rendezvous

After Clyman joined Fitzpatrick, the parties probably trapped together until the first trappers' rendezvous on July 1, 1825. The exact location of this first rendezvous is still debated; it was at or near the junction of

Henry's Fork and Green River. Fred R. Gowans, in his *Rocky Mountain Rendezvous* locates it on a bench between Burnt Fork and Henry's Fork. Here the parties came together—Jedediah Smith and John H. Weber, Fitzpatrick, Ham and Clyman from the upper Green River basin, and some deserters from Hudson's Bay company. The trappers sold their furs to Ashley, probably for supplies.

Don Berry, in *A Majority of Scoundrels,* makes some interesting comparisons between prices paid by suppliers in St. Louis and those paid by the trappers in the mountains. In St. Louis, coffee was $1.50 per pound; in the mountains, $2. In St. Louis, powder was $1.50 per pound; in the mountains, $2.50. Of course, these prices varied from year to year; in some years the markup was up to 2000% on goods brought to the mountains for trade.

In the spring of 1826 Clyman took part in a feat that seems incredible—not the first or the last of his feats to do so. With three companions, he circumnavigated Great Salt Lake in skin canoes. His diary of June 1, 1846, mentions this fact casually, but it impressed his friends in Wisconsin, who often referred to it in later years. It's uncertain who went with him, but Camp thinks it may have been Louis Vasquez, Moses Harris, and Henry G. Fraeb. All off them suffered from thirst, found no beaver, and didn't find what they were looking for: an outlet from the lake, by which they hoped for a route toward the West. There is no outlet.

In the fall of 1826, William Sublette probably saw Yellowstone Lake, since the lake was named for him on early maps, though surely John Colter had already seen it. It's likely that others in Sublette's party included Clyman, as well as David E. Jackson, Robert Campbell, Jim Bridger and Daniel T. Potts. Potts later wrote the earliest authentic description of what is now Yellowstone Park. Jackson later wrote of trapping, with Sublette, the forks of the Missouri, the Gallatin and the headwaters of the Columbia, and this may have been when Jackson Hole was named. We have no way of knowing exactly where Clyman was during this period, but he often traveled with Sublette.

In January of 1827, Sublette and Black Harris started for St. Louis after supplies. As soon as the river broke up, the rest of the party started on a hunt on the Green. Probably Clyman was along. Sublette met other members of the party at the head of Bear Lake in the spring of 1827; in July, Jedediah Smith showed up too, returning from his first California expedition. With James B. Bruffee and Hiram Scott (who later died at Scott's Bluff) commanding the party, Jackson, Sublette and Clyman headed for St. Louis in the fall of 1827. Clyman had "the honorable post of being pilot," and it was probably his first chance to see St. Louis since he'd joined Ashley.

————

Clyman Escapes Blackfoot Camp

General Randolph B. Marcy later wrote of meeting Clyman in the winter of 1835 and hearing a tale that may have occurred during this period. General Marcy said he found Clyman "a very pleasant traveling companion and he very kindly whiled away the monotony of our long and solitary ride through that dense wilderness by relating to me several thrilling incidents in the history of his highly eventful career. As his character for honor and veracity are fully established and will, I dare say, be vouched for by the early settlers of Milwaukee, the reader may rest perfectly assured that every word of his narrative has the impress of reality and truth..." (Marcy: *Thirty Years of Army Life on the Border,* 1866, pp. 412–15.)

According to General Marcy, Clyman and a companion, while trapping in hostile Blackfoot country, were wisely visiting their traps only at dawn and late in the evening, hiding out during the day. They'd trapped for some time in this way when, riding through some heavy timber, they found themselves in the middle of a Blackfoot camp. Clyman, who Marcy says was "under all circumstance, cool and self-possessed," rode straight up to the chief's lodge, made signs indicating friendship, and claimed that the two had ridden into camp deliberately to pass the night. Clyman apparently reasoned that his bravery, coupled with his appeal to the chief's pride, might protect them.

The chief wasn't exactly friendly, but the women did serve food to the two trappers; unfortunately, their appetites seem suddenly to have deserted them. They ate a little and then lit their pipes. Clyman, who understood some Blackfoot, heard the chief tell some of the warriors that the two trappers should be killed. He warned his companion, and as soon as it was almost dark, and the Indians off their guard, Clyman leaped to his feet and ran for the river. His friend—and most of the Blackfoot—were close behind, the latter firing both balls and arrows after the trappers. Clyman got to the river, swam across, and hid under a bank on the opposite side. There he waited until the Indians had given up the hunt and gone back to camp. Once all was quiet, he emerged and tried to find the other trapper, but he was never heard from again.

This story bears a close resemblance to several others from the fur trade days, but that doesn't mean it's not true, and it certainly has merit as one of the few tales of adventure we have from Clyman. Camp speculates that Clyman's companion was Pierre Tivanitagon, an Iroquois, who was apparently killed by the Blackfoot in 1827. Ogden's Journal, quoted by Morgan (*Jedediah Smith,* p. 294), mentions the killing of "Old Piere," and Ashley also mentions it in a letter to Benton. Pierre was a deserter from Ogden's party in 1825, and had evidently joined W. L. Sublette's party to trade with the Blackfoot in July, 1827. It may be that Clyman was with this party. If so he, and possibly Sublette, must have left it late in the summer to return to St. Louis, where Clyman arrived before October 17, 1827.

Chapter 4
Return to the Settlements, 1827–44

Clyman returned to St. Louis from the mountains by way of the Platte-Kansas River route, according to his 1844 diary. His pack of high-grade beaver fur was sold to Wilson P. Hunt, the former Astorian, at St. Louis on October 17, 1827—278 pounds of "mountain beaver" at $4.50 a pound, a total of $1,251. (Morgan, "Ashley Diary," *Bulletin of the Missouri Historical Society,* April, 1955, p. 298.)

With this money, the equivalent of a couple of years' wages, Clyman bought land near Danville, Illinois. Residents of the area who knew him at this time have furnished descriptions of this mountain man, now 35 years old, a man in his prime, a man who had survived the mountains, but had been changed by his experiences. He was about six feet tall, rawboned, slender, and a little stooped. One friend mentioned his "firm and elastic tread," and said he was "deliberate in all his movements." He spoke clearly and distinctly with a slight Southern accent as a Virginian would, and his manner was courteous and dignified. He was not inclined to be garrulous or overly sociable; he was a little cool to strangers, and especially so to Indians.

G. C. Pearson, a pioneer who knew Clyman in Illinois, wrote in more detail of Clyman in his history of Vermillion County.

One well remembered by the writer was Captain Jim Clyman, a

genuine frontiersman, hunter and trapper, tall, spare in flesh, keen deep-set blue eyes, face and hands as bronzed as the color o smoked buckskin: hair that fell upon his shoulders: mouth that closed like a steel trap, surrounded by a heavy beard which with his hair was the color of dried grass. Habited in a composite dress of linsey-woolsey wamus [shirt], buckskin pants, and footwear, a coon-skin cap worn when in the settlement. His long full stocked flint-lock rifle, tomahawk and knife were never out of reach except when he was in the house of a friend which was seldom...Clyman's remarkable individuality attracted all who came in contact with him. At times when in the conversational mood he could keep listeners spellbound by narrating his personal experiences among the Indians: of the many hairbreadth escapes from capture, which meant death by torture, practiced only by the Indians; of his contests with mountain lions, panthers, grizzly bears, and other wild animals which furnish the furs so much in demand and are captured at such hazard to life." (G. C. Pearson, *Past and Present of Vermillion County, Illinois,* Danville, Illinois, Public Library, n.d.).

Clyman established two of his brothers on the farm near Danville, but he apparently didn't settle down there himself, at least not for long.

Congress had declared the Big Vermillion River navigable, and the stream was supposed to be kept free of mill dams and other obstructions. Clyman and William Reed, the first sheriff of the area, were authorized by court order in 1829 to proceed against a violator of the Act. In 1835 Clyman was called up to help Sheriff Thomas McKibben transport state prisoners.

Other records show Clyman entered business in a general store with Daniel W. Beckwith, setting up in one of the first log stores in Danville. Later Goulding Arnett took over Beckwith's share in the partnership and the firm continued under the name of Clyman and Arnett until 1839. Lands belonging to Clyman were then sold in order to pay off overdue notes.

The Black Hawk War

It is difficult to picture Clyman as a storekeeper after his mountain life, and perhaps he didn't spend much time behind the counter. When the Black Hawk War broke out, Clyman probably wasn't unhappy to join Capt. Jacob M. Early's Company of Mounted Volunteers, though it is hard to understand why such an experienced Indian fighter was not an officer. He enlisted as a private on June 16,1832 and remained until July 10 of the same year. During this period he served in the same company with two men, James Frazier Reed and Abraham Lincoln, who were to become well-known for different reasons in later years. Muster rolls in the James Frazier Reed papers show "James Climan" as No. 34, with Lincoln as No. 4 and Reed as No. 5.

Reed, who must have grown tired of settlement life, helped lead a group of people named Donner toward California; he and Clyman were destined to meet again during that fateful trip. And, as Clyman later said, "Abe Lincoln served in the same company with me. We didn't think much then about his ever being president of the United States."

Clyman's first campaign of the war was short, and details are well known. The company marched from Dixon's Ferry on June 27th to Whitewater River and searched the country for Indians. They found mosquitoes instead, as Lincoln later mentioned in his reminiscences. Perhaps typically, on the day the company was mustered out, "James Climan" was listed as "Horse Hunting."

Clyman was commissioned a 2nd lieutenant of Mounted Rangers July 23, 1832, and joined Jesse B. Brown's company in Major Henry Dodge's battalion. After the capture of Black Hawk the rangers moved down to Rock Island. There, on September 23, Lieut. Clyman was appointed assistant commissary of subsistence for the company.

The troops spent the next year removing the Winnebago Indians from their ancestral home in Wisconsin. On September 19, 1833, Clyman was transferred to the First Dragoons, and accompanied the command to Fort Gibson and finally to Missouri. From Missouri Clyman sent in his resignation, accepted May 31,1834. Two years later, he was appointed Colonel of the Wisconsin Militia by Governor Dodge.

When Clyman returned to Danville and his business, he was considered liable for past-due military accounts, some of which went back to the time of Clyman's predecessor in 1832, from the Commissary General of Subsistence at Washington. These notes requested the return of vouchers and abstracts of ration issues made during campaigns in the field; Clyman was charged on the books with over $400, and there is evidence he paid part of this sum during the next year.

Pioneering in Wisconsin

Presumably, Clyman operated his store and stuck to his business for about a year before adventuring again, this time to the north with a friend, Hiram Ross. Ross later reported that he and Clyman went to Wisconsin on horseback early in January, 1835, and recorded claims on government land. They stayed about three weeks in Milwaukee and then went back to Danville together. Late in February they started for Milwaukee again, with two teams loaded with provisions, spending seven or eight days on the trip. They built a sawmill on the Monomonee River about four miles from Milwaukee in the spring and summer of 1836. The mill, later known as the "Ross Mill," was located in the town of Wauwatosa, and built for the firm of Clyman and Arnett. Clyman furnished $200 to start the work.

In March, like any good citizen, Clyman paid taxes on his property in Milwaukee County; the lots he held are apparently now inside the city limits.

But Clyman soon became discontented with his Milwaukee claim, perhaps because so many settlers rushed in, and he headed north again, this time with Ellsworth Burnett. The adventure the two had was told by James S. Buck, in his *Pioneer History of Milwaukee,* (Milwaukee, 1881, Vol. 2, p. 13.)

On November 4,1835, the two headed toward Rock River to look for land. On the second day of travel, they reached the river and found an Indian wigwam. From the woman in it, they bought a canoe for 50 cents, put their baggage in it, and headed down river. They were hardly out of sight when the woman's husband and son returned home. They immediately chased the two white men, both to recover the canoe, and to avenge the death of the woman's brother, who had been killed by a soldier at Fort Winnebago two years before.

When the Indians caught up with them, Clyman and Burnett had landed and were preparing to spend the night in a deserted cabin. Burnett was inside building a fire, while Clyman was gathering wood nearby, without his gun. The two Indians moved in so quickly the white men had no notion of hostile intent. Clyman heard a shot, followed by a scream. Looking up, he saw the older Indian standing in the door of the cabin, waving at him to come quickly, saying that Burnett had accidentally shot himself. Clyman started for the cabin and had nearly reached it when the Indian raised his gun to shoot Clyman. Alerted (and one can only be surprised that an old mountain man had been taken in at all), Clyman began to run, zig-zagging to make himself a poor target.

The old Indian fired, hitting Clyman's left arm, and breaking it below the elbow. At the same time the son came out of the cabin, grabbed Clyman's own gun, and shot him in the thigh with a full load of buckshot. Then both Indians started chasing him. (Clyman later said it made him "mad as hell" to be shot with his own gun, but he wasn't in a position to do much about it right then.) Once he had gotten a little ahead of his pursuers, he hid under a fallen tree. At one point, they stood on the tree, discussing his whereabouts.

Once the Indians had given up the chase, and darkness had fallen, Clyman bound up his arm with his handkerchief and started walking toward Milwaukee, fifty miles away. He had no gun, and no food. He held his left arm in his right hand, and traveled all night during a hard rain. In the morning of the second day he came out near the Cold Spring. There he met an old Rocky Mountain trapper friend, John Bowen of Wauwatosa, to whom he reportedly said, "Oh John, how I wish we had taken you along. Wouldn't we have fixed them red devils!"

One can only imagine what else he probably said that historians of his day did not see fit to record. He was probably pretty disgusted with himself for not being more suspicious of the local Indians, not to mention his temper after walking two days on a leg filled with buck-shot from his own gun. Bowen took him to the house of William Woodward at Cold Spring, and dressed his wounds.

Buck, who recorded the story, said "As an exhibition of physical endurance, this had seldom if ever been equaled; and as a specimen of skill in wood craft, never." Buck probably never went west or trapped in the Rockies. Had he been on the spot at the time to listen to Clyman and John Bowen talk over shining times in the mountains, he might have heard reminiscences that would have altered his ideas about what was physically possible and what constituted "wood craft." Bowen, though Clyman never mentions him in his journals, must have been an intriguing character. He was apparently with Ashley in 1827, hired on at $110 a year, according to documents in the Missouri Historical Society. By the end of the year, the salaries of men hired at a given rate were reduced by advances enroute, and the sum each man was actually paid is also recorded. John Bowen was paid $109 at the end of the year. Don Berry, who quotes this information, says, "I'd give a lot to know what he spent that buck for in transit. It must have been a soul-rending decision."

The Indians were captured and put in prison, tried at Milwaukee, and pardoned by Gov. Henry Dodge—under whom, in Jesse Brown's company, Clyman had served when Dodge was just a major.

Local history has it that neither Indian was ever seen in Milwaukee again, and that no other Indian would stay in town more than twenty minutes once Clyman arrived. The shot was removed from his thigh by Milwaukee surgeons, but witnesses said he limped for a long time afterwards. He is said to have returned to the scene for his gun, a "double barreled stub and twist shot gun, large caliber," according to John Hustis, who was annoyed to discover later that Clyman had borrowed his pistol for the trip.

As a climax of this whole series of events, forty-nine settlers petitioned Congress to grant Clyman a square mile of land as a bounty since, they said, he'd lost $350 and use of his arm in the fracas. The petition called him "one of the most honorable and worthy citizens" of Milwaukee, and noted that it was not signed by Clyman "nor by any person in his name or in his behalf." The claim was not granted.

From 1836 until 1840 Clyman was apparently involved in his business at Danville. Some time later he took out a contract for the "placing of milestones on the old state road, laid out by authority of the legislature of Illinois, from Vincennes Indiana to Chicago."

At this time, Clyman was a Whig politically, and was marshal of the day at the January, 1841, celebration of Harrison's election. On July 4, 1842, he was listed as a colonel for a procession in Milwaukee.

Clint Clay Tilton, writing in the *Centennial Book of Vermillion County, Illinois,* in his description of the funeral of Dan Beckwith on Christmas Day, 1835, says this of Clyman: "Jim Clyman, hunter and fisherman for sheer love of the kill, sometime partner of Dan in his Trading Post in the 'Hole in the Hill,' and whose boast it was that razor never had touched his face nor shear snipped at his flowing hair, armed with pick and shovel, wended down to the old Williams Burying Ground and dug a grave in the frozen soil. There were other willing hands to help, but Jim, with the Soul of a Poet, wanted in this way to pay last tribute to his friend."

of The Review.

was obtained at a later gate, perhaps in my visit to S. Louis before
embassy of the Oregon Bill for the first time.

Notes on Chapter Four

If he'd sold them in the mountains, Clyman's furs would have brought
no more than $3 a pound. Since a mature beaver pelt weighed about
1¾ pounds on the average, Clyman brought in only about 167 skins,
presumably the part of his catch for the year 1826–7 not owed to the
company for supplies. This record is one of the few available as to the
returns from one man's trapping during this best decade of fur
hunting.

Clyman's rifle was left to his heirs, who still had it in 1960 when
Camp was working on his second edition. A percussion-cap rifle, not a
flintlock, it was inscribed "J. & S. Hawken." Its total length was 54
inches, with an octagon barrel, weight 13½ lbs., muzzle loader, with a
barrel 38 inches long from the firing chamber, 1⅝ inches in diameter
between flat faces, bore 17/32 inches, spiral rifling about ½ revolution
in total length of barrel, 7 lands and 7 grooves, double-set hair trigger
—a modified Kentucky rifle. Camp says the stock had been painted red
by Clyman's descendants for the Fourth of July parades in Napa, and
the ramrod was missing.

Clyman had lost one rifle in the fight with the Arikaras, and at the
time he was shot in Wisconsin was carrying a shotgun, so this Hawken

was obtained at a later date, perhaps on his visit to St. Louis before going over the Oregon Trail for the first time.

Chapter 5
Memorandum and Diary, 1840

This Clyman journal was originally the property of Hiram J. Ross, a friend and partner of Clyman's in the Ross-Clyman mill at Wauwatosa, near Milwaukee.

The diary may be typical of Clyman's activities during this 17-year period of a relatively settled life in Illinois. No other diaries of this period have been located. He may simply not have kept diaries, since his everyday life was less active than his trapping or later travel on the Oregon Trail, or they may have been lost.

The end of this short diary, with its list of accounts, is interesting because of the values given to various products, especially in contrast to the costs Clyman later found in the gold fields of California.

It is fascinating to speculate that there may be other Clyman journals, lost in a dusty archive somewhere. Clyman said in his conversations with Montgomery that he thought he'd sent a copy of his fur trapping adventures to the "Historical Society of Milwaukee" but no record of it has ever been found.

———

1840 Jan 1st

Light showers of snow a light wind from the NE—I am nearly all pealed with some kind of inflamation so as to scarcely be able to sit-up.

Mem—Heard yesterday that the stat[e] bank of Illinois had surrenedered her charter to the Legislature

Good Sleighing—Ross is making a sleigh in yard

Contracted with John Plum for Building a frame House 42 ft long 14 ft wide with a porch on—the S. Side 14 ft by 10 Plumb to cover and enclose.

Paid Plumb in advance for the work

John Plumb Dr

To 1 yoke steer $65—5 Bush potatoes $6750

Barrel pork 20$ 20 $97.50 [sic!] of all People it seems to me those are the most tiresome who never convers on any subject but their misfortunes.

1840 Jany 2nd

Morning overcast with light clouds pleasant winter weather.

It snowed moderately nearly all night last night Fine winter weather snow 5 or 6 inches deep.

Two things Infinite Time and space Two things more appear to be attached to the above infinity (wiz) Matter and number Matter appears to prevade the infinity of space and number attempts to define quantity of matter as well as to give bounds to space—which continually Expands before matter and number—and all human speculation is here bounden in matter and number leaving space at least almost completely untouched.

About the year 650 from the fowning [founding] of Rome the difficulties commenced Between Marius and Sylla from which I date the commencement of the decline of the Roman commonwealth.

1840 Jany 4th

Fine fair day.

Sent to Town for Midicien [medicine] have been confined to the house for 2 weeks.

During the years from 1823 to 1827, I passed my time with furr traders on & about the Region of the main chain of the Rocky Mountains and had frequent oppertunities for observation and have frequently thought that the great Quantities of mud Brot down by the Misourie was owing to the whole Region of the main mountain Chain h[a]ving at some remote period been burned and Torn to pieces by interval volcanic eruptions & as in that high and Dreary region there is continual and never varying strong west wind blowing the ashes emited would be continually carried and Lodged on the eastern verge of the mountain owing to its dry chimical and vitrious Qualities it never yet has been sufficiently saturated to give it solidity but is carried away continually in pr[o]digious large Quantities in the spring season when the snow thaws the water on many large tracts being almost as thick as it can move.

184[0] Jany 5

This morning has some appearance for a thaw.

Sent some [Illinois paper] money to Town yestarday & got it Exchanged at the Brokers office paid 15 per cent for exchang.

Cash 111. Paper 110$ Dr

To exchang By Broker 16.50

Bo[ugh]t Medicine of Doct Castleman Unpd

Every person that has ever passed through the western country must have observed the Quanty of granite Boulders that lay scattered all over the vast extent of country north west of the Ohio River and which seem to grow larger and more plenty in allmost Regular progression as you traverse the Region northward from the mouth of the Ohio as none of this rock is found in regular strata it has been a matter of much speculation to know how they came situate whare they are as likewise whare they came from and as all Speculation on this head must be mere conjecture my oppinion is that remote period the whole of the Missisippi valy was covered with water at which time those.

1840 Jany 6

Snowed lightly all day yestardy and last night still shews like thawing Bot. of Mr Eggleston 3600 feet of oak lumber at 5$ per M. 18.00 rocks were brought from the base of the Rocky mountains in the ice and carried southward wore let loos as they progressed by the thaws and sunk whare they are now found some have thought that they ware seen lying in Regular parirs on the prairies of Illinois But from my own observation I see nothing to confirm that singalar idea.

In our passage from the headswaters of White River of the Misouri to the Shiann [Cheyenne] River we passed over a high and most singular Tract of country of about 15 or 20 miles from East to west how far it extends N. & S. I cannot tell it is almost Completely bear of vege- tation nothing growing except here and there a stinted prickley pair the soil beng of a mast loose sterrile nature posible and the appearance extremely singular it having been all carried away by the thawing of the snows and shows of rain in to ravines of extreme depth leaving the plain verry uneven.

1840 Jany 7th

Qute moderate.

And standing full of rounded conical hillocks of pyramidial form some large at the Base and upwards 100 ft hig[h] and all sizes from that down to ordinary hillocks not more [than] three feet high From its present Shape I would Judge that at about the depth of 50 feet below the common surface of the earth the top being carried away to that depth from some cause or other perhaps from a greate accumila- tion of moisture a slight formation of sand stone occurs which shields the tops of all the larger mounds and from which cause retain their present elevation the earth being of all shades from height gray to a dark brown an becomes remarkably easyly saturated on the surface Mixing in large Quantities with the water the water where filled with earth has a sweet taste causing those that are under the necisity [of] using it to be remarkable costive [constipated].

1870 Jany 8

Cloudy and warm for the season.

After passing through this last Discribed Tract you arive at the foot of the Black Hill[s] a region of hills or rather rounded knobs and valies but without timber and a great scarcity of water allthough they are finely covered with nutricious grass and herbs.

The Black Hills are the first or most Eastern range of the Rockey Mountains and are generally well wooded with the various species of Pine Timber here we observed a picular feature in the substrata not found to my knowledge in any other part of this vast range of mountains the formation of Slate Rock in a verticle pile with a regular stratification of from 4 to 12 feet high & I observed in some deep ravines from 10 to 18 layers on top of each other in nearly a porpendicula pile some strata having a small inclination one way & some another with the horizon.

The anniversary of the Battle of New Orleans

This day the anaversary of Battle of N. Orleans appears to be allmost forgotten no firing salutes the rising day no gay parties of pleasure.

1840 Jany 9

Cloudy warm and thawy.

No military parade no rich dinners no splendid Feasts of Chanpain no high sounding patriotic toasts no gay cotilion parties no Bacanalian revelry—all still and quiet save only the common affairs of life no Bustle no hurrying to & fro no anxious and inquisitive looks—no stir save now & then the sound of the woodmans axe or the lonely team-ster calling to his slugish oxen as he slowly drive along.

How different to the days I have before seen so hath passed many of the greate days of Festivity now forgotten and given place to others like the retiring sound of some ancient forest oak which when first uptorn makes a tremendous crash but as it passes the echo grows more dull more distant untill it is lost in the surrounding forest.

1840 Jany 10th

Cloudy thawy misting with rain.

After passing the before mentioned Black Hill range of (of) Moun-tains we came into a uneven vally in which the heads of the Shianne and Powder River rises the former passing the Black Hills and taking an eastern direction falls in to the Missouri and [latter] taking a northern Rout falls in to the Yellow Stone River in their vally and on the hight of Land dividing the two river we found a great quantity of petrifactions Mostly of the vegatable Kingdom and on the North side of a ridge we pased allmost an entire forrest of petrified Timber apear-antly of the pine species the stumps of which were standing thick one of which I rode up to and which required some exertion for me to reach the top sitting on horseback the trunk of which lay scatered along in large chunks the Branches Broken up more small these petri-factions are very hard and Bring fire from steel The whole of this forrest of petrifactions appear to have been deeply embeded in the earth By ancient convulsion of the earth and the continual washing away of earth are now bringing them again to the light of (of) day the stumps stand some nearly perpendicular But mostly in an inclining posture some one way & some another.

1840 Jany 11th

It rained and snowed allnight last night this is Terrible stormy with [rain] & snow from the East.

I do not recolect that I saw any primitive rock in this place except some granite Boulders all the rock that I saw being secondary Lime rock although all the petrifactions and even pebble stone are verry hard and flinty and in fact all the rock formation in this region is Trasition and secondary Except it may be the state [state] before mentioned.

I have thought here it would not be uninteresting to give a discription of the Buffaloe with is habit althoug they have been so frequently described by other—The Buffaloe are of the gregarious Class and the females and all the young under three years old go sometimes in immense herds particularly in the fore part of winter whin they colect in the lower valies and most sheltered parts of the vast plains they inhabit whare they remain all winter if not interrupted The female keeping quite fat untill the spring thaws commence when all at once they become verry poor and lean in the course of a few days.

1840 Jany 12th

It froze considerably last night.

This is probably owing to the pecularities of this climate which is remarkably dry through the summer and fall months the vegitation having come to full maturity by the fore part of July The winter snows having nearly all gone by that time the shower all on a sudden cease to fall and the vegetation immediately dries up the earth becomes dry parched the vegetable matter remaining dry and unbleached untill the next springs thaws the winter commencing without rain the first fall being snow which usually commences about the first of November By this peculiarity of climate the grasses retain nearly all thier substance through the long Rockey Mountain winters But to return again to the Buffaloe in spring the thaws having commenced the animal becoming poor rapidly the hunter thin is looking daily for white Liver so called in the hunter phraze this white liver is allways fown [found] in female that [are?] forward with young which peculiarity is no way accounted for The liver instead of Being red and bloody as usual becomes of a pale light ash colour.

1840 Jany 13th

Cloudy, cold, and freezing, and so tinder that it hardly holds together and is a complete lump of fat and is considered the most delicate mess ever found in the animal.

In the later part of April and through the month of May the female brings fourth thier young which are all of a red colour and verry helpless for a few days frequently if the herd should be interupted and leave the (the) immediate place the females leave their young an fallow [following] the main herd never returning.

Immediately after the grass begins to spring the Buffaloe Begin to scatter from the lower plains and assend the more lofty parts of the mountain region in small heards the males generally solitary and alone find their way into the small mountain glens whare they remain feeding on the young and tender vegitation and when satiated continually rubbing off the old winters coat against trees rocks Banks or any hard body they.

1840 Jany 14th

Cold and clear.

Come across making a low grunting nois not much unlike the grunt of a hog the males which come through the winter nothing but skin and bone now Begin to [shed?] remarkably fast and in 5 or 6 weeks after the young herbage begins to spring then are fine fat fleshey and good beef as are the females likewise that do not give suck and from a weatherbeaten light brown they all now become a fine sleek black about the middle of July they again begin to assemble in large heards their running time haveing commenced a short time previous.

The apears to be the night the time of sleep and rest for the vegetable kingdom leafless and frozen they are now taking their rest and matureing the subsistance they recieved during the last summer it apears as if the revolution of the earth around the sun was the day & night for the vegetable as is the earth's revolution on its own axis.

1840 Jany 15th

Clear and verry cold the time for activity and rest to animal tribes.

Sleep is a curious and singular phenomonon in the more active animal as likewis in human species Nearly all the animals that prefer night time for collecting thier substance seems to have the peculiar adaption to the taking of a long and torpid sleep in the winter however many animals that would seek subsistance in daylight in their natureal wild state are so timerous and fearefull of man that they are compeled to take the night for what they would prefer the day and therefore seem to prefer what is entirely contrary to their natureal inclination.

The velocity of light seems to be the greatest of all known principals unless electricity should be greater some have thought that Electricity is instantaneous throughout all universal space I can hardly think this to be the fact but if it should.

1840 Jany 16

Clear still more cold.

It puts to rest the difficult question of infinity of space For if any known and palpable principle is instantaneous through eternal space then eternal space may be infinite as to bounds and duration and mater may likewise be infinite as to quant[it]y and duration. But on the contrary if no known palpable or impalpable principle or matter can be found but what is limited by size or time then infi[ni]ty means nothing more than such an imense mass of space matter or time as becomes immeasureable and incomprehensable to all means of comparison for instance.

We may comprehend the globe we inhabit pretty fully and even the sollar System but a million of such systems becomes incomprehensible allthough even a million such Systems may fall verry short of the quantity of matter in existance throughout the universal Kingdom.

1840 Jany 17th

Verry cold but appears to moderate alittle.

But notwithstanding this immense quantity still Finity becomes a part of infinity and the globe being Finnite or measureable so by comparison of one measurable part or particle of infinite matter occupying a speck of space may we geathur some crude Idea of infinity itself although this Idea may ammount to nothing more than to say all things have thier Bounds and Limits space has its bounds and time has its limmits mater ocupies all space and time wears out all things some seem to think that infinity means something that cannot even have a beginning nor an end and that if it were possible to move with the velocity of light for millions and millions of years and even time without limit that you then have not more than set out But admit all this and say that after you have floun [flown] with the speed of light for as many years as there is particle of sand.

1840 Jany 18th

Quite moderate.

Included in the whole Solar System even at that immense time and immense swiftness if you have advanced a quarter of an inch comparatively you at once give imaginary Bounds to space although it may not be posible to measure or comprehend but a verry small quantiy of Space or matter.

The Jewish History of the beginning and formation of matter gives definite bounds as it ware in respect to time but not so definite as respects Quantity. It says in plain words that the grate universal and eternal esence of matter was six days in making or rather in collecting and araingeing three of the greate globes of our Solar Sustem (viz) The earth the sun and moon The sun however as the center should come first the earth second and in this we have a Tolerable fair history First chapt of Cenesis [Genesis] 1st verse In the beginning God created the Heaven and the earth.

Now here appears to be three distinct Periods.

1840 Jany 19th

Clean and pleasant.

The first as to time which is—in the beginning T[he] second as to space—The Heaven— the third as to matter—the earth.

Now as to time allthough there could be no time much anterior to the begining nor no Place anterior to space which I take the word— Heaven. Here to mean in fact their could be no measure for time as we now understand the term untill some matter was brought into actual motion and the first revolution of the first globe of matter would be the actual beginning of all things but in the second verse we read—*the spirit of God rested upon the waters*— which I take to mean that the water then existed in that part of space now oncupied by the Earth.

1840 Jany 20th

Warm and thawing a little.

1840 Jany 21st

Cold strong wind from the W.

1840 Jany 22nd

Clear and Cold.

1840 March 10th

Oliver P Nichols Dr to 1 Barrell Pork $15.00.

Chapter 6
Clyman Takes the Oregon Trail, 1844

By 1844, 17 years since Jim Clyman left the mountains, sold his furs in St. Louis, and bought land in Illinois, one would assume he'd successfully made the transition from restless mountain man and trapper to farmer and businessman. But, as Buck said, "Colonel Clyman belonged to that class of men ever to be found in advance of civilization, who form the advance guard, the pioneer proper. Consequently the country had no sooner began to settle up, than he was away."

Once again, Clyman seemed to see the country "settling up" around him, and—probably in spite of his best intentions—he was ready to move on again.

He was fifty-two years old, no spring chicken by the standards of any age, and definitely getting old by the standards of the 1840s. He should have been bouncing grandchildren on his knee, but as far as we know, he didn't have any children yet—a curious point. Most of the trappers took Indian women as wives, or at least companions while in the mountains; consequently, most had a tipi full of half-breed children somewhere in the mountains. But no record has been found that indicates Clyman ever lived with a woman during his trapping days, or married back in the settlements.

More than one trapper left his Indian offspring behind with her family when he left the mountains, and quite often married a white woman as soon as he returned to the settlements. Some traded the woman off to another trapper; that's how Joe Meek won his Mountain Lamb. But Clyman doesn't seem to have been the type to abandon responsibility quite so lightly. Perhaps he confined his search for companionship to brief relationships, and steered clear of the responsibilities of children. Perhaps he was celibate—hard to believe, given what we know of Clyman and the life of the mountain man in general. Since he didn't see fit to discuss this aspect of his life in the journals, we simply don't know, and probably never will.

Since Clyman remained in the settlements so long, it's unusual that he didn't marry and settle down during that period. Again, the diaries we have don't mention the subject, so anything we might say is sheer speculation. Clyman's diaries show him as a man of emotion on several occasions, but also seem to indicate his awareness that he might be writing for publication. On several occasions he omitted happenings from his diary because they disgusted him, and in some instances he lists the names of men who participated in events of which he clearly disapproved. (For example, on June 24, 1845, during his travels in California, he mentions the capture of a "female" Indian by two men in his party, who also took her horse. There is no further mention of the Indian woman, but Clyman carefully notes the names of the men responsible for the capture.)

So perhaps he simply left out of his journal anything he felt would not reflect to his credit with later readers.

With no family to hold him, in the spring of 1844 Clyman packed up and headed down to Wisconsin and beyond on horseback to "see the country and try to find a better climate." He later told a reporter he was looking for a better climate to rid himself of a cough that had troubled him during the cold winter just past. "Did not improve in health —had a cough in winter. In winter of 1842–43 was very unwell— weather was very cold—perhaps in consequence of the great comet that year, near the sun," he said.

He might also have been, like most mountain men when they

return to the settlements, just restless. Managing a store and presiding at parades were a bit tame after life in the mountains.

Horseback, he rode through Arkansas and back into Missouri where, at Independence, he found emigrants assembling for the passage across the plains. The promise of free land in Oregon, and a paradise for settlers in California—still a Mexican possession—had inspired practically every farmer in sight. From Missouri, Illinois, Indiana, Kentucky, Tennessee and points east came a new class of pioneers, packing great quantities of household possessions into covered wagons, buying oxen with which many of them were unfamiliar, and heading west to the promised land.

This had all been going on for several years, but perhaps Clyman had not really seen it so clearly before. At Independence, he may have found old mountain friends who gathered to watch and laugh at the innocents who thought they could cross the plains carrying great grandmother's grand piano, or who were hired as guides. Mountain men made the best guides available for emigrants crossing the plains, because a clear knowledge of the lay of the land was necessary to their profession. In addition to knowing how to cross the country, they knew good streams, and spots where they could hide from Indians—knowledge essential to saving their hair. Trappers had mental maps of the country that map makers didn't catch up with for fifty years.

Perhaps Clyman was simply caught up in the excitement and wanted to cross the plains again, see the rest of the western country for himself. Perhaps he remembered how alive—in spite of Blackfoot arrows, lurking grizzlies and setting traps in freezing water—he'd felt in the mountains. Or perhaps there's no need to search for an explanation that sounds logical to modern ears. Clyman had been pioneering since he was a child in Virginia; he wasn't ready to sit on a barrel behind a store counter and get fat. Always keenly interested in what was happening in his world—even on the plains his journals mention presidential campaigns—he wanted to keep right on pioneering.

Clyman couldn't go back to trapping, even if he'd wanted to; after 1840, the demand for beaver fur almost ceased to exist, and hundreds of trappers had depopulated the beaver streams Clyman helped find with Ashley's men. Times were slow for former trappers, many of whom simply couldn't adapt to "civilized" life and stayed in the mountains with their Indian families, disappearing from the history books. The American Fur brigade had rendezvoused for the last time on Green River in 1840.

About 1500 persons started west in 1844, the largest number in a single year. Five groups started, and the three largest of these went through to Oregon—companies led by General Cornelius Gilliam, John Thorp, and Colonel Nathaniel Ford. Clyman joined Ford's group of about 500 persons at Independence, and seems to have acted as treasurer for a part of the outfit, according to his journal.

Chapter 7
Notebook One
The Oregon Trail, Independence to Little Blue River

May 14 to June 30, 1844

1844 of May the 14th

Left Independence & proceded on to West port Roads extremely bad owing to the Leate greate rains 15 at Westport morning dull slight rains about 10 left West port continues to rain all day passed the head of Blue River [Indian Creek] came to camp at Elm Brook [Mill Creek] passed the methodist mission [at Shawnee, Kansas] and Several Shawnee Indian Formes in the course of the day made 18 miles [to Cedar Creek].

16 It rained all night last night in one continued and rapid Shower This morning the whole prairie covered in water Shoe mouth deep no wood to be had except what we had hauled in waggons Started throug the rain about 8 miles over a roling prairie covered nearly knee deep in mud and water camped about ½ mile from timber [N. E. of Gardner] packed some up to camp on our mules it continued to rain all night Slightly.

16[17] Got up our teams and put to the road again made 9 miles to Black Jack creek [Captain Creek] amuddy desolate looking place about non to day left the Sant a fee trace [Santa Fe Trace] these are two of the longest roads that are perhaps in the world the one to Sant Afee and the other to Oregon doubled teams nearly all the way Both teams Swamped down and had to unload our team breakeing an axeltree.

17[18] About 9 oclock it begain to rain again it [rained] all day so much that we could not finish our axeltr[ee] continued to rain all night and our beds ware overflown in water nearly mid side deep 19 Sunday a dismal rainy thick morning, all Brot to Stand about 11AM after a Tremendeous Shower it Slacked up for the rest of the day got a new axel tree in and reloaded our waggon Saw & picked a considerabble fine mess of ripe Strawberies.

20 Thick and foggy the women & children are coming out again haveing been confined to the waggons for 2 days past went to a camp of 4 waggons in the fore noon returned and crossed the western-Branch of Black Jack country high roling Prairie interspersed with numerous small groves of Timber Five wagons left encamped a ½ mile Behind us Two men returned this morning after some cattle that had strayed away.

Afternoon doubled teams and moved 4 miles camped on a high ridge in a small grove of Brack oak 2 fine looking yong Ladies in camp.

22[21] Laid at camp all day to wait for the falling of the waters and drying of the roads 2 teams that ware behind came up this evening.

22 Moved ahead 8 miles over roling hilly Prairie 6 miles crossed dirty muddy Brook [Cole Creek north of Sibley] camped on the waukarusha Quite a fine little rivulet with a fine dry bank on the East Side Several Shawnee Indians pased our camp yesterday and to day a fine clear day with brisk south wind dug a kind of a road down the bank &c.

23 A fine clear night and a pleasant morning the small river Waukarusha (to) yet to ford with teams walked out through camp observed all sizes and ages Several fine intelegent young Ladies engaged one of them to make me a pair of Pantaloons picked some strawberries a handsome country fine land but timber shrubby 5 waggons came up to day 2 men from the mountains stoped an hour at our camp from some of the trading Stations on the arkansas a Lot of pack mules Likewise passed us on their way to Fort Larrimie.

We have been passing through lands sofar belonging to the Shawnee nation or Tribe of Indians nearly all of which Tribe have Quit hunting and gone into a half civilized manner of living cultivating small Lots of ground in corn Beans Potatoes and grains and vegetables their country is almost intierly striped of all kinds of game but is fine and Productive in grains and Stock both horses and cattle Timber is scarce but finely watered in part the trail passes through The company of pack mules and ponies that passed to day are a part of Mr. Bissenettes [Bissonette] and will [follow] 7 or 800 miles of our rout.

24 It rained all night by day our teams ware moving to the river which we had been expecting [to] fall but which began to rise again we let down by cords over a steep rock bluff through mud knee deep an[d] in the rain pouring in torrents me[n] women and children dripping in mud and water over Shoe mouth deep and I Thought I never saw more determined resolution even amongst men than most of the female part of our company exhibited The leaving of home of-near andear friend the war whoop and Scalping Knif The long dreary Journey the privations of a life in a Tent with all the horrors of flood and field and even the element seemed to combine to make us uncomfortable But still there was a determined resolution sufficient to overcome all obsicles with the utmost exertion we crssed over 20 waggons by about 10 o'clock when the waters became too deep to cross and in about an hour it rose so as to swim a horse it continued to rain in rapid Thunder Showers all day with a strong S.W. wind

25 It slacked raining about dusk and did not rain any during the night tho river rose 6 or 7 Feet during the night about 8 the sun made a (a) faint glimering appearance all hands Buisy in contriving ways and means to cross the teams remaining on the oposite side We had a kind of an election which resulted in the chois of Col [Nathaniel] Ford for our capt or leader By a considerable of a majority all seem to enjoy good health not with standing our extremely disagreeable Situation and a Mr [L.] Everhart who is taking a trip for his health swam his horse several times since [coming] here and is making rapid impovements in his health one verry ordinary conoe being all we have for a ferry boat our crossing progresses verry slowly and the water continues still riseing

26 A fine pleasant night and a clear morning the Ladies passing from Tent to Tent Early our ferrying continues to progress Slowly Some young men got a hymn Book and sung a few familiar reformation camp meeting songs last night which had a peculiar Symphonic and feeling Effect in connection with the time and place. a call was made this morning for a regular organization.

The before Mentioned men 19 in number in 7 waggons formed in to one mess for mutual assistance in traveling and encamcamping near togeather about 2 oclock we got all our Teams waggons and Baggage over & assertained that there ware 92 men present made some regulations to prepare for keeping of a night and day guard as we are now not more (the) [than] 2 days easy travel from the Kaw Indian villagis the first of the wild roveing tribes that we meet with on our way this evening two waggons that ware in the rear came up opposite side & we ware told that 12 or 15 Teams are yet comeing on it has been fine and clear & the evening pleasant the Ladies gave us a few hymns in the afternoon which had a pleasant meloncholly affect

27 A great stir commenced early & a little after sun rise waggons began to roll out at 7 in morning we made 8 miles in an Northerly direction over a picturesque and rather hilly prairie The waukarusha that has given us somuch trouble & consumed so much time is about 12 rods wide running from S. W. to N.E. & Entering the Kanzas or Kaw river about 8 or 10 miles below our last encampment for the first time we have this evening encamped on ridge of prairie & in the form of a hollw squair early in the afternoon it commenced raining again & rained in thunder showers all night.

28 The earth completely covered in water at 7 got under way although it continued rain a thick fine rain 2 gents and myself started for the Kanzas river with a view of examining the roads and the

[Papan's] ferry proceeded on about 18 miles to acreek & found it verry high and rapid being swolen by the last nights rains turned loose our animals to graze and consult remained about an hour saw a heavy shower coming up from S.W. Saddled our mules & after finding the creek was swimming, (and) started back for camp a tremendeous shower came on before we fairly got saddeld and in 10 minuits we ware completely drenched with rain it continued to rain all the way to camp the roads being deep and heavey thee teams ware Scattered about 2 miles in length along the open prairie ridge on which they ware traveling each one pressing on to some shelter through mud and rain became discouaged one by one and stoped on the ground whare they happened to be many without fire or cooked provision to nurrish them after a verry tidious & toilsome d[a]ys drive I arived at my mess wet as water could make me and found them all sheltering themselves in the best way they could about the waggons they ware fortunate enough however to have furnished themselves with a fair supply of wood & now commenced the tug of war for the rain again renued its strength & fell in perfect sluces as though the windows of heaven had again been broken up and a second deluge had commenced intermingled with vived flashes of Lightning and deep growling thunder which continued until about dark when it slaked up for the night, and here let me say there was one young Lady which showed herself worthy of the bravest undaunted poieneer of [the] west for after having kneaded her dough she watched and nursed the fire and held an umblella over the fire and her skillit with the greatest composure for near 2 hours and baked bread enough to give us a verry plentifull supper and to her I offer my thanks of gratitude for our last nights repast Billitts of wood ox yokes Saddles and all kinds of matter now Became in requisition to raise our bodies above the water and we spent a verry uncomfortable night in all the forms of moisture short of swimming.

29 Truged around through the mud and water Shoe mouth deep got a bite of Breakfast and put to the road again our whole distance yesterday being about 12 miles again made a scattering drive 6 miles to the Tunga Nunga the creek spoken of yesterday in the afternoon all the

teams came up encamped on a fine dry Bluff on the S side had a clear
night and fine.

30 Morning rode over to the Kanzas found it verry full and S.
Bank overflown several teams crossed to day the day fine & fair saw a
number of the Kaw Iindians a misrable poor dirty Lazy Looking Tribe
and disgusting in the extreme To lazy to work and to cowardly to go to
the boffaloe whare they frequently meet with their enemies get a few
killed and return to dig roots Beg and starve 2 or 3 months then make
another effort which may or may not be more successfull our ferrying
goes on Slowly it being difficult to get to the boat on account of the low
grounds being overflown.

31 A fine clear night and a pleasant morning Mr Texes Smith
mess leaving for the Ferry & Capt Ford followed our mess remain to
give the women a chance for washing pased on to the Kanzas about 16
waggons having passed over the river without much difficulty.

1844 June the 1s Satturday

Made 4 mils yesterday Encamped on the Bluff near the Ferry
performed a singular and Farcicle operation of guarding our stock
running loose on the Prairie & found them more scattered this
morning than if we had let them roam at (at) large a warm morning
with the appearance of rain went out early to get in our horses could
not find my horse and a mess mates mule both fine animals slept rest-
lessly rose early.

2 Started in search of my horse & comrades morins mule rode
around our encampment several times and back on our trail 3 or 4
miles at last took the track down the course of the Kanzas on an
Iindian trail followed our anamals about 8 miles when they lef the trail
and went in to a thicket whare our anamals had been tied [to] a couple
of large trees and saw the bed whare one of the Kaws had Spread his
couch near by and taken a happy and no doubt pleasant repose over
his rascaly and ill gottin treasure after examination we followed on
again over rocky bluffs smoothe prairies and Brushy thickits untill no
doubt we ware discovered for our anamals had been put to the keen
Jump and run 3 or 4 miles when caution again was taken and hard

rockey Bluffs again taken untill we became discouraged and nearly lost orselves arived at 5 evening at camp.

3 Put to stand to know what measures to take to recover our Lost animals crossed over the river hired two Indians and made another Trial to find our animals went back to whare we left the Trail Last night followd it 5 or 6 miles to whare we came to the main waggon Trail about 15 miles East of our encamp 9 Teams having passed a few hours previous we could not follow any further Returned to camp tired and dijected with fair prospect of making the remainder of our long Toilsome Journey to Oregon on foot and here let me remark that this is [the] third season that a considerabbl emegration has pased right through the Kaw village and crossed the Kanzas at this place yet I have not heard that Maijor Cummings or any other agent or Interpeter has ever been here at the time they passed which is certainly a great deriliction of the duties of an agent Last year I understand that the Emigrant[s] lost that never ware returned 3 or 4 horses & 20 or thirty head of neat cattle and a considerabl amount of other property and we have Lost 200 Dollars worth or horses mules and other property which might be mostly recovered if time would permit and we had an intirperter that would look to our intrest but as it is we must submit without recourse the Kaws are now starting on their summer hunt and our Stolen horses cannot be obtained untill they return which will not be untill some time about the first of august or latear.

4 A thick foggy morning 9 cle[red] off fine & pleasant all hands still engage getting our stock across the river which is begining to fall one of our Indians returned without finding our animals nine Teams came up on the oposite side of the river I am inclined to think that there is a much better Raut than the one we are taking By crossing the Kanzas at ferry on the Military road leading from Fort Levenworth to Fort Scott and Taking the high lands between the Kanzas and wolf river still Keeping west after passing wolf river between the Nimihaw and Kanzas untill you pass the heads of the Nimihaw you gain the main high land between the Kanzas & Great Platt whare insted of Swiming rivers you will heave to shape your course so as to strike water once or twice a day and bear on to the Great platt near the head of the grand Island.

5 Crossed over the river went 10 miles up the river to the village of the head chief a tall lean wrinkld faced Filthy looking man with a forehead indicating deceet Dissimilutoin and intriegue and more like a Beggarly scape gallows than a Chief but nodoubt these fine Qualities are higly prized by the Kaw nation after telling him through an interperter that whites wanted nothing of the Kaws than a passage through their country the water thy drank and the wood thy kooked their victual with all other things that thy injured or used they would pay for and that I took it verry unkindly of him to allow his young men to steal our horses and cattle He talked with great energy assuring me that if he could See his rascally scamps with our horses he would immediately bring them to us and assured us that in three days he thought we might expect to see our horses I how-ewer put but little confidence in his asseverations a clear warm day and a warm night.

6 Returned to camp awarm clar morning all waiting for the rear of our camp to cross the river about dusk in the evening Jo a kaw who speaks pretty fair English came up to our camp & told me that 2 young men had been down to the Shawnees and came back with three ponies Suspicions had rested on these two scamps for some days past that they had stolen our animals and now the thing was explained.

7 Three of us and two friendly Kaws started to overtake the two horse thieves who had followed a party that ware starting out on a Buffeloe hunt it commenced raining early & continued all day late in the afternoon after swiming two creeks & wadeing three more breast deep I arived at [the] village in the midst of a Tremendeous hail storm And found about 20 Drunken Indians in a dirt covered lodge half knee deep in water Judge of my feeling a rapid hail Storm out[side] a hog wallow within all in unison the Thunder Lightning & hail the schreems an yells within and my object to recover stolen property being insantly known all eyes ware directed on me a loud angry Quarrel commenced between my Friends and enemies and my situation was far from being envious for Knives ware soon drawn and one Flurrished over my head the indian that held it was soon grappled & a half dozen ware as soon wallowing in the mud on the ground floor of the Lodge.

8 Returned to camp which had moved about 12 miles up the river did not reach the camp till after midnight in a tremendious thunder Shower lay down dripping with water and as soon as I Became warm fell asleep and slept soundly untill day light though the water raised in a perfect Spring in under us.

9 Sundy. No guard last night and two horses and two mules missing walked up the creek a little and saw the Moccosin tracks under a steep Bluff all explained the animals ware Stolen after a considerable search found whare they had swam the creek Capt Ford and 10 men went in persuit could not move camp on account of high water in the afternoon Capt Ford Discovered two indians on high points in the prairie on approaching them he found they were in possession of his lost animals and he brought them to camp the Kaws said that they found the mules & horses in possession of an Oto Indian whoom they beat and whiped and took the stolen horses from him and ware returning to us with them when capt Ford first saw them but this story did not go down with many of us.

10 It commenced raining about an hour before or 2 before daylight and rained all day without a moments cesation the creek on which we are encamped bears the dignified name of Knife river and rose 15 feet during the day the [Kaws] that had Capt Fords Horses went away to day verry much disadisfied not getting as much pay as they expected Several of us tried to make them understand that we had sent to Fort Levenworth for an escort of (of) dragoons & hope it may have a good efect.

11 It continued to rain all night and is still raining the prairie has become so soft that it will [not] bear the weight of a man in many places Several persons are becomeing discouraged on account of our slow progress and it is almost enough to discourage the stoutest and bravest amongst us I now see the water spreading on all the low grounds & if it was not for the strip of timber it [would] have the appearance of an extensive Lake.

12 No guard last night it rained all night but not so rapid as to keep the creek up as it fell about 3 feet 8 oclock we saw a watry glance of the sun for about a minuit all camp regulations are lost & each individual seeking a dry Sheltered spot to stand or lie down on our Tents beds blankets clothing provision and every thing almost rotting and no prospect of drying them and even our cattle are Scarcely able to walk the mudy weather having given them the fouls. It still continues to rain moved camp a ½ mile to escape the mud which resembled a brick yard on our old encampment without the least strech of immaginution.

13 It rained all last night verry rapidly & the creek rose again 6 or 8 feet 10 A.M. we saw the sun & a general shout was raised through all the camp after 80 hours steady rain we saw the Kanzas river from the Bluffs & it shews 8 or 10 miles wide the sun shines pale and watry with no fair prospects of clear weather.

A great Dijection in camp as it is imposible to overcome natures obsticles & many are brooding over fine houses dry beds & pleasant Society all of which are scarce here on the bluffs of Knife river & the distance and circumstance allmost seem to forbid our ever regaining any of the comforts of civitization and verry little encouragemet can be given to the fearefull and Timerous.

14 A thick foggy morning but Some prospect of Better weather sadly disappointed we barly saw the sun through thick foggy showers aand the day closed in without drying our clothes & provisions.

15 A dull Foggy morning without any pospect of clear weather a disaffected camp without unity or concert in any matter except Sleeping which is performed by the male part of the camp to the greatest perfection several complaining of the chollic.

Ten oclk Maijor Richard Cummings arived on the oposite side of the creek on his way home from running some lines between The Kaws & Pawnees the maijor is goverments agent for the Kaw & Several other tribes of Neighbouring Indians & we ware well pleased to see him so near us.

16 (Sunday) The clouds braking away with a prospect of fair weather to dry our Baggage one clear day the first we have seen for 8 drid all our Baggage and commenced making a raft to cross the creek the camp looks Quite cheerfull this evening and our prospects have a better appearance for Traveling.

17 Commenced early to make preperations for crossing the creek about [?] it commenced hailing from the west but soon changed to rain one hour more of fair weather would have seen apart of us on the other side but such was not our fortune and when we will be able to leave the Bluff on which we are encamped the Lord inhis provedence either of Mercy or anger only knows.

At 2 P.M. the rain slaked up & all hands to work again we By active exertion crossed over 19 Teams and encamped on a miserably dirty muddy Bottom that had been overflown 6 or 8 feet deep only 24 Hours previous.

18 Thunder & an apearance of more rain a warm sultery disagreeable morning & no better pospect of dry weather than there was a month since when the rains commenced against all expectation the day passed without rain and all hands moved out about 1 mile on the Prairie & the sun set clear for once at last.

19 How Sadly are we freguently mistaken when we depend on our own calculations for the sun had hardly shot its last rays over the western horizon when a small Black cloud shewed itself in the S.W. and the grumbling thunder began to growl & in ten minuits a rapid thunder Shower was desending in torrents on us which however was not of long duration for it passd off to the S.E. & about dark gave us a Splended natural meteorick Exhibition the electrik fluid Sparkling and flashing in front & byond the dark heavy masses of fleecy cloud which shewed like frowning mountains Stupendeous rocks & deep chasms & dark raviens illuminated with dazzeling brileancy too bright & glancing for the eye to dwel on & might be truly be called the Sublime aweful.

Rolled out early through the rain which continued untill 12 o'clock when the sun broke out had several views of the Kanzas river which was overflown from Bluff to Bluff 8 or 10 miles wide made 10 miles encamped on a narrow ridge ½ mile from timber a Bright clear evining and a fine view of extensive uneven Prairie pospect.

20 A fine fair morning rolled out along a ridge Northwardly on account of the back water from the Kanzas made 5 miles and halted to look for a passage over the Black vermillion Several returned after some hours of fruitless search the Teamsters becoming tired of waiting took a S.W. Ridge made about 5 miles & encamped a good ford having been discovered on the best course we returned to camp the day haveing been clear & bright the highlands are becoming firm.

21 Some for Rafting near the mouth of the creek some for returning to the ford discovered and some for hunting another ford after about 4 hours search another ford was discovered and we rolled out to it Distant 3 miles and immediate set to work to prepare the banks (which are verry steep and muddy) for crossing in about 2 hours we commenced crossing & more than half the teams passed over the river Jordan (or vermillion as it is called) and if Jordan more black & muddy than this stream it would hardly run, observed several marien shells in flint rock and some pieces of pettrified wood (a fine clear day).

22 A clear night & a fine Beautifull morning yestardy Mr. Robinson Mr Morin & Mr [Isaac W.] Alderman Returned withour Sloten [stolen] animals which ware taken on the First of this month after Swimming Sawping and wadeing and enduring inumerable hardships almost Beyond discription we once more gladly hailed our messmates to camp They Likewise brot us some news From civilization The streams South and east being all overflown ennumerable damage Sweeping Fences Houses Barns & in fine distroying all kinds of Property on the intervales so far as heard from And Likewise information from the Political world As it appears there to there has been a great Troubling & Striving of the eliments the mountain having at last brot forth J. K. Polk Capt Tyler & the invincible Henry Clay as candidates for the Presidency. go it Clay. Just whigs enough in camp to take the curse off, made 14 miles along a narrow Prairie ridge and found fine water in a little grove of Elms.

23 (Sunday) A Fine clear morning noticed a great many granite Boulders some of a Fine vermilion Tint verry compact & handsome scattered on a limestone Strata At 10 A.M. Struck the Oregon trace on Cannon Ball Creek greate Joy at finding the trail and a good ford

Crossed over without delay or diffculty except the breaking of an axel-tree whiich was repaired in ½ an hour made 12 miles and encamped on a small Brook with a Plentifull scarcity of wood (made 12 miles) the country verry uneven and broken in an immence number and veriety of conicle noils all Beautyfully covered and clothed in grass But we found the ravine soft and deep & many Teams doubled over.

24 Rolled out at sun rise and at 11 reached Burr oak creek a deep dirty stream about 10 rods wide all the Banks and bottoms having Been overflown found the date of Mr Gillhams [Cornelius Gilliam] company having crossed 4 days previous crossed over in 2 hours although we had to let down our wagons down a steep Slipery bank by hand to day struck our old trail made on our return from the mountains in 1827 when I had the honorable post of being pilot Some points look quite familiar allthough I never passed but once & that time nearly 17 years ago our evening camp in particular game is verry scarce but one deer having been killed made 14 mils.

25 A thunder shower came on early & continued at entervals all night found Middle camp creek overflown and it still raining. Rolled out at 1 oclock through the rain & went up the creek 2 or 3 miles to a shallow ford crossed over with out difficulty made 5 miles by the old trace & encamped on the Smoky fork or Blue fork (of Kanzas) [Big Blue River] found two canoes left by those ahead.

26 A dull Cloudy morning rolled up to the place of embarcation this stream is about 80 yards wide and has fine intervale and prairie lands based on a fine white Limestone but timber is rather scarce Here we had an awfull time in crossing our Stock the Bottoms and [word omitted] being so soft from the over flowings of watter that we had to Litterly drag our animals several rods to swiming water and again from it and in all probabillity the everlasting hill never since the deluge experianaced such a superabundance of moisture particularly the immediate countery through which we have to pass got more than half our wagons over & cattle enough to drag our wagon to dry land about ½ mile distant by hitching all to one wagon at a time.

27 A thick foggy morning it rained yestarday which is so common that I neglected to mention it got all our camp over before night Mr

[Andrew] Sublett & party arived on the oposite side Mr. Sublett party consists of 20 men 11 of whoom are Sick and traveling for health one of which died and was Buried this morning about 15 miles East of this Poor fellow Marshall by name his fair companion accompanied him from St Louis and tenderly watched over him to Indipendence whare thy seperated Kind companion her worst fears are realized her Husbands bones rest Quietly forever on the bluffs of oak creek whare no noise disturbes his rest but the carrol of summer wild birds and the nightly howl of the lonely wolf the day proved to be one unusualy fine.

28 Left our encampment early which was in several respects the finest we have made consisting of a nice little little grove of Hackbery & elm timber a beautifull Spring of cool clear water runing past well stored with goosberry shrubbery some of which we had for coffe Tea I cannot call it as we had none the rest was covered with an uneven ridge of Limestone rock on the east runs Blue river meandring throug a grove of Hickory walnut oak and cottonwood timber capd with fine conical green noils and ridges to South lies the wally of Blue revir a fine prairie soile & handsom little Brooks passing through our rout to day lay north westwardly ovie rathe uneven Prairie ridge Beetwen the main Blue & the wesst fork of the sane made 16 miles & encamped on the east of the ridge.

29 A Strong South wind all night with thunder Showers passing for once they mised us weather very warm & the road soft & heavy but fine Black rich soil Tried to Stand guard last night a good deal of grumbling & discontent amongst those that have horses & those that have none some not even wanting a camp guard our pilot Mr [Moses "Black"] Harris. 22 years experianc and advice is perfectly useless in this age of improvement when human intelect not only strides but actually Jumps & flies into conclusions Traveled 16 miles over uneven prairie & circuitous crooked road Some miles migt be saved and a better track by following the main ridge 3 or 4 miles South of the wagon trail corssed rock Creek late and encamped on the W. side [of] it a rapid shower of rain fell in the afternoon & 4 or 5 Teams came up so late as not to cross the creek raised and at dark was swiming another heavy shower fell at day light.

30 The creek still rising and verry rapid this creek is branch of Little Blue or west fork of Blue river & affords some usefull Timber fine grass & good soil a verry warm day almost to suffication The trace we have been traveling follows neare the dividing ridge between the main Blue & the west fork and is the higest land in the country one or two teams that had been 2 days behind came up to day Laid still to day to await the falling of the creek that all the teams might get to gather our camp is on rather a sandy soil the first we have seen on upland since we passed the waukarusha.

Notes on Chapter Seven

Some of the place names Clyman uses might have been confusing even to readers of his own day, and not simply because of his spelling. Shunganunga Creek was evidently named for a Kaw Indian, Shonga-Tonga (Big Horse); Waukarusha (Black Bear Hill) was the Kaw name for the wooded hill now called Blue Mound. A contemporary map excellent for tracing Clyman's journey and others of the era is reproduced in Dale Morgan's *Overland Diary of James A. Pritchard, 1849* (Denver: Rosenstock, 1959.) This work, which Camp calls "superbly edited," contains information on the trail, its landmarks and history.

Writing to Col. Elisha Starr, editor of the *Milwaukee Sentinel* on May 30,1844, Clyman gave a bit more coherent detail on the unusual flooding the train faced. The train, Clyman said, numbered about 100 wagons, and from 500 to 700 people. At the time he wrote to Starr, the crossing of the Kansas River had begun, and the entire train was not expected to be collected again for eight or ten days.

"The traveling," said Clyman, "has been the worst possible...at all prairie encampments, without wood and wallowing in mud, swimming creeks and rivers. But all, thus far, have got along well, and without serious loss or accident. The ladies in particular have evinced an uncommon degree of fortitude and resignation under all hardships and privations incident to traveling in mud and water." Though he apparently did without the close companionship of a woman for some time, he *did* notice them, especially when they demonstrated fortitude.

Clyman was apparently serving as clerk of a segment of the train, and lists those in his mess at the end of this journal. Camp's footnotes give various identifications for the list of men, since not all have been identified by historians.

Moses Harris was an old mountain man hired to guide emigrants in the 1844 migration. He spent the next five years pioneering new emigrant routes across the Cascade Range and into California and northern Nevada. Harris was famous for his love of a good joke or tall tale; he is credited with spreading the story of the "putrified" forest in its various forms. He was also known for his solitary travels carrying messages for the fur trade from the western side of the Rockies to Fort Laramie. DeVoto calls him "a specialist in solitary travel"; his habit was to ride all night and hide during the day, carrying dried meat to avoid making fires.

He was probably with the Ashley-Henry party of 1822, and may have been in the mountains even earlier, if we can believe Beckwourth on this point. William Sublette chose him as sole companion on their trip out of the mountains in January, 1827, when the two were reduced by starvation to eating their pack dog. In 1829–30, the two repeated the journey, taking along "a train of pack dogs"; some early travelers were astonished at how excellent young dog tasted, so perhaps the pack train was along as emergency provisions, as well as carriers.

Ruxton mentions a dog feast in a camp of French Canadian and Creole trappers and Indians on Horse Creek. "A coyote, attracted by the scent of blood, drew near, unwitting of the canine feast in progress, and was likewise soon made *dog* of, and thrust into the boiling kettle with the rest." He was pronounced fully as savoury as the canine ingredients.

By 1840, when the trapping business was in decline, Harris was one of the best known trappers, and easily turned to guiding emigrant trains. He stayed three years in Oregon, exploring and helping to build roads, and was active after that in various guide jobs.

Harris died of cholera in Independence, Missouri, in 1849 during a plague of the disease that claimed large numbers of emigrants in the camps along the trail.

Clyman's verse on Harris is a fitting memorial:

Here lies the bones of old Black Harris
who often traveled beyond the far west
and for the freedom of Equal rights
He crossed the snowy mountin Hights
was free and easy kind of sou
Especially with a Belly full

Chapter 8
Notebook Two
Little Blue River to Red Buttes near the Mouth
of the Sweetwater

[July 1 to August 14, 1844]

Oregon Emegrants Camp

Rock creek July the 1st 1844

The above named rock creek seems to be almost arbitrary there being but one rock seen & that one a loose boulder but Lying right in the middle of the ford the sun rose nearly clear while the grumbling thunder was heard to the South the road very heavy and several wagons stuck in the low grounds & raviens small groves of Timber seen either to the right or left some sand Shews itself in the trail to day which is hailed with delight as being our Saviour from mud in which we have ate drank Traveled slept and breathed continually ever since we left the settlements & about 2 weeks previous made 13 miles & encamped on dry sandy ridge near Cotton creek which runs S. West-wardly into the west fork or little blue.

2 A thick foggy morning walked about ½ a mile back on the trail to see a mountain of Petrifactions this mound is 150 or 200 feet above the level of the small streams passing to the south of it & is formed [of] grey lime rock near the top which rock is intirely composed of shells & other manrine matter greate portions of it is broken up verry fine near the surface every fragment of which shews a shell of various sicess [sizes] and shapes & at least a dozen differant kinds another Shower of rain fell this morning rode out saw deep ravine washed out of marly lime stone about 8 feet deep which was intirely composed of Shells in a solid compact form remained in camp to day on account of high water the afternoon clear & fine.

3 Foggy cool with an East wind Cottonwood creek fell four or five feet Last night many of the small Brooks in the Neighbourhood completely choked up with slides of earth froom the contiguious Bluff the Bluffs & banks formed of round was[h]ed gravel & Shell rock Based on a strong clay bed 10 A.M. a Shower of rain Turned out to Bridg the creek but returned to await its falling Mr. Subletts again came up having buried one more of his invalids Mr. Kechup by name three days since at his camp called by him Ketchums grave 10 miles West of Blue river Mr Ketchum was [a] yong man his Brother came with him and attended him to his grave in this greate wilderness of Prairie which streches in all most all directions beyond the field of vision.

4th of July The sun rose in pale misty magesty and was salutd by Several guns forom thoes owt on the morning watch Soon after the Stars & Stripes floted in the Breeze the american Jubilee was but little further noticed than that the star Spangled Banner floated from Esqr Rolands waggon throughout the day crossed cotton wood and left Fossil Bluffs with all their once numerious animated family and made 12 miles crossed Sandy a Broad Shallow Stream with sand barrs and Isleands running nearly S. W. into west fork or little Blue our rout to day was near the ridge dividing Cottonwood and West fork and was dryer and firmer than any 12 miles previously traveled over allthoug the rains have been frequent and rapid.

5 A verry warm Night & a wam morning the Musketoes troublesome Several persons compaining of the Rhumatism & Dyentery it thundred and Lightned all night allthough it did not rain made 14 miles over uneven Prairie crossed 4 shallwo sandy Brooks all Tributory of west fork & encamped on the last mentioned stream which stream

is about 40 yards wide and runs rapidly over a Sandy bed course From
N W. to S E. large intervales as much as 3 miles wide no timber except
cottonwood and willows The wind from the S & air extremely warm at
about 5 P.M. the wind suddenly shifted to the N & it insantly became
cooll enough to want our coats saw severall antelop to day & for the
first [time] & some of the men killed one of them.

6 A fine cool morning the wind from North for the first time since
we left the Settlement a cool N.E. wind all day made 17 miles up the W.
Fork mostly on the interval encamped on a low bottom a Tremendious
thunder shower came up before sundown which lasted untill 9 oclock
two or 3 dozen of fine catfish was caught & in fact all the tributaries of
the Kanzas seem well stored with that Species of fish and have been
easily taken when ever the water has been low enough to permit us to
approach the main Banks of the streams which however has been
seldom Mr Subletts party passed us to day and we are now in the rear
of all the different parties traveling over the western praries passed
some fine Bottom lands to day but little timber and that not valuable
the wolves howled vehemently around us last night.

7 **(Sunday)** The creek bank full this morning wind N.E. a thick
drizzely morning the road laid out from the creek at the heads of the
ravines about 12 The sun broke through the misty clouds & we stoped
to water & graze on the reshes which have been plenty in patches for
several days horses & cattle feed on them voraciously 2 miles Brot us
up to Mr Sublett party of invalids whane they had Just finished
intering Mr Browning who left this troublesome world last night at 11
oClock the season has been the worst posible for Sick persons generally allthough the 3 or 4 consumptives travelling with us are mending
slowly made 16 miles to day the afternoon near the crek which has
diminished since we first came on its banks saw some Beaver cutting
for the first observed the earth is becoming much firmer
notwithstanding the rains.

8 Another Foggy morning we are beginning to camp in Tolerable
order running the wagons on a level piece of ground and forming a
Square round or oblong Krale the tents Pitched on the outside the fires
still on the ouside of the tents and the guard outside of all the horses &

other valuables in the Koral a little afternoon passed the great Pawnee Lodge trail leading South came near Splitting camp there being Several trails and as many nominal pilots but all but one wagon came up to camp in the evening the Bluffs and ravines shew a great flood at some time more vilent than any I ever observed in the states made 18 miles and encamped on a brook Tribitory to the West fork nothing but willows for fire wood But we are told that we need not expect any better verry soon our course to day South of West.

9 It thundred & Ligtned all night & Several Showers of rain fell during the night the morning fair several patches of Short Buffaloe grass made its appearance about our camp made 10 miles N.W. over deep cut ravines in a loose soft clay intermixed with fine sand encamped on the bluffs of a small Brook Lying deep below the surounding level of the country wood and water scarce & difficult to approach Several Teams remained at last encampment to await the appearance of a young emigrant who came on & overtook us at 5 oclock P.M. in riding this forenoon a Short distance south of the trail we fell in a deep vally amid the bare clay Bluffs which realized allmost all the fabled scent of the much Fabled Spice groves [of] arabia or India for more than 2 miles the odours of the wild rose & many other oderiferous herbs scented the whole atmosphere But the groves ware wanting nothing but gnarled cotton woods ware seen.

10 A sight shower of rain fell about sunrise roled out across the devide between the head of Kanzas & the great Platt and from the eye I should Judge that the main platte is as high or higher than the Kanzas near our last nights encampment a narrow row of low sand hills running paralel with and not more than 6 or 8 miles from the platte being the only deviding ridge. all the water South of the sand hills runing into the Kanzas and none at all runnin into the platte this last named stream being the most mudy & in fact a grate deal more muddy than the Missourie itself the father of mud made 17 miles & encamped on the Platt near the middle of the grand Isleand the country as far as the eye can reach is as level as a pond except the low sand hills before mentioned.

11 A cool Pleasant morning no wood but a few dry willows and

Quite small made 18 miles up the south side of the River over a level Prarie no timber except a few cotton wood Trees & them all confined to the Islands in the river which are numerous but generally small the Prairie ponds are wells[t]ored with wild ducks [these] with a few antelope constuite all the game yet seen & but feew of them precured a rapid shower of rain about sun down This river Platt has a channel not much less than three miles wide and the intervale from Bluff to Bluff as much as 12 miles wide the bank from 2 to 4 feet high above the water whare it is 4 feet high it is remarkable dry ana hard formed of a fine pale tenacious clay and fine dead sand remarkabel hard and smoothe.

12 A clear morning and a fine day but verry warm the same Level country the want of wood and water except the river and the long grass on the lowlands made 20 miles and encamped near some low willow Islands from which we obtained dry willows sufficiant to make fire for the night Several antelope ware killed to day and a number of wild ducks seen— had a fair view of our camp traveling as seen from the Bluffs abut a mile distant they made Quite a picturesque [appearance] First came a few stragling foot & horse men ahead & on the left flank the right being on the river next a thick squad of horsmen in front followeed by a long string of white looking wagon covers flanked with gentlemen & Ladies occasionally in the rear a long string of Loose cattle horses and mules the tout assemble being rather uneque.

13 A fair day started early & made about 20 miles over a level Planies & a heard smoothe road To day the sand hill which have lain to our left disappeared and ware succeeded by dry clay Bluff cut into deep narrow ravenis which do not reach far back into the (the) country as no streame that brings any running water has yet been seen the high level country South of the ravines are Beautifull Beyond discription handsomely roling and thickly set with fine Buffalo grass and Blue stem almost as soft as a bed and luxuriously covered with wild sun flowers and several other speces of yallow Blossoms which are now in full Bloom and scent the air to a considerable distance with a verry fine perfume as plasant as a flower garden.

14 (Sunday) It rained a light Shower last night & a thick cloudy morning Mr Hinman who [went] south into the Bluffs to shoot antelope did not return turned [out the] men this morning to hunt for him no place in the world looks more lonesome and discourageing than the wide Prairies of this region neither tree bush shrub rock nor water to cherish or shelter him and such a perfect sameness with a alusive ridge all around you meeting the Horozon in all directions you Suppose your course to lie over some one of those horizontal ridges when after several hours anxious fatigue you suppose you are about to assend the highest pinacle and some Known Land mark what is your diapoimtmint to find ridge rise beyond ridge to the utmost extant of human vision.

15 Rold. out unusually early found the road quite sloppy The weather close and warm and the mosquetoes thicker than I ever saw in any place to continue for a whole day as they (as they) did here until dark when they eased off & we had a fair nights rest the course of the river nearly due west [down] the valy [to] the extensive level plain Timber still more scarce and for miles nothing seen but now and then a Junt of shrubby Cottonwood or a dwarf willow made 20 miles recent Tracks of Buffaloe seen in Quanties but the animal himself Kept out of Sight rode out south onto the Bluffs and saw an undiscribeable country of hills Bluffs and deep cut ravines through a pale yallow clay soil some of which are 100 feet perpendicular the great reservoirs of mud which lie here in reserve for the next rain.

16 A clear morning all though it thundred and Lighned in all directions Throughout the night all the companis of Oregon Emigrants mountaineers & califoronians &c &c ahead of us had had buffaloe for several days & being anxious my self to get amess I laid my couse S.W. over the cut Bluffs nearly perpendicular and passed main rang[e] the country became more regual and level found the Buffalo in great Quantities Killed one verry fine one loaded my mule and started for camp had hard riding to pass the cut Bluffs & obtain the open plain through which the river passes before sundown But here commenced our Toils the camp having made 18 miles at 12 of which we had to ride after night the moketoes with uncommon Blood thirsty appetite commenced & ware Litterly so thick that with all our exertions we could hardly breath.

17 La[s]t night we passed Mr Gilhams company & they repassed us again in this morning we have now arived at the dry & thirsty clay soil which is always hard or if soft melts & runs with the water so thick that you can not see aparticle of the whitest matter the ½ of an inch below its surface Made 12 miles & passed the Junction of the S & N Branchs of Platte which Junction is in a verry low wet country & only a fieu inches above the surfac of the water Several Hunters ware out to day all returned Brot Quantities of meat some verry fine & all good I am sorry to Say that I was mistaken about the Hunters all returning 4 men did not return and great anxiety is [felt] on account of them 3 with families & 2 of the women driving the Teams for 2 days past arived at our supposed ford and making preperations to cross over.

18 It rained a light shower last night after which the (the) wind changed to the N. & we had afine coll night & a pleasant fair morning. Cooked our Supper last night with Buffaloe dung called chips in a modest way Such an article as wood (being) not being found 18 [miles] Crossed the S. Fork of the Platte river without the least difficulty over a loose sandy shallow ford and encamped on the smoothe level Prairie about 2 miles form our last nights encampment the bluffs in the contigous contry in many Places shew a fine loose limestone which gives it a white appearanc at a distance Soil dry and hard bearing the fine Buffaloe grass but no timber had a pleasant cool day for July the [valley] narrowed down to about 4 or 5 miles in width but level as heretofore.

19 A cool clear morning all it Thundred and Lightned in several Directions last night our 4 lost hunters returned after wandring 3 days & 2 nights over the boundless Prairies and allthough the summer is far advanced our prosspects wore a bette[r] face for crossing the mountains before winter made 5 miles and encamped on accoun of one of the Ladies being to sick to travel Rode out on the hills devideing the N. & S. Forks (which in appearance are nearly the same vollume of water) Found the ridges dry & hard composed mostly of rounded granite gravel undelaid with strato of soft marly Limestone several male

Buffaloe ware see[n] from camp and one large herd containing Several hundreds on the opposite Side of the river nothing in the character of a spring or Brook of running water has been seen since we came on the platte.

20 A beautifull (clear) clear cool morning the finest we have yet seen a Light west wind and clear atmophere imence heards of Buffalo seen from the hills near camp on the plains Beyond the river 4 days since we overtook Mr Gilhams company of Oregon Emigrants & yesterday an arangement was entered into for the traveling in the neare vicinity of each other & encamping no further apart than necessary for the good of our stock so that our entire company makes 96 Teams wagons & occupies with loose stock & all more than two miles of tolerable close collumn 16 [miles].

No preceveable alteration in soil or river or apeareance of country except the uplands are dryer & harder & on the Bottoms a fair appeareance of salt mixed with several other mineral substances.

21 A slight shower of rain fell about sundown yestarday evening & several others during the night a clear morning cole & pleasant made 14 miles up the N. Side of the S. Fork of Platte over dry Prairie intervale as fine a road as any in the union or even the world great Quntitees of Buffaloe seen a few miles from the trail but verry few imediately on the rout owing to several small companies of malcontents going ahead and driveing them away But our Hunters have been able to keep our camp well supplied with the finest kind all Ladies Gentleme[n] Children and all with the greatest uninimity agree that this is the finest richest sweetest living of any they have ever experienced and all hope that they may last far long & broad without stint or diminution.

22 A warm evening last and a warm morning this the mosquetoes verry troublesome the first time we have been much troubled in camp allthough they cover a single individual horse and all in a few minuits of evenings & mornings for the last 10 days if he happen to be out alone Quantities of Buffalo in sight all day to day made 7 miles to the point whare we leave the S. Fork & cross over the ridge to the N. Fork a verry warm day without scarcely a breath of air to keep down the flies

& Moketoes country the same except that their has been a Tremendious Shower rain not long since which has flooded all the ravines & given life & vigor to all Fly & Moketoe tribe & the warm weather has given them keen appetites.

23 Contrary to all the k[n]own rules of Traveling in this country a number of horses & mules run loosse last night & Likewise acording to a well known Phraze 15 or 20 came up missing this morning a fine cool day for crossing the interminable Prairies rolled out early nearly a north course found by good luck and unexpectedly several ponds of water about noon Likewise passed an extensive prairie dog village containing 3 or 400 acres of Land thickly settled with an active population living remote forom every thing but grass & weeds which constitutes their entire subsistance made 22 miles & encamped at dark on (on) the South bank of the N Fork in excelent grazing which is verry extensive the intervales being 6 or 8 miles wide not a stick of Standing timber in sight in any direction The Bluff down the river formed of Lime stone.

24 The coolest morning we have experianced with a brisk N wind all pleasan & animated on account of our late good roads & rapid traviling did not travel to day an odd Butle [Bustle?] of washing shaveing cleaning & repairing it being the first since the 4th when we left Fossil Bluffs to the east risis steep Limes[t]one cliffs all most perpendicular near 100 feet high worn into all manner of Shapes by the action of the wind This stream is a Counterpart of Stream we left at our last encampment Except that it is not so muddy being more than a mile in width generally shallow & running rapidly over loose floating sand no place more than 5 feet deep Quantities of Saline Substances making their appearance on the surface in Evenings of clear days the opposite side of the river shew high rounded sand hills.

25 Fair with a light east wind and plesanly cool moved of at an Early hour Singular as it may seem this Stream like the last has no tributarys falling into it from either side the Loup or wolf fork falling in below drains all the immence Sand plains N. to the Shianne which is the first stream nothe that takes its waters from the highlands or mountains made about 18 miles partly loose Sand & partly a Tenacious light coloured clay verry fine & close & in places white as pipe clay the Limestone ledge nearly dissap[ear]ed Toward evening and was succeeded with clay and Sand bluffs but not near so high in the evening passed the Broad channel of a brook with a little shallow water rippling over the sand the first water we have seen running into the Main Platt or its Branches since we struck that river no Buffalo seen on the N Fork.

26 A light shower of rain fell about dusk last night a clear warm morning Pased one mud hole the first on the Platte made 17 miles over the usual level Prairie one or 2 Shrubby hackberry trees seen through the day and passed some scattering clumps of pine to the South of our track theat at the distance shew rough uneven and rocky the Bluffs shew close to the water on the oposite side of the river in many places the day clar and warm throughout and the evening Remarkably light and pleasant with a bright moon the (the) chimny rock was said to be visable but I did not see it allthough I watched close No Buffaloe seen since we left the S Fork.

27 A clear cool morning the Ladies pleasant animated and in fine Spirits which make a fine contrer part to the morning Early we came in sight of the noted chimney rock at the supposed distance of 30 miles it rises perpendicular and alone and looked like an old dry stub not larger in appearance than your finger 4 or 5 miles from our nooning raises a bank of clay & rock having all the appearanc of some old castle of circular shape the spire having been Blown down the main walls and dome roof in a good state of preservation and still shewing the even range work of rubble rock of which the structure was formed made 20 miles over the level intirmenable Prairie But not so tiresome as their was Quite a veriety in sight the chimney rock changed its appearance & Shewed like a large conicle fort with a Tremendeous large & high flag staff & top taken off with out towers and (&) various fixtures of defence.

28 (Sunday) Fine and dry not a drop of dew fell last night which circumstance is not uncommon in the region of country we are now approaching all our sick of old cronic disorder begin to ware a healthy appearance & active elastick movement nooned opposite the chimny rock Scotts Bluffs in full vieu ahead on the whole the vieu in all directions Singular and Picturesque emmence level plains east the river a mile wide meandring along but your eye can not tell at a short distance which way the water runs the chimny rock with rugged Bluff from which it has sometimme or other been parted south Scotts Bluffs like a walled and fortified city with immenc out works west a ruged chain of Spercely pine timbred hill in the back ground the river a broad vally & a distant chain of Barren hills to the North made 22 miles.

29 My Page being entirely full yestarday I had not room to say That A light shower of rain fell in the afternoon which collected & commenced falling not more than ½ a mile ahead of our camp Keen claps of thunder with a profusion of Electrick fluid playin in all directions in a dry clear sky set the dry grass on fire in several places in sight of our traveling caravan which was soon extinguished by the rain Just mentioned Left the River and struck S. of W. 14 miles and encamped in the midtst of Scotts blufs By a cool spring in a romantic & picturisque vally surounded except to the E. by high & allmost impassably steep clay cliffs of all immagenary shapes & forms supped on a most dlecious piece of venison from the loin of a fat Black taild Buck and I must not omit to mention that I took my rifle and (and) walked out in the deep ravin to guard a Beautifull covey of young Ladies & misses while they gathered wild currants & choke chirries which grow in great perfusion in this region and of the finerst kind.

30 Roled out over the last ridge of Scotts Bluffs which is a ridge or connetion of highland commencing on the river & running Southwardly as far as visably rising in many places from 600 to 1000 feet high formed of clay & a verry fine dead sand & occasionly a thin layer of Soft Limestone which last mentioned layers protects the Softer parts from the ravages of Storms of wind & rain The whole range apears to have been once the common level of the country but owing to solible Qualities of the earth the main Bulk now forming the low grounds have been carried away with the water which opperation is still in active opperation these hills are finely stored with game Such as Black tailed deer antelope mountain Sheep & some times Buffaloe Elk & grisled Bear I must not omit to mention a singularity on a vally we pased yestarday which was covered in all parts with Quantities of dry logs & wood the only reasonable conjecture with me was that the vally some 10 or 12 miles in [l]ength & 8 or 10 wide has no channel for the discharge of the water from the surrounding hills [which] occasionally in winter become deeply frozen considerable snow falling which goes off with a sudden thaw all the mountain torrents come rapidly down charged with drift the water filling the wally diposits its drift on the Shores & Islans of the newly formed lake which soon finds a pasage through the sandy soil on which it rests we had a destinct & clear but distant view of the Black hills from the hights this morning made 14 miles & encamped on the river crossed horse creek about noon.

31 A fine clear cool morning a dry camp clear cool water and fine grazing the moon Shone clear as day allmost during the whole nigt about one third of our company remaind to recruit their lame Stock the Prairies ware on fire in Several directions last night and all the uplands look dry and parched made 14 miles over dry & verry dusty road We have been following A recent lodge Trail of moveing Indians for some days But have not been able to overtake them several persons went ahead to day to await us at the fort supposed to not be more than 20 or 30 miles considerable Quantities of cottonwood made it[s] appearance on Bottoms & islands to day as Likewise drift pine along the Shores Several flocks of wild [fowl] seen to day on the dry bars of the river the mountains do not change their appearance.

Thursday the 1st of August

Dry clear warm day cool Beautifully fine nights with Scarcely any dew or moisture to dampen a blanket of those that sleep out in the open air Soil a fine whiteish clay mixed with sand usually verry fine but sometimes moderately coarse about 4 oclock in the afternoon we hove in sight of the white Battlments of Fort Larrimie and Fort Platte whose white walls surrounded by a few Sioux Indian Lodges shewed us that Human life was not extinct this being the first we have seen since we left the Kaws the various Emigrants Excepted crossed the Larrimie river a clear fine Streean about 80 yards wide only about half of the channel filled with water 2 feet deep Several persons getting scant of Flour Some to be had here (at) Superfine at 40 dollars a barrel Spannish at 30.

2 Clear cool nights & mornings verry warm days Remained in camp to day trading and waiting for Blacksmith and other repairs went down to the fort after writeing to my Friend Starr of the Milwaukie Sentinell and found no prospect of his receiving my communication verry soon but I left the letter hoping that he m[a]y recieve it Soon I tried to trade some but found even the products of the country verry high I puchased a dressed deer skin for 2.50 cents and returned to camp satisfied that money was allmost useless while all kinds of grocerys & Liquors ware exorbitantly high for instance sugar 1.50 cents per pint or cupfull and other things in proportion Flour Superfine 1.00 dollars per pint or 40 dollars per Barrel Spannish 30 no dried Buffaloe meat could be had at any price so our stores of provision did not increase.

3 Roled out over the parched hills and soon lost singht of the white washed mud walls of Fort Larrimie & her twin Sister fort Piearre [Platte] made 12 miles over the dry parched hills which make a verry Singular appearance dotted all over with Shrubby Junts of dark looking Pine and cedars rootted in the white dry weather worn Lime rock which in many places shews like chalk banks & appears to be formed of Strong white marly clay dried by the sun and formed into rough Solid masses of rock without much form or regular Stratification and affording but feew Springs and no brooks as the water rises and Sinks occasionly along their gravelly beds encamped by one of those Springs which is a fine Strong rapid Spring but disappears in less than ½ mile amongst hight white rocky clifs which Surround us in all directions.

4 (Sunday) Tt thundred and lightned consideraby about dusk & rained a few drops but the sun rose in beautifull majesty over her parched cliffs this morning as it rains but little in this region Made 8 miles over the same Kind of dry hard thirsty country as yestarday and encamped on the dry sand barr of Sandy creek a little rill of warm muddy mean tasted water was all that dignified this broad channel of more than 100 yards broad crossed over the Bluffs & hills with our guns after camping to the river which here runs through a deep cut channel of Solid Lime stone more than 1000 feet deep 7 or 800 of which is perpendicular and not more at the top than 3000 feet wide coming up from the south with allmost level Prarie I neglected to mention that the Junction of Platte & Larrimie is immediately below the back hills Both isuing from deep cut rocks a Short distance above through which they pass for more than 40 miles with a few intervining small vallies or open spaces.

5 Shortly after dark their came on a thunder Shower with such a Squall of wind that allmost all our Tents ware fluttering on the ground in a moment the large cold drops of rain pelting us furiously all over & not even sparing the delicate Ladies & small children which ran helter skeltter in all directions seeking for shelter from the storm which was of Short duration Passed up our Shallow stream west & soon came to a beautifull running brook with a fine intervale well clothed with timber & much the handsomest place we have yet seen well clothed with green vegetation & is one of the green spots so sldom seen in this arid scorched region but this beautiful vally did not last long for after passing about 6 miles up we left it & turned up north along a dry sandy bed of what is sometimes a brook and assended up it to its extreme eastern head whare we assended a beautifull smoothe roling ridge covered with scattereing pines from which we had the finest view which can be had in this romantick country the immediate country dry & beautifully smooth & roling into Knobbs to the south a distant & extensive view of appearantly smooth level prarie turning your head to S. W. & W. an extensive view of the roughest & most raged mountain in all this rough region mellowed down by the distance into smoothe sharp pinecles with others rising in the back ground to a great hight turning to the north a large uneven vally makes its appearance filled with finely rounded ridges & butes intermingled with vallies to the utmost reach of vision turning to the East is perhaps the most singular of all you have an extensive view of the greate Kenyon Through which the river passes and in the distance is a crowded view of rounded butes & would resemble the larges assemblage of Arabian lodges that ever encamped togather and of nearly all the shades of colour from red to white & occasionally black being covered with the tufted pine and cedar all handsomely exhibited in light & shade by a clear afternoon Sun made 20 miles the last 4 or 5 rather rough & heavy on account of the deep sand at our camp on horse shoe creek we over took all the differant companies of emigrants except Hitchcocks and encamped in a Jumbled mass of Stock tents people &c &c.

6 Turned out early from our camp on Wagon Hound creek and had Some Steep pitches to raise before we got clear of the creek then some fine rolling country was passed with several brooks of clear water several miles of desent brot us into the vally of wagon hound creek whare we encamped for the night haveing made 15 miles in this vally we saw Quantities of Buffaloe but few of them were taken owing to the lateness of the day when we arived & the number of hunters out which drove them from one another which is envariably the case when a great number of anxious men turn out (out) to hunt after any discription of game the mountains discribed yesterday are of a light grey granit & are the frst seen on our assent from the vally Below Scotts bluff as before mentioned.

7 Clear as usual in this region of (of) allmost cloudless Skies moved out of our dry grassless camp crossed clear fine little Brook at the distance of 5 miles on both sides of which the utmost confusion exists vitrified earth clay & rock of several kinds in banks hills Knobs mounds piles & mountains ly & stand in all angles from horizontal to perpendicular but mostly in an angle from 20 to 45 all seem to have been hove up from the N. E. for that is the Slanting direction & the S. W. being nearly perpendicular—and the ranges running from N. W. to S.E. formed of grey granit red Sandstone blue lime stone clay red as brick and some black looking Substance resembling decomposed Slate or Something blackned by fire made 14 miles & encamped near a fine spring our camp once again largely supplied with Buffaloe beef.

8 The same as yestarday a clear Bright sun & cloudless atmosphere on the road again passed a number of Beautifull little clear Brooks cool & remarkable sweet comeing out of the grey granite mountain lying only a few miles to the South of our rout & in many places the strata rises nearly perpendicular & allway at (at) least 40 degrees with the Horizon Made 17 miles and encamped on a fine little stream almost in sight of N Fork of the Platte in the vally of which Stream we have been traveling ever since leaving Larremie but seldom in sight our encampment is the best for stock we have yet seen since passing the Forks and a number of Scaffolds are arected well covered and smoking with fine Buffalo Beef to dry for the road as well as the Board which is finely stored for supper with the choisest Kind.

9 The same Beautifull clear Sky concluded to remain in our prsent position on Boxwood creek which is thickly set with that kind of Timber well Stored with current and choke cherries & a number of Large grissly Bears to feed on them as is plenly seen by their numerious pathes through the brush the Bear feeds on all kinds of fruit but the red willow berry which is extremely Bitter seems to be their favourite food all hands busied in preparing and drying the finest kind of Buffaloe Beef as we are fearfull that they will not be many on the road ahead walked up to the mountain about 4 miles distant found the top ledges 4 or 500 feet high composed of a whitesh grey granite then a strata of rough red sandson 5 or 200 feet thick based on blue & red Lime stone intermixed with red vitrified clay the water of the brook running over loose rock of all the above descriptions.

10 Moved off forom our encampment on Boxwood & crossed over about 5 miles to the river crossed Several small Brooks and dined on deer creek made 15 miles and encamped on the river Same hard granite gravely rounded hills the mountains keeping close on our left and (and) running paralell to our rout along the river the weather fine as usual the uplands dry and parched

The mountains lying to our left are not verry high perhaps not more than 3 or 4000 feet above the vally of the river but they are extremely ruged and Steep the(y) rocks standing in many places nearly in perpendicular strata the range is narrow an uneven vally lying beyond then another paralel range Beyond which is an elevated table land distitute of Timber & Tolerable Smooth Turfed.

11 (Sunday) A beautifull morning Roled on up the river crossed several fine Brook considerable timber or Junts rather of cottonwood the Bottoms covered with dry fallen Timber which in this region never decays but wares away in Slow degrees by the weather the Buffaloe verry fat and excelent eating and still found in great abundance made 18 miles and encamped on the river grass scarce and nearly dry even on the most moist Situations & we begin to find our delay on Kaw river was a great detriment to our traveling here bringing us through this dry region in warmest and dryest part of the Season our Stock begins to look bad and loose their activity and yet we have not arived at the worst part of our long tiresome Journey our own subsistance dose not look so precarious as the forrage for our stock our horses in particular.

12 Moved up the river 4 miles to the place whare we leave the river and cross over the red Bute mountain and encamped a few miles below the lower Kenyon the cliffs on this Kenyon are for more than half way up of a fine deep brick red appearantly of burned Slate and a marly clay lime.

13 Made an early start and raised the rounded dry hills of the Red Bute mountain which falls off to moderate hills without timber to the north of our rout but rises again on the head of the South Branches of the Big Horn and Toungue and Powder rivers this range I could not understand was Heretofore named or laid down on any map of this country the tops of thise hills are fine sand and clay lower down a rough sand stone Based on a whitish coloured Slate which with a little change from Black to red makes the lowermost Strata or bed to be seen and in many places stands edgeways or in perpendicular form made 12 miles of crooked woorming Travel and encamped in a small valy a dry Brook a Brackish [spring] rising near (near) it(s) Buffaloe chips wild Sage and Prairie thorn forming our Stock of wood 4 miles to the South resis The Red Bute which give name to the awfull Kenyon both above & below the Bute on Standing on the cliffs near the edge of the Poicipice you see the river both above & below on two bends of the river which is much narrower at top than at the water the continual waring Below haveing fully doubled its once width through the solid granite & its perpendicular depth being over 1000 feet the stream looking not larger than your finger seemed to be at an angle of 40 at least and clear under your feet.

14 Left our encampment early and again took to the rising hills which we nearly toped in about 2 ½ hours from which we had a distinct view of Wind river mountain standing in bold raged cliffs directly ahead and about a N.W. course a few rods to the left of the road breakes up a fine oil spring from in under a rounded Knoll of whiteish Slate & appears to be much frequented by the Buffaloe & other animals numerious ledges of different kinds of rock all standing edgewise and nearly perpendicular one in particular of white Sand Stone which extended to the utmost reach of vision in a narrow Straight line nearly north over ridge and hollow now rising then sinking from 3 to 20 feet in hight no discription of mine will give any adaquate idea of the Barren dry Sterility of the dry land of this region Made 20 miles & encamped without grass but had fine water and plenty of good dry wood our rout to day was verry crooked & 6 or 8 miles might be Saved by taking a more Southern route.

Notes on Chapter Eight

Note how often in the preceding pages Clyman mentions the "ladies." Perhaps he was, even now, searching for someone with whom to settle down; in fact, that may have been part of his object in agreeing to accompany this train, or in leaving Wisconsin in the first place; perhaps "traveling for his health" really meant "hunting for a wife."

Chapter 9
Notebook Three
Red Buttes to the Blue Mountains

[August 15 to September 30, 1844]

August the 15th 1844

Left our contracted encampment at willow Spring near the top of the Red Bute mountain & in ½ an hour reachd the top of the ridge had a fair view of the east end of the wind river mountain the numerous rough granite peaks on Sweet water & those around Indipindance rock But it soon became So smokey that our fine viws ware intirely obscured the ridges vallys hallows & all (all) the whole region near our rout these last two days have been the (the) most Sterile Barren land imaginable haveing but little vegetation except the wild sage and that not more than Six or (or) eight inches high curled down & level & stiff makeing a good seat Soil granite gravel & sand intermingled with rounded granite Boulders some of considerable size Made 16 miles and encamped on Sweet water ½ a mile below the rock indipendence.

16 Moved on up the creek saw the notable rock Independance with the names of its numerious visitors most of which are nearly obliterated by the weather & ravages of time amongst which I observed the names of two of my old friends the notable mountaneers Thos. Fitzpatrick & W. L. Sublette as likewise one of our noblest politicians

Henry Clay coupled in division with that of Martin Van Buren a few miles furthe[r] up the creek pases through the South point of a most ruged & solid looking granite rock by a verry narrow pass after passing which we entered a valy Surounded by low ruged mountains except to the West whare a defiel Shews itself the lower vally of this creek is well clothed with short grass the upper with sand & sage the mountains with short scattering pines but in many places nothing but the bear rock in large steep Surfaces made 8 miles & encamped for the night on a good plat of grass.

17 Smokey But the sun rose over the Eastern mountains in its usual majesty Some recent Signs of a war party of Indians ware discovred yestarddy which caused some uneasiness but verry little more caution roled up the Stream on the South side arang[e] of the most ruged bare granite rocks lay along the North side close to the water & a range of Blue mountains to the S. at the distance of 6 or 8 miles the sides bear the tops pretty well clothed with pine Timber saw some fine herds of Ibex or wild sheep some of which ware taken and (&) found to be verry fine eating saw great flocks of young wild ducks many of which ware unable to fly not having their wing feathers stiff enough.

This region seems to be the refuses of the world thrown up in the utmost confusion rocks without strata forming mountains others standing in perpendicular strata made 13 miles & encamped.

18 Left our encampment near the granite rocks and moved up the creek & passed several points of the same range of cliffs untill we entered a close Kenyon the cliffs nearly approching the water from either side giving bearly room for the teams to pass which opened out into a fine wally at the distance of a fewe miles above up which we passed and encamped 14 miles from our last camp the grass had been pasturd verry close by the Buffalou all through the rout up this creek and we found them in greate abundance near our encampment a slight Shower of rain fell after which the wind blew quite cool for august which in fact has been the case for several nights allthough the days for several hours near noon was verry warm.

19 Left the creek immediately after starting and laid our couse

south of west and allmost directly from the creek which course we traveled most of the day over a barren tract of country nothing escaping the appetite of the Buffaloe except the wild sage which is left for the antelope & mountain grouse the only animals known to feed on such bitter herbage the Brarren Sterelity of this region must be desolate in the extreme in the winter as it has nothing inviting now Made 18 miles and struck the creek again and encamped without scarcely aparticle of grass the earth dry and completely parched to dust which moves in perfect clouds around us during the day when on march it is a little remarkable that all the native animals get so verry fat in dry parched region so bare of vegetation.

20 Crossed over a narrow ridge and struck the creek again above the rocks through which it passes made 7 miles and encamped clos below another Kenyon through which the creek passes and near to whare we encamped in January 1824 at which time we under J. Smith and T Fitzpatrick first traversed the now well known South pass and campd on green river on the 19th of march 11 days of which time we never saw a drop of water except what we thawed from Snow The mountains look quite familiar allthough I have not seen them for 17 year and it appears as if the 17 summers last past had not in the least diminished the snow that then crownd their lofty heads which still ware the white appearance of old age.

21 It had the appearance of rain last nght and a few drops fell But the sun arose this morning with its usual brightness moved up the dry parched hills crossed a number of ranges of perpendicular rocks black and (&) appearantly vitrified passed numerous small brooks & springs verry fine and cool & appearantly clear of lime or any substance whatver being nearly as pure distiled passed several fine small groves of Aspin the first seen of any consequence Made 14 miles and campd on the creek again that we had left this morning now reduced to a small Brook & damned up by the beaver Likiwise confined between steep rocky Bluffs the strata of which rises in perpendicular form Mr. Barnette who has been confined 5 or 6 days with a fever has the appearance of being quite dangerous and has been delerious during the whole of the night.

22 Left our thick willow camp and after raising the bluffs Had a fine undulating road across the ridges to another Branch of Sweet water the wild sage the only vegitable seen on the ridges Hardly exceeded two inches in hight so completely are these hills formed of dry gravel and deprived of Moisture added to the intense coldness of this high region in sight of the eternal snow that Scarce a week passes without frost and we had a fine one this morning which caused us to hover close to our willow brush fires and [those] out after cattle & Horses complained of cold toes made 7 miles & camped in a pretty faced vally covered with copses of willow and thin short grass many wearing our coats all day without feeling uncomfortably warm.

23 Remained in camp to day on the account of Mr. Barnett who we did not expect to live being verry low with a Typhus Fever several teams however went on & Mr Gilhams company passed our encampment all Buiseed in mending washing and preparing for Tomorow poor Mr Barnetts prospects bad our circumstances not permitting delay & he not being able to travel.

To our right and but a short distance Isued a considerable branch of Popo Azia [Agie] the most Southern water of Wind River which Brakes out between a rough pine clad range of mountains and the eternal snow capt. range which rises here from an uneven high plain which forms the dividing ridge Between the waters running into the yallowstone and the platte all portes of which Shew the remains of great convulsions at some remote time.

24 A dull cloudy morning the camp made early preparations For moveing & all roled out except ourselves who remain to take care of Mr Barnett whose prspects for living seem a little better than yestarday all though yet quite small every preperation seemed dull & melancholly & many bid the sick man their last farewell look a Spade was thrown out & left which looked rather ominous The ravens came croaking around us and the Shaggey wolf was seen peeping from the hills to see if the way was clear to contend with the ravens for the Fragment of the camp Early in the afternoon Capt Shaw and Morisons company hove in sight and the hills and the vally became the seene of life and animation again for the evening they camping about ½ a mile below us Several came to visit us Mr. Harris staid though the night.

25 (Sunday) Clear and Bright no change for the better in Mr Barnetts Symtoms rather worse allthough medicine seemed to operate well Found it verry Lonesome to be clear of the noise and Bustle of a large camp and to remain Stationary with a Sick man in one of the most prominent Indian passes of the country in the afternoon However Perkins and Scott came up with the rear of all the Emigrants on the rout & we had their company during the night which intirely relieved the lonsomeness of the Place and many of the Ladies seemed emulous to see which should be the most active in giving us advice & assistance for the relief of our appearently dying friend the Perkins family in particular.

I noticed several vegetables now in full Bloom & do not seem to be the least affected by the cold allthough we have had frost & Ice for 4 nights in succession.

26 Usually fine and bright Mr Burnett to all appearance Still wareing away under a verry Strong nervous excitement never being Scarcly one minuit still at a time Mr Scotts company remain here to day and Several of the Ladies are verry kind in doing all they can to make the sick man comfortable about noon Mr Barnette commenced with severe Spasms & seemd to be in the gratest agony imaginable continually driving his teame or calling on some friend to do something or other all those called being absent late in the evening howeveer he became at spells more camlm & even Stupid & about 10 oclock he departed this life verry easy without a struggle or a groan & all his troubles ware in Silent death having nothing better we cut a bed of green willows & laid him out on the cold ground & all of us seated ourselves around our camp fire & listned to the hair beadth escapes of Mr Harris & other Mountaineers.

27 Early we ware up and making preperations for the enterment of the deceased when after Burying him in the most decent manner our circumstances would admit we made ready for leaveing Sweet water on which now rests the Body of Mr Barnette the first white man that ever rested his bones on that stream leaving our willow encampment we soon rose the deviding ridge Between the waters of the Atlantic & Pacific which is nothing more than a plasant assent for about 23 miles & decent of the same distance to afine grassy Spring Brook which pours it's crystal waters through green River into the gulf of California rode 25 miles and campd on little sandy likewise a tributary of green River.

28 Made an Early Start & in a few hours came in sight of a large grassy vally through which runs Big Sandy which unites with the stream we encamped on last night a few miles blow & continue nearly a South course untill they mingle their waters with Green river our general course a little West of South yesterday & to day we had a number of fine views of Several of the pinicles of the wind river mountains the country dry & dusty cowred with wild sage & Praerie Thorn & a few other hardy Stinted vegetables traveled down the west side of Big Sandy Several miles from the Stream as it runs in a croked deep Channel Rode 25 miles and campd on Big Sandy During the day had one or 2 views of the utaw mountains Several Snowy point being directly South and bearing Southwest.

29 In about 2 Hours ride we came to green river a beautifull clear crystal Stream about one hundred yards wide & nearly Belly deep to our Horses running East of S. through a Sandy parched dry country but little of it clothed with grass some groves of Shrubby cotton wood growing on its banks after crossing we rode down the vally of this stream about 6 miles East of South then South over the Bluffs 12 miles to Black fork which Stream likewise runs into Seetskadee [Green River] about 20 miles east of whare our trail struck it all the high ground dry & dusty & covered with the Eternal Sage which can live without rain from June untill October on a clean pure granite gravel after coming down into the vally of Blacks Fork we turned Short to the West up the same rode 5 miles making about 30 miles and encamped with our former mess once more.

30 Moved up Blacks fork and in an hour crossed Hams fork coming in from the N.W. through a fine grassy vally crossed Blacks fork & made a cut off of a long bend & struck the river again in the afternoon we had the Singular phenominon of Seeing a Shower of rain in the vally & after the light cloud passed off the peaks of the Eutaw [Uintah] mountain ware covered white with a fresh fallen snow which however ware partially covered with the snows of former winters made 18 miles & encamped on the Stream we left this morning numerous Butes Mounds & ridges occurring all through this vally formed to all appearances by wash of water consisting of Red brown white & green clay formed in many places into Soft rock but still washing away by the water at ever[y] freshett Made 14 miles.

31 Moved up the vally of Blacks Fork & early in the afternoon arived at Bridger & Vasqueses trading house [Fort Bridger] a tempory concern calculated for the trade with Shoshonees and Eutaws which trade is not verry valuable this place is likewise the general rendezvous of all the rocky mountain hunters & Trappers that once numerous class of adventurers are now reduced to less than thirty men which Started out under the command of Mr Bredger yestarday on an excursion thrugh the mountains of Northern & central Mexico this small Trading post is also within the limmits of Mexico but can be no great distance south of the U. S.tates Boundary line this Establisment has a fine grassy vally arround it but of no greate extent we here met Mr Robedeau [Antoine Robidoux] from the arkansas with horses and mules & other articles porposely to catch our trade.

Sunday the 1st of September 1844
Moved out north across the hills from Bridgers Trading House found the road rough & hilly & perfectly bare of grass crossed Several steep & deep ravines one of which had some pools of poor Brackish water standing in it in the afternoon passed a low range of hills covered with cedar to our left and encamped on a creek called [Little] muddy emtying into Hams creek our rout through this Green River vally has been verry crooked & might be easily made to save about 50 miles by keeping more westwardly as the rout is equally level & the only object of this zigzag road is to pass the trading hous which however is some convenienc as we ware able to trade every extra article we had for mokisens & leather clothing exchanged of all our worn out mules & horses 20 miles.

2 Fine & dry moved westwardly up the vally of [Little] mudy creek which is entirely bare of grass made 12 miles & encamped in a Loose Scattering manner grass Scarce & dried all up pased Several ranges of volcanic hills rocks standing nearly perpendicular running as usual from S.W. to N.E. But differant from any I had before noticed the perpendicular Bluffs being on the eastern side & the gradual slope on the west the sides of many of the ridges are covered with scatering cedars but most of them are bare having Scarcely any vegetation on them not even the wild Sage which seems to be the hardiest vegitable in this cold dry region & I can now see severall Bunches Just dropping the Bloom allthough we have had but few nightis without frost since we came in sight of the snow capt mountains game antelopes grouse & Rabbits.

3 I let my Horses loose a little before day & they took the road ahead & I did not come up with them for about 4 miles whare they stoped to graze on a small valy of fine grass whare we all Should have encampd last night all Subordination and controle haveing been broken up for several days thinking ourselves out of danger at least danger of life But all savages will Steal & so will the Shoshonees a partiy of which are now passing while I am writeing Made 5 miles & encamped at a fine Sping of water the head of the North branch of [Little] Muddy on a fine platte of grass the rout to cross the Second mountain or devideing ridge between Green river & Bear river Several of us are preparing to go through on Horses & are Buisily preparing for our departure tomorrow nothing for fire but Sage.

4 Left our encampment Early 4 of us on packhorses for fort Hall & In a few hours we arived at the top of the ridge or mountain deviding the waters of green river and Bear riiver which last Emties in to the Greate Salt Lake from the top of the ridge we had a fine view of Green River vally which at this season of the year Looks Bald rough & desolate the Bear River vally ahead not quite so Bad but bear & Bad Enough every thing looking dry and parched the road up the East side follows a ravine whose sides are finely clothed in many places with aspin groves and the assent not verry Steep or difficult several fine Springs breaking out Just below the assent the asent westward is steep in several places & some sideling ground that requires some care & a good spring

Breaks out on Left of the road made 30 melis & encamped on Bear river.

5 Packed up & moved North down Bear River vally a brad fine well grssed vally with a steep range of volcanick mountains on each side but these ranges are not so regular as those noticied Hertofore but the rocks & earth Shew more the marks of eternal heat about noon we passed Smiths river running into Bear River the former a rapid Stream about 20 yards wide running rapidly over a round gravelly bed clear as crystal & cool as spring water made 24 miles & encamped on the North bend or as the hunters say whare Bear River comes around the point of the mountain this vally is the early Rendevous of the mountain Trappers & hunters But in the last 7 or 8 years the Buffaloe have entirely left this country & are now seldom seen west of Sweet water 20 miles Travled.

6 Started Early on the road following the bends of the River which was here during the forenoon verry crooked running at allmost all points of the compass early in the afternoon the road Steered out from the river & crossed over a steep ruged mountain which howevir is not wide the decente being very steep & about a mile in length from the top of this mountain we had a view of the N. end of sweet Lake [Bear Lake] which lies in a vally South of the river the river pasing through this mountain opens out into a much larger vally below the mountains bordering this vally have the same vitrified volcanick appearance as yestarday If it was not for the intire want of Timber this vally in many places might bear cultivation to some extent made 27 miles & encamped on a cool mountain Brook destitute of Timber.

7 Packed up before Sunrise and made off down the rever a N. W. course through a fine level vally for Several hours the mountains keeping thier usual appearance about noon we again had to cross over a mountain not verry high or ruged We did not Strike the river during the day but crossed several Brooks of good water & encamped at the Soda Springs a company of hunters from Fort hall had Just arived & Likewise a few persons (to hunt and make dried meat) For California.

These Springs are a greate natural curiosity the immediate vicinity of Springs are covered with Shrubby Cedars and pine timber & near the river a Shelly rock makes its appearance a little further out a fine white clay which appeared to have been blown up with a Substrata of rock which lies immediately beneath a thin Layer of caly [clay] this appears in dry times to form Quantities of the Salts of Soda then it becomes Quickly moistened and produces a Quanty of gass which is confined below & Bursts up the rock & earth to give it vent. the Strongest Spring is about ½ a mile North from the river which is so highly charged that it almost takes your Breath to drink acup of it Quick from the Spring But the most Singular one is below near the river Spouting as much as 6 feet high & a heavy collumn I had not more than one hour to make my examinations I regrett much that I was so hurried Several Large Spings of fresh water Break out in the viceinity of these & one hot Spring the rocks Strewed over the Lower plain has once evidently been in a State of fusion & resemble the Slag thrown out of Lead furnaces I mean the rock Strewed over the lower part of the vally.

8 After taking several hearty drinks of Soda water we left the Soda Springs went down the vally of the River about three miles when the river & us took different directions we turning Short to the N. & the River to the S a fine looking open vally Shewed itself before us but we ware Sadly disapointed for our appearant Smoothe road was rough & rocky all covered with Cynders of the hardest kind and broken into chasms & deep holes in all directions & the forenoon was wholy the worst road we have seen the afternoon proved to be better Traveling made 17 miles & encamped on Portnuff a Stream haveing Some curoisity about its heading in (in) the mountain deviding Bear & Snake Rivirs and taking a Southern course into the vally of Bear River it turns short into the mont[ain].

9 Made an Early Start on way up Portnuff & at noon Stop to graze on the top of the mountaines deviding the rivers we found this mountain pass verry cold & windy leaveing our Nooning place we wound around from Knob to ravine a few hours and began [to] desend on the ravines of Rosss. Creek toward Snake River Saw Some good Soil on these mountains but it is so dry & cold that it is useless made 25 miles and campd. The Prairies haveing been burnt recently our horses fared rather poor the ranges of these hills or mountains are not so regular as some others we have passed But are burned blacker and harder than any yet seen & are thrown up in a more confused manner Saw no kind of game Save a few covys of mountain grouse.

I fear the whole country West and South of us will be burned over as it keeps verry Smokey.

10 Moved on down the creek N. W. & Soon came in sight of the broad extensive vally of Snake river which for Several miles was entirely covered with wild Sage & deep blackish Sand after a fatiguing [ride] we at length reachd the Low vally & found plenty of grass & good water whare we unpacked to graze Made 16 miles & encamped on Snake River abut 2 miles above Fort Hall as we understood the grass was poor Further down this vally is wide & the Northern Highlands are invisible perhaps on account of the Smoke which lies thick in this vally the land appears to be poor & cold with great Quantities of Springs & Brooks in all Directions with the finest Kind of Trout but they ware Difficult to be Taken I did not go down to visit the Fort as I had no Letters for that place a good stock of cattle is Kept at the fort & a Large Quantity of Horses.

11 One ½ hour brot us oposite to the white washed mud walled Battlements of Fort Hall and as I had no Buisiness to transact I did not go inside But the outward appearance was pretty fair for a comfortable place for all that the present trade admits of Flour plenty at $20 per cwt. as nothing was purchased I cannot give any other prices but I presume they are as cheap as any of her Sister establishment in this region about noon crossed Portnuff here a Swift Stream 60 yards wide & Belly deep to our horses haveing plenty of T[r]out in it Made 18 miles & encamped on the river about half of a mile above the first falls during the whole of the afternoon we ware passing large bottoms of grass which would Support a considerable number of cattle & other Stock but no land fit for cultivation the uplands are covered with wild Sage.

12 About Sunrise we ware again on the trail and passed the falls whose musick luled us to sleep last night these falls have but little perpendicular pitch but fall about 16 or 18 feet in a verry short distance the water comeing rapidly down a raged rock is torn all into white foam Several rapids occured this forenoon and the whole country appears to have been once in a complete fusion of Liquid matter the rocks are all of a dark Borown & Black vitrified colour & some resembling Black glass in every particular a fiw Scattering cedars appear along the Bluffs which only help to give the country more of a melencholly appearance the Eternal Sage plains appear as extensive as formerly Cossed one singular creek which came tumbling down rapidly over a continual Succession of diposit damns made from the water made 27 miles.

13 Last night contrary to our expectations we came to a brook with a broad vally of fine grass this brook is called cassia [Raft River, says Camp] & is the place whare Mr. Hitchcock left our rout & went South with 13 wagons in company for California this days Travel is the most Barren Sterril region we have yet passed nothing to disturb the monotony of the Eternal Sage plain which is covered with broken cynders much resembling Junks of pot mettal & Now & then a cliff of Black burned rock which looks like Distruction brooding over dispair found a filthy pond of water at noon made 28 miles & encamped on the river which we left yesterday & again had fair grazeing No animal Seen no fowl Save a few mountain grouse which can live in any region whare vegitation can grow our couse down this river so far has been S.W.

14 Left our camp on the river & Steered S. of W. across a Barren Sage plain corssed one brook of water & Saw 2 Antelope the only animals seen in some days The earth is the driest I ever saw it & the dust rises in perfect clouds every particle of moistness & adhsion is obliterated & lost & currents of dust is frequently seen rolling down the path & Spreading like hot embers that have been well Stirred came to the River to noon & grze the River running through cliffs of Black volcanic Rocks which grew Steeper & higher as we decended down the River at length we left the Bluffs of the River being 1000 or more feet of Perpendicular Rock standing from the plain to the water & the river pressed to 20 or 30 feet in width after 20 miles of fatiugueing ride we encampd haveing made 30 miles at fair grass & water.

15 (Sunday) Left our camp on the brook & moved off west over a Sage plaine as usual Kept down the course of the creek we encamped, on last nght soon saw that it fell in to a Kenyon of Steep Black Rocks after following 8 or 10 miles we crossed..over the Kenyon at a favourable point & Struck for the River over the usual Kind of Sage plane & late in the afternoon we desended the main Kenyon on Snake River The Black battlement cliffs of this river remind one of the Fragments of a world distroyed or at least distroyed for all human purposes on the river we found a Small fishing party of Ponacks. [Bannocks] who had plenty of Small fish of the Sucker mouthed Kind Several Tremendious Springs come Pouring out of the rocks oposite Made 20 miles & encamped on the River confined in Between high & impassible rocks.

16 Pased down the Kenyon to the mouth of a Small river & over the ridge to the little or upper Salmon Falls whare we found a number of Indians encamped who offered us plenty of dried Salmon cheap & almost for any thing we offered them these falls are Surrounded with high inaccessable Clay & rock Bluffs the vally norrow & Broken up with ravines Sandy without vegitation except Sage & some of the Same Kind of useless hardy plants Made 25 miles over Sage plains deep ravines clay Bluffs &c &c it being the most uneven roade we have yet had for so greate a distance & the most Barren county of grass Likewise as well as an intire want of water except in the River [which] runs in such a precepice that only a few places can [be] desended even on foot & then to return to the summit is ½ a days hard labour.

17 Left our position & went down the River whare it was with difficulty that our pack horses could Travel on account of the steepness of the way at length about 10 A.M. we came to the ford or upper crossing of the river & saw a few Teams on the opposite side that had left Fort Hall 6 days before us. Soil since we left portnuff Slaked & unslaked lime volcanic rocks & fine & coarse sand Sometimes simple & pure & other times mixed in various porportions vegitation Sage prarie Thorn & Liquorice plant all Shrubby but thick set with Scarcely any grass on the uplands Some lowlands are Sometimes well set withe Short grass made 24 miles & encamped on a Small Brook with Several

Wagons & found Some Ney Percee Indians with them & a few Snakes Some difficulty was likely to grow out of a Stolen horse. the [matter] was easily settled.

18 After crossing the River yestarday we Steered north Several miles We raised a high bluff & crossed an uneven sage plane on a western direction & at Starting we Steered N. W. to the point of a low Mountain intirly destitute of Timber But Plenty of Sage & the ground Strewn thick with Cynders & other volcanic Rock verry rough & Sharp to travel over passed a verry hot Spring & grazed at a muddy Brook overgrown with canes.

The afternoon about 10 miles was the most Rocky rough road we have yet seen made 25 miles & encampd on a Small Brook running through a deep kenyon the mountains again made their appearanc on the South Side of Snake River which had disappered for Some days past the Rocky cliffs to our North of us appear verry dry & Rugged.

19 A few hours from our last nights encampment Brot us to an entire chang of Surface & we gladly exchangd the rough volcanick rocks for good hard gravel road but Quite uneven and the Burnt earth & rock entirely disapeared & was succeeded by the rough grey granite Standing like Stumps on a fallow or more like a monumental church yard this singular appearance lasted in groups for several hours & we saw but little sage during the day Made 30 miles & encamped at the first possible chance we found to desend to the River Gross Boise or Bigwood which here comes rushing out of the most uneven Ruged Mountain I had yet seen & passes rapidly down through a Steep Kenyon which cannot [be] assended or desended even on foot except in a few places this is a rapid Stream about 40 yards wide & is fine for Salmon.

20 Set out down the river west the mountains to our right and the perpendicular rock Bank to the left both receding & deminishing a fine wide vally opened to our view & we pased down through the dust which was almost past endureance but not much wose than it had been for Several day past This stream has more Timber & Brush than most of the streams of this [region] allthough this vally is wide yet it has scarcely any grass & the land is as dry as ashes & would not produce any Known grains or vegitables made 20 miles & encamped on the river which is as clear & fine as a mountain Torrent which it is of the finest Kind ourselves & animals are completey tired out with dust & burned Prairies which has generally been the case since we left the devide between Bar River and Snake River.

Campd with 2 Teams that were ahead Made 28 miles.

21 Left our camp & Took to the dust again in a few miles we passd 9 wagons in camp about 4 miles further passed 14 or 15 more all making a move for the road crossed over the river to the north Side & made our way down a dry dusty plane untill noon this river so far has but little grass & what is is dry or Burned close to the ground to day we are almost out of Sight of Mountains only the tops of a few being visable The country we have passed over will be distressing to the teams in the rear as it is already bare.

Afternoon again Bore down the vally found in verry dry & dusty But better grassed course North of West a little Before Sundown came in sight of Fort Boisie & encamped for the night a beautifull clear evening & the sun went tranquilly down behind the Blue mountans without a cloud to be seen.

22 (Sunday) Left our camp 2 miles above Fort Boise & passed the mud walld Fort of Boise & the clerk was Kind enough to make us out a Sketch of the rout to walla walla crossed Snake River a Short distance below the Fort found the ford good & Smoothe but rather deep for wagons unpacked on the opposite Side Several Families of Ponacks [Bannocks] & Sauptins [Nez Perces] ware encamped at the Fort it being Sunday the sauptins refused to trade with our men on account of the Sabbath Packed oup & put N. of W. Snake River running N. The Trail carried us over another Sage plain 14 miles to Malure [Malheur] River a dirty deep Stream running to the N. E. with a fine large dry vally covered in strong coarse grass & small willows a hot spring comming out on E. Shore under a high cliff of volcanic rocks Made 28 miles.

23 Left our camp on Malure & Struck out N.W. up a vally the eastern branch of which we assended to the head & decended another dry ravine beyond the ridge the entire country covered with sage which

from some cause or other is nearly all dead passed the Birch Spring
and encamped on Snake River which here comes out of a rough
looking mountain to the east & makeing a Short curve goes off into the
mountains again to the North our camp is verry poor for grass which
has been the case for Several days & no appearance for the better many
of our horses are nearly exhausted & several afoot this evening we
raised our bread with saleratas picked up a few miles east of indepen-
denc rock on sweet water.

   24 Clear as usual for it has not rained Since we left Fort Larrimie
passed a ridge & soon Struck by what we Supposed to be Burnt River
Quite a small criek Bound in by steep high Lime rock Mountains
almost impasible for our horses yet the wagons have gone this rout
these mountains as well as those passed yesterday shew all the visible
effects of fire Some red some yellow Brown white & green mostly of
decomposed rock & remarkable fine clay all dry & dusty even to the
touch Made 17 miles through the worst mountains and over the worst
road we have yet seen the sides of these mountains are nearly pependicular & composed of granite & rough Slate rock without any timber
or any other kind of vegitation except Short grass and in many places
entirely bare.

   25 Left our camp in the slate mountains & after making two or
three curves in the hills we came out on an open country comparatively & Struck Burnt river again in a vally north of which stands a
singular conicle Knobb crownd with several pinicles of rocks resembling horns no game of any kind seen not even the appearance of a
rabbit which are so plenty on snake River Made 18 miles & encampd at
a Spring amongst rounded Knobs well clothed in Short grass as all the
country in sight has been all the afternoon there seems to be an entire
change of Soil from any we have passed over Lately all the streams are
likewise (are) slightly skirted to day with willows alders & a Species of
Birch & other Shrubery but no valluable timber has been seen since we
passed the Black Hills.

   26 Left our camp at the spring & took the trail bearing N. up
though the hills arived at the top of the ridge Saw to ou left mountains
clothed with pine or othe[r] evergreen timber a few hours brought us

to another detested sage plain that vegitable being Scarce for the last 2 days Nooned at what is called the lone Tree in the middle of a vally & a fine one it has been of the pine Spicies now cut down & all the branches used for fuel the day verry Smoky & I Begin to doubt Mr. Espys theory of produceeing rain by any phisical means as the whole country has been on fire for a month past & no rain yet a range of mountains lying close to our left seem to be all enveloped in Smoke Made 25 miles & encamped on Powder River which runs (when there is Plenty of water) through a fair vally of grass the hills Likewise are generally well covered with the Same, our selves & animals are becomeing tired of travel.

27 Came to our camp last night Mr [William C.] Dement and 4 Indians going to meet the wagons their object I did not assertain but some (some) speculation no doubt Passed through a beautifull vally this fore noon well grassed but to dry for cultivation a Timbred mountain close to our left the same seen range yestarday morning As we caught our horses for our aftenoons travel Some Indian as is their habit when they discover Strangers in their country set fire to the grass about a half mile ahiad of us our rout being N. & a strong south wind blowing the fire kept ahead of us though the hills about 6 or 8 miles and when we overtook the fire we had some difficulty in passing it but all got through nearly suffocated with smoke & dust & entered the grand Round vally the whole mountains which surround this vally completely enveloped in fire and Smoke neare Sundown we discovered a man rideing rapidly toward us which proved Mr Watters [James Waters] from Willamitt waiting for his family which he expects to come in this seasons imigraton made 26 miles and encamped close under the Bleue Mountains in company with Mr. Watters & Mr [Rice?].

28 Concluded to ly still to day and rest ourselves and horses before taking the Blue Mountains which we are informed will be two days without grass this is a well watered well grassed vally but the thick smoke preventes me from seeing the probatile Size or extent I think however it is not large Remained in camp to day which was Quite warm although we had a white frost last night as we have had for several nights past. Encamped in this vally are several hudred Indians of the Skyuse nation now amalgamated with Shehaptin or Pierce nose nation 30 or 40 of these people visited us this afternoon & from whoom we traded a little cammerce thy bringing with them some peas & Squashes of their own raising they seemed to be anxious to see our wagons & cattle they being anxious to trade horses (for) of which they have great Quantities for cattle & appear to be rapidly advancing in civilization this vally is also verry favourable to the groth of the (root) Cammerce [Camas] root a root much esembling & onion in appearance but of a Sweet rich tast when roasted after the manner of the Indians the smok appeared to encrease.

29 (Sunday) Left our camp in the grand Round vally and took up the Blue Mountains which are steep & rough but not so bad as I had anticipated from Previous information came to the grand round creek in about 10 miles the mountain so far is mostly Prairie & fairly covered with g[r]ass some parts However espicially the ravines & vallies are covered with pine & spruce timber the rocks all shew the effects of internal fires Left our nooning & proceeded on N. Westward Pased some remarkable wild & lonesome groves of pine & firr that had a dark appeearanc & the more so on account of the thick smoke that enveloped the mountain in such clouds as to nearly hide the sun at midday continued untill dusk along bare rocky rough Sides of the mountain extremly bad for wagons & encamped with out water there being but little water in these dry vitrified ridges made 26 miles saw but little sign of any wile animals Except Pheasants which are plenty in some parts of this range & live upon the berries of winter green which grows in Quantities in many places saw likewise a specees of Laurel or Ivy on the Ridgis.

30 Saddled up at day light and proceded on our way found the trail tolerable for hosses in about 8 miles came to some pools of Standing water whare we took Breakfast these mountains are partially covered with Several Kinds of evergreen timber the South sides of the ridgis are bare or thinly sit with grass all the rocks & they are plenty shew the effects of fire at some remote period the caly [clay] is of the same kind as that found on the plains verry fine and Soluble in water but of a yellow colour Some a verry deep yellow with all Shades down to a pale grate Quantities of coarse pummice stone laying strewed over the ground particularly near the western desent of the mountain the western desent of the Mountain is much more easy & grduel than the easterm so far I have seen but little land that would be called fit for cultivation in any of the Western States allthough there are a fiw Spots that would bare cultivation Made 25 miles & encamped on a Small brook or rather Spring to the right of the trail & close to the foot of the mountain.

[Inside back cover]

Madison Gilmore	|	tell these
Joel Walker	|	Gentlemen
Peter H. Burnett	|	that Gnel [General]
Anarson [Anderson] Smith	|	Gilham is on the road
James Watters	|	and scarce of Provision

Notes on Chapter Nine

Clyman seems well aware, in his notes for August 20, that his party under Jedediah Smith and Tom Fitzpatrick was responsible for bringing South Pass to general knowledge.

Apparently Clyman carved the headstone for the unfortunate Mr. Barnette, whose death is recorded on August 26. Clyman had developed a distinctive carving style when he chiseled the milestones on the Vincennes-Springfield turnpike as a surveyor in Illinois. A photograph published in L. V. Loomis' *Journal of the Birmingham Emigrating Company,* (Salt Lake City, 1928), shows the inscription on Barnette's grave carved like Clyman's milestones.

Chapter 10
Notebook Four
The Blue Mountains to the Valley of the Willamette

[October 1, 1844 to January 31, 1845]

Tuesday Oct 1st 1844

A beautifull morning & fine clear nights I neglected to mention yesterday that this vally was nearly covered with horses when we came down the mountain but no Indians came to our camp this as well as the grand round vally being one of the great Stoping places of the Kyuse tribe of Indians & from them we obtained Some Potatoes Corn Peas & Squashes of their own raising they likewise are verry anxious to obtain cows & other cattle for which they exchang horses of which they have great Quantities There is no climate finer than this if dry weather constitutes a fine climate & indeed the days remind one of Byrons discription of Italy not a cloud to be seen neither day nor night for months togather

Left our encampment & proceded on the Trail 2 or 3 miles when we came to a Kyuse farm Krailed [corralled] in with willows and planted with corn beans potatoes &c &c here we left the wagon trail which turns to the right & goes to Dr Whitmans said to be 40 or 50 miles further than the rout we took which goes down the Utilla I here observed that the wild Bunch grass of this country was intirely eat out near the Indian farms and does not seem to grow again Traded some potatoes of the Kyuse Women & proceeded on down the Utilla a fine mill-stream made 16 miles & campd on the creek at the head of a Kenyon through which the creek passes during the day saw several large roads leading in different directions.

2   I neglected to mention that I forwarded all the letters intrusted to my care & directed to Mr [H. H.] Spalding & Dr. [Marcus] Whitman to Mr Gilbert who left us in the grand round vally to go directly to Dr Whitmans & I hope they went to their proper directions Last night about 8 oclock & while we ware all siting by our camp fire talking & thinking ourselves one niight safe for horse thieivs we heard an unusual tramping of our horses When I arose & walked out in the direction of our horses what was my surprise to find my fine but most st[a]rved mare being driven off by an Indian on hose back not haveing brought my gun with me I called to him to halt at which he put off at full speed leaveing the mare & 2 mules that ware following so much for the Kyuse who are said to be the most honest Savage people on the continent our fore noons travel has been mostly down the utilla through a very dry country the stream confined amidst a black wall of volcanick rocks & over a dryer upland thinly coated with short grass made 26 miles & encamped on the utilla several Indians made their appearance but did not come to us this afternoon passed some small patches of cultivated land in a small but rich vally near the creek the weather contines verry smoky allthough we have not seen aney fires for several days this creek does not afford any valuable timber ther being nothing but cotton wood that grows to any size & that is verry shrubly.

3   Left our camp amidst the walla walla camps there being 3 of their fires in sight none of them came near us during the night & as several men ware robed by them last season we ware glad to [see] that they kept at a distanc our party being now reduced to 4 men the others some haveing gone to Dr Whitmans and some having preceded us on leaveing camp We likewise left the timber which extends no farthe down the utilla the stream running over black burned rocks to whare it enters the columbia came on the banks of the great river about 11

o'clock which shews no change but runs through sand planes & rocky banks so far as we went without timber or drift wood except here & there a small clump of willows & those scarce passed several encampments of Wallawallas sutuate on sand bars along the river which came out & gazed at us as we passed.

Made 24 miles over mostly sand plains covered with sage & prickly pears bothe of which we thought & hoped that we had passed at our camp we found it difficult to gather as much Brush weeds & sage as would boil a fiw potatoes & a cup of coffee the river looks Beautiful & the water clear and good but nothing else can be seen to change the sight of the detested sage & and sand planes.

Greate Quantities of Salmon are taken in the utilla when the water is up in June and their appears to be plenty of that Fish in the stream yet as we could hear splunging on the ripples all night but they are [not] considered good at this season haveing become Quite poor from their long stay in fresh water as the smallest kind of a fish could not assend this streame at this season of the year the upper vally of this stream would make some handsome farms if their was any timber to be had but none is seen except cottonwood & willow.

4 Had a Quiet nights rest and a Beautifull clear morning Left our camp on the great river & proceed down the River passed several Indian villages all on the oposite side nothing seen but rocks sand & a shrubby stinted groth of vegetation with here & there [a] Bunch of short grass the north side of the River appears to be closely Bound by a ridge of Black frowning rocks current of the river rapid.

The ridge of rocks mentioned in the fore noon closed up on the sauth side in afternoon and gave us an uncommon bad road even in this steril region and we had to travil over sharp rocks or deep sands & sometimes both the rocks being covered deep in sand so that our horses sunk half leg deep in sand & then stepd on unknown sharp rocks at the bottom makeing the way extremely tiresome & bad.

Made 26 miles & encamped on the (on the) River again before we had packed up three men with thier guide & enterperter came up from willamette on their way to meet the emegrants one of them general [M. M.] McCarver was expecting to see his family on the road but we could not give him any information concerning them we soon parted they proceeding up & we down the river.

The general seemed to speak in raptures of the Oregon Country and even went on to say that on the top of the cliff of Black rocks under which we ware encamped was a fine grazeing country this may be admitted but certainly their was not the amount of one cord of wood in the circuit of 25 miles & perhaps not a drop of water in the same distance except what flowed in the Columbia & many other extravigancies.

5 Left our camp once more after haveing 28 miles of the most tiresome Travel we had yet found on account of the Quantity of sharp fallen rocke which filled the path over which we had to travel the [path] leading near the water in under a cliff of dark perpendicular rocks the fragments of which had fallin down & choked up all the narrow wally far in to the water some times disending to a considerable hight immediately under the cliff & then acsending back to the water edge along a narrow path which one animal could scarcely travel in over sharp rocks made the road tiresome in the extreme & we traveled steadly all day without stopping the afternoon being windy & Bo[is]torows the dust & sand nearly choked us when about sundown we came to a small open vally & encamped for the night tired and glad to find a resting place larg enough to ley down on these rocks remind one of emmense walled cities castled forts & ruins of tremendious magnitude but this is the last place in the world to enjoy any such scenery whare nothing is to be seen but rocks Sand & Savages.

6 Crossed Johndays River early which like all the country in this region comes in through steep rocks & is difficult to cross on account of the rocks being very steep passed severall steep cliffs all of which may [be] said to be dangerous on account of the loose rocks of which they are composed & the high perpendicular cliffs below jetting over the river Late in the afternoon passed the river De Shutes made 44 miles in the 2 days.

7 Yestarday evening after passing the River De Chuttes took a guide who conducted us a short rout over the hills to a small rich vally with handsome little Brook running through it whare we encamped

for the night this vally would bear cutivation but has no timber in sight
saw mount hood nearly west covered in snow nearly halfway dow[n]
its sides this weather continues thick & smoky.

Every device and artifice is used by the natives of this river to
obtain ammunition & other manufactoried articles of the whites & the
following was used by some natives to day 5 or 6 natives came leaping
& yelling gaily from behind the sand hills one [had] a small piece of
dried salmon an other a few handfulls of corn a 3d some dried roots
each bringing something & insisted that we should eat we continued
moveing on & they running along side offering ther subsistance
without price untill reaching a bend in the River we stoped to let our
horses drink when one of them spreading his blanket on the sand they
spread out the repast for us, & obliged us to taste the provision which
gave them a fair right to beg and importune us for tobacca Lead
powder and in short every small article they could think of after giving
a part of what they wanted we rode on they seeming well pleased.

Reached Mr [H. K. W.] Perkins missionary station in the fore noon
now occupid by Mr [Alvan F.] Waller delivered to him a letter taken
from the office at west port Mr Waller apears to be a gentleman but I
do not recolect that he thanked me for the care & trouble of bringing
the letter but the reverend gentleman must be excused for my appearance certanly did not shew that I could appreceate any civilities not
haveing shaved for about 15 days or changed clothes for more than 30
and the Reverend gentleman pricking himself verry much on outward
appearances as I have since understood.

8 Started up the steep ridge west of the creek & in ½ an hour
reached the top our selve & horses in a foam of sweat on account of
the steepness of the path but the cool mountain Breeze soon relieved
our lungs this like all the ridges of this mountain was soon crossed &
we had a longer & steeper decent than any previouly crossed but after
a pack horse or two pitching thire loads over their heads we at length
reached not the bottom but smoothe going which fell into deep ravines
to the right passed over an uneven plain covered with the pines &
largest kind of Fir & pine timber interspersed with stented oaks this
continued for some 9 [?] miles with several small Brook passing

through made 18 miles & encamped near the bank of rapid tumbling mountain torrent immediately below the forks the eastern branch from its colour & appearanc being a part of the weepings from the white summit of Mount Hood which is covered in snow more than half way down its sides.

The ridges over which we passed are verry steep and high being about 2 miles & about the same distance down the opposite side.

From the missionary establishment passed yestarday there is a grand view of the Columbia pushing its course through the black Frowning rocks which stand in thick profusion in over & about the stream with the wildest mountain scenery in all directions & of all kinds surmounted in the north west by a conicle summit of a mountain caped in Eternal snow.

9 Proceede early up the East side of the stream we had encamped on & soon crossed the Eastern branch the water being very rapid tumbling & roling down amidst the rocks which lay so thick that it was difficult for our horses to keep their feet pased up the stream some miles through allmost impervious thickits of veer[y] green shrubery of to me new & unknown kinds crossed over to the W Branch through the same kind of Shrubery & passed up the East side of the W Branch through immence groves of Fir timber the tallest & straites I ever beheld some supposed to be nearly or Quite 100 feet high & not more than 18 inches through at the ground immence mountains covered and crouded thickly with timber apearing in all directions in the afternoon we assended an open ridge the large timber having (havein) been killed off by fire & from this ridge we had a splendid view of mount Hood & various other ridges & pinicles some thickly timbered to their summits others nearly bar or covered with under brush shewing at this season a greate veriaty of [colors] some covered with a species of dwarf maple wore a deep red appearance others yallow & Brown contrasted with the deep green Firr of othe[r] points & the white snowy summit of Mount Hood gave us all the veriety of shades allmost between green white & red But soon we took down the steep sides again & all views ware lost except now & then a perpendicular peep up an immence Firr tree which seemed to have no reasonable stopping but went on to a dizzy hight.

Made about 25 miles & encamped after sun down tied up our horses not having seen a hanfull of grass during the day.

10 Saddled our Starved animals and proceed up the couse of one of branches of the same creek we followed all day yesterday the same immence Quantity of timber continueing & not in the [least] diminished in Size & hight in about 4 hours winding around & jumping over logs we (we) assended the highest ridge of the cascade mountains over which the trail passes but the timber prevented us forom having any view in any direction turning short to the west we began our desent down the western declivity & following the course of a ravine through which ran a clear Brook of cool water we desended rapidly and found going down hill more pleasant than going up especially when one goes on foot as we all did our horses not being able to carry us in about 3 hours we came to an open sandy vally through which ran a rapid Brook called Sandy the vally being more than a mile wide & covered with sand & Loose rock.

This vally appeared to have been a deep mountain ravine at no distant period from the greate Quantities of dry Firr that [were] standing on each side and lay strewn over and intermingled with the rocks and sand and as the Stream takes its rise from the summer weepings of Ice & snow on the western declivity of Mount Hood I conclud that some tremendious avalanch must have decended into the vally carrying every thing before it rock sand gravel timber & all in one confused mass the whole being carried down filled up the narrow ravine & forming the present vally now Just begining to shew a stented groth of young Firrs or that some internal heat must have melted off the ice & the immence flood of water broke over all its original bounds tore away from the lower part of the mountain [the] mixed mass that now fills & forms the vally.

11 Left our camp on sandy & proceded along the blind trail down the stream at a slow gate untill nearly noon the brawling mountain torrent haveing assumed Quite the appearanc of a river we left the stream & turned short to the right & soon came to a kind of Brushy opening of rich soil & some grass whare we stoped to graze an hour saw some male Fern growing here nine or 10 feet in hight moved on the trail along a narrow ridge amongst the tall Firr and the emmence large Hemlock timber grate Quantities lying down & more standing Several small Brooks crossing our path untill near sundown we came to an opening or Small Prairie whare we encamped for the night going nearly ½ amile down a steep declivity for water to cook our Suppers during the whole of today the country had been burned some still on fire & some had been burned last year the under Brush being killed & the larger [timber] haveing fallen in all directions made the travelling verry bad & tiresome as our horses had to leap over all the logs filled with sharp snags & limbs to the greate danger of letting out their entrails.

Made about 18 miles & we ware glad to find a spot of green grass for our animals to feed on during the night these mountains do not appear to have much game on them as we saw nothing but a few small Squirrels & some Pheasants the latter plenty in (in) some places & several ware killed to day which proved to make a fine Treat and ate well being fat and finely flavorured passed several small spots of land that appeared to have a deep rich soil of pale redish coloured clay mingled with decomposed rock and gravel and generally covered with an emmence thick and large groth of firr timber.

12 Again under way before Sunrise a stiff white frost covered the grass & weeds in an hours travel we came down a Steep hill into a low ground completely strewn over with logs & brush a late fire having passed over in many [plaes] the smoldring logs ware (ware) yet smoking after leaping logs & Braking Brush we succeeded in gaining the Banks of sandy the stream we left to the south of us yestardy & crossed to South side whare for a mile or more we encountred the same difficulties as on the North side after greate exertion to our Jaded animals we at length gained the top of the Bluffs whare the pathe became more opin and traveling more pleasant crossing two or three handsome Brooks & passing as many thickets we at length gained an open highland of fine Soil covered thickly with fern & dug thickly with holes by some Burrowing animal what kind I did not asertain.

Made about 15 miles and encamped at a small Spring whare we found fair grazing for our animals and we made preperations for Shaveing & prepareing ourselves to see our countrymen tomorrow allmost wearied out with the continual watching it requires to tarvel through an unsettled country such as we had now passed our little party felt lively and happy and [it] Bcame a pleasant task to once more wash shave and bathe ourselves in the cold clear running little brook that passed our present encampment and we spent a Jovial evening around our camp fire in the anticipation that for a while at least our constant toils ware about to ceas as we knew the setlements ware not far distant about dark two Indians of the Walla walla tribe came up & campd near having been to willhamett trading they remained with us & in the morning we parted each [going his own] road.

13 (Sunday) Early we ware again on our saddles and Kept down the valy of (of) some creek or river [of] which we heard the water rippeling but did not come in sight of the stream, the trail leading along through a kind of firr opening whare the grass in places looked green as summer in spots but we soon passed over all the fine places going up (and) steep banks through brush & logs allmost impassable the woods haveing been rcently burned & many old logs yet smoking and again crossed sandy haveing increased to a small river still running rapid over a rocky bed the low grounds being litterly covered with logs and brush after tearing through brush and leaping logs about an hour we at length assended the bluffs & found an open trail comparatively crossed Several fine running brooks of clear water steep guters &c &c About 2 oclock P.M. came on the top of ridge & saw some cattle feeding on the vally of the clackimus River & soon came in sight of a cabbin the first of the settlement of Willhamett and on enquiry found we ware within 4 miles of the Falls of Willhamett the Seat of government & the main commercial place for all the settlments of the Teritory of Oregon crossed a rough rocky Ridge & came to a small farm or two on the bottom land of the Clackimus crossed the river at an old Chinook village and in ½ an hour we ware on the banks of the Willhamett River and at (on) the lower part of the town or city platt.

as soon as I entered the village I shook hands with a Mr Ware [J. W. Wair] a young man of my acquaintance from Indiana who came out with the last years emigration 20 miles.

————

Along the Willamette in 1844 and 1845

It commenced raining on [Oct.] the 21 which is earlier than usual From the 13th to the 22nd remained at the falls of Wilhamett or in the near vicinity when Three of us precured a skiff and made an excursion down to Fort Vancouver.

This great depository of goods and peltries for all the Indian trade west of the main range of the Rocky mountains stands on a gravely plain on the north side of the Columbia River and about five miles above the upper mouth of the Wilhamet and is situated bearly above extreme high water mark.

The Fort itself is a wooden stockade and contains in its inside the companies store all the officies of the company and a complete Quadangular row of Buildings for servants &c which like the outer works can be closed by port doors at pleasure all in a good State of repair & kept clean and neat.

The present incumbent Doct. [John] McLaughlin received us verry hospitably and intertained us in the most kind genteel and agreeable manner during our stay at the Fort giving all the information desired on all subjects connected with the country but seemed anxious that greate Brittain might retain the north of the Columbia river saying that it was poor and of little use except the Fur and peltries that it yealded this may or may not be the fact.

25 On our return from Vancouver the morning being pleasant I took my gun and left the skiff to the management of my comrades and landed on the western shore of the Willhamet I soon found a stripe of open Prarie land overflown in high water but now dry and pleasant walking with here and there a pool of mud and water which has stood the drough of summer These pools or ponds are now overgrown with several kind of vegitation and (and) litterly and completely covered over with water fowl of various kinds from the nobl and majestick swan down to the Teal & plover For miles the air seemed to be darkened with the emmenc flights that arose as I proceeded up the vally the morning being still thier nois was tumultuous and grand the hoarse shrieks of the Heron intermingled with the Symphonic Swan the fine treble of the Brant answered by the strong Bass of the goose with ennumerable shreeking and Quacking of the large and Smaller duck tribe filled every evenue of Surrounding space with nois and reminded one of Some aerial battle as discribed by Milton and all though I had been on the grand pass of waterfowl on the Illinois River it will not begin to bear a comparison with this thier being probably Half a Million in sight at one time and all appearantly Screaming & Screeching at once.

   26 Arived at the Falls again the las week being showery.

   27 Sunday Fair and warm wrote to H J Ross.

Clyman's letter to Ross

COL. CLYMAN.—Most of our readers in this vicinity, and particularly those who are old settlers, remember Col. James Clyman, one of the earliest settlers of Wisconsin, and they know also that a year ago last spring the Col. started with an emigrating party to Oregon. A few days since Mr. Hiram Ross received a letter from the Col. which we subjoin. We are confident that we could not give place in our columns to any thing that would be more acceptable.

Willamet Falls, Oregon,
October 27, 1844.

   I arrived here on the 13th day of the present month, having been on the way 151 days from Independence, Missouri, which was at least one month longer than were the last year's company of emigrants.

This was owing to the unusual rains that fell during the first two months after our departure from Missouri.

My health is good and has been during the whole route. The health of the small party that accompanied me is also good. The last thousand miles no interruption from the Indians took place, nor did even a shower of rain fall to lay the dust.

None of the families have yet arrived. The foremost are expected to reach this neighborhood in about a week. The last range of mountains, called the Cascades, have never been passed with waggons. We were five days passing over this range of mountains, and found it by far the most difficult and fatiguing part of the journey, both for ourselves and our horses. The mountains extend to within a few miles of this place. The range runs nearly north and south. The Willamet is on the west side of the mountains. The Columbia breaks through from east to west; it has a number of dangerous passes, and two falls that cannot be passed by the lightest canoe. Our families, waggons and baggage were carried around the falls; the portages however are not lengthy.

The settlements of this Territory appear to be in a good and prosperous condition. Even the last years' emigrants, some of whom have not been more than 9 or 10 months on their new farms, have plenty for themselves, and some to spare for their countrymen now on the way. Of bread, beef, fish, and potatoes of a superior kind, we have plenty. The three first mentioned articles are exported. The Brig Columbia is now freighted with wheat and flour, and will sail in a few days for the Sandwich Islands. A probable trade with the Islands is already commenced. From us they receive wheat, flour, beef, pork and lumber. In return we receive from the British, Chinese & American manufactured articles; and molasses, sugar, coffee, and rice, the growth of the Islands.

Standing in the door of my present lodgings I can count sixty-two buildings. They form the present village of the city of Oregon. Timber and lumber lay scattered about for more buildings, say 8 or 10. Several other villages, (one or two of them I have seen) have some pretensions to future greatness, but are quite small as yet.

The Hudson Bay Company transact nearly all the foreign and domestic trade. The Company derive great profit from the business, and at the same time accomodate the inhabitants of the Territory, who are all agriculturists and mechanics without capital sufficient for commercial pursuits. On our arrival we found the country dry and parched. We have recently had a week of warm rainy weather. The grass has commenced springing up and looks much like our Wisconsin prairies in May. The leaves of such trees as shed their foliage are yellow and beginning to fall. The kinds shedding the leaf are oak, a species of maple, alow [willow?], box wood, hazel, elder, &c, all small and scrubby, compared to those in the states except elder and alder, which here grow quite large. Notwithstanding the ease with which the necessaries of life are acquired, I never saw a more discontented community, owing principally to natural disposition. Nearly all, like myself, having been of a roving discontented character before leaving their eastern homes. The long tiresome trip from the States, has taught them what they are capable of performing and enduring. They talk of removing to the Islands, California, Chili, and other parts of South America with as much composure as you in Wisconsin talk of removing to Indiana or Michigan.

Almost the first man I met on my arrival, was J. M. Weir formerly of Indiana, who served with me in the Rangers. I also hear of Lancaster Clyman, who is married and settled some 40 or 50 miles up the Willamet. I expect to see him this week. It is said that he is doing well.

You recollect the large stories we used to hear respecting the immense size and height of timber in this country. The largest timber I have seen is an evergreen of the fir kind. One tree that I measured a few days since, is six feet four inches in diameter and 268 feet long. The tree was felled with an axe last summer. The firr is of two kinds, white and red; both good for timber and lumber, and generally splits easy, making the neatest rail fences I have ever seen; it has the appearance of being durable. This is the season for sowing wheat; all the farmers are busily employed, it having been heretofore too dry to sprout the grain. The farmer can sow wheat from August until June,

with a certainty of reaping a fair compensation for his labor. The
straw of that sown in May grows very short which renders it difficult
to harvest. That sown early and in good order grows large and long,
measuring 5 and 6 feet, and in some extraordinary cases, it has been
known to measure 7 feet in length, with a proportionable length of
head. The grain or berry of all that I have seen is remarkable for its
round plump form.

The small Canada corn comes to perfection; oats likewise grow
well; Irish potatoes are of a fine quality and yield abundantly. The
streams I am told never freeze over, nor does the snow cover the
ground more than 3 or 4 days at any one time during the winter. The
open or prairie valleys are small, almost all the uplands are covered
thickly with the loftiest firr. The earth is thickly covered with bogs,
underbrush, and the male fern called by some brake. It grows in
many places up to my shoulders, and so thick that I found it impos-
sible in some instances to break through it.

I have crowded all I could on one sheet which I send by Mr.
Perkins of the brig Columbia, bound to Oahoo on the Sandwich
Islands, whence I hope it will find its way by the whalers to Boston or
some other port in the States. You may not hear from me again until I
reach California.

JAS. CLYMAN.

28 The morning Foggy day Fair.

29 Slight Showers through the night and in fact continued all day.

30 Rained all night slight showers through the day.

31 Riany and windy most of the night the winds so far from the S.
W. morning still and foggy. But cleared off in the Forenoon &
continued clear & warm all day.

1844 Friday the 1st November
Fair and warm the Hazel & willow begining to shed their Leaves.

2 Left the falls & rode out westwardly 20 miles to the Twalitine
Plains over an undulating Firr Plain in many Places Quite open soil a
dark red clay the planes themselves are fine open Prarie of good deep

clay Loam solil Staid with a Mr Pomroy [Walter Pomeroy] who has a farm of 180 acres in cultivation this day was fair.

3 It rained several Showers through the night But cleared away in the morning Passed nearly through the Twalitine settlements containing about Sixty families all appearing in a thrifty condition thiere farms on rich smoothe clay Prairie Had a Beautiful view of Mount Hood clothed in his white mantle of snow & Looking out far above a girdle of clouds that wrapd. his icy sides.

4 Pased through several Beautifull small Praries most of which are claimed & on [which] some fair sized Farms have commenced which shew that the occupants have been handsomely Rewarded for their labour crossed the three Branches of the Twalitine River all narrow streams but deep as our horses had to swim and we passed over on some (of) long Firr trees which had been felled across them Pased through the Chehalem vally a high open vally about a mile wide extending from the South Branch of Twaletine to the Yam Hill river which is likewise a Tributory of the wilhamet this vally is bounded on the east with high rounded rang of hills well set with fine green grass and covered thinly with short Junts of shrubby white oaks on the west it rises up into a much higher range of hills thickly cowered with tall Firr timber.

5 Crossed a range of high rounded hills covered with excelent grass and whare it had been burned 16 or 18 days it was now green and fair pasturage that which had not been burned of was likewise green & good grazing crossed the Yam Hill Rivir about Twelve Rods wide deep & navegable for smal Boats haveing a range of new farms both up and down on the Prairies near the stream came up in the evening at Mr. Mannings who came out with the last years emigration but who has a fair start for farming haveing raised about 300 bush of wheat sown in May last on new Broke Prarie In crossing the Hills spoken of we passed immediately through several clouds or banks of thick misty fog so thick that we could not see scarcely two rods around us and nearly dark as night & when all at once we passed out into open Sunshine immediately around us the Fog being above below and all around us in thick dark fleecy clouds arising into the upper atmosphere and passing off to the N. E. and reathing around the lower parts of Mount Hood while the top appears to enjoy almost an Eeternal sunshine to give Beauty to its glaziers.

6 Spent the day with Mr Manning it rained all the afternoon walked around with our guns But had no success in hunting the deer appear to be plenty But confined themselves to the thickets which are allmost impassable through this whole region of country.

7 Showers of Rain fell during the Day.

8 Cloudy without rain a white frost last night.

9 Some rain last night with slight showers through the day— visited several Neighbours all buisy and appear to be doing well though several are dissatisfied and talk of California.

10 (Sunday) A dense fog covered the whole vally of the Yam Hill & Willhamet rivers and fell almost like a rain about noon the fog arose & we had a Bright sunny after noon walked out over a fine rounded ridge covered with green grass now springing up Beautifully & haveing the appearance of wheat fields in the states at this season of the year from the top of this ridge I had a Beautifull extensive view of the yam Hill Streching away to the N. W. untill it mingled with the Brown roling oak hills rising into the dark green Firr mountains beyond the vally itself covered in a young growth of green grass the old haveing been burned off not exceeding Thirty days [ago.].

Turning to the East N. E. . & S & S. W. lay the wally of the wilhamet skirted with irregular Stripes of green Prarie lately burned off white not burned Brown oak timber yallow cotton wood the leaf not yet shed & deep grien the Firr an evergreen all handsomely Blended and extending Beyond vision near the cascade mountains whare a Blue Streak of Fog lay impenetrable to the sight.

11 Morning thick with light Shower of rain greate Quantities of wild geese seen flying & feeding on the young grass of the lately Burned Praries which are Quite tame & easily approached on horse back Light showers of rain fell during the day.

12 Still continues showery The restless waves of the Pacciffic ware distinctly heard at early daylight distan[ce] I could not assertain In the afternoon Several rapid Showers of rain fell.

13 Continued Showers.

14 A strong south wind blew all night with rapid shower of rain continued to rain but slaked off in the Evening.

15 The fog hung aroud the Hills until about noon when it arose and the sun broke through the mist I again walked over the green hills which ware here and their dotted with cattle and horses feeding on the young grass now about three inches high and thick and as thrifty as the summer groth of the western Praries Likewise greate Quantites of water fowl seen on the low ground such as geese duck Brants and Cranes makeing fine amusement for the Sportsman.

The grass does not coat as thick no[r] as deep on the earth as in the western Praries but on the contrary turns up fine and loose after the Plow it is Likewise loose and soft to walk over and greately worked up by moles and mice and in many place by Burrowing squirrels which are now laid up being an animal that lies torped through the winter none are now seen although their has scarcely been frost enough to kill the tenderest vegitable The alder begining to shed the leaf.

16 It rained moderately all night and continued throughout the day.

17 **(Sunday)** Lowry in the morning greate numbers of Snipe seen on the marshes Continued Showers of Rain all day.

18 A strong south wind blew all night with rapid showers of rain which continued at interavails all through the day the water Fowle continue to come in in great abundanc Scarcely a day has passed since the rainy season commenced that the Rain Bow has not been seen & some days have given us a shew of Ten or Twelve in the course of a day and at times Three or Four in one hours time large and Beautifully curved and coulored.

19 As usual it continued to Rain at intervals through the night the wind however veered to the west.

20 The night Passed off without rain the morning a thick [mist] covered the vally with Fog about noon It commenced raining moderately and continued to rain the rest of the day.

21 The Bats seen flitting about seeking their food every evening The wind from the South it rained all the latter part of the night Scattering portions of our Emigration comeing in through the rain mud and water completely prostrated and tired out.

22 It still continues to Rain.

23 Still continues to Rain but more moderately than the two preceding days in the evening the wind veered to the west and it ceasd raining.

24 (**Sunday**) Thick and cloudy without rain the cranes leaving for the South rode out five of six miles throug the vally of the yam Hill river in many places the young grass was waveing in the wind thew hole country clothed in young green grass.

25 A strong south wind with thick mist desending at intervals from the souhern mountains.

26 As usual a strong south wind with rain.

27 The south wind with its regular attendant rain still continues the waters much swollen and all the Lowlands overflown and covered with water Fowl fine for the sportsman I had been led to believe from previous information that the winter rains had not yet commenced on the 21 of October But all the old residents ware mistaken for once.

28 A Bostirous stormy night the wind shifting to westward Blew a perfect Hericane nearly all night with rapid showas of rain This morning however the sun shewed his countanance mild and pleasant after his long absence a few light showers of rain fell during the day.

29 The sun shone nearly all day and the green hills shewed to greate advantage A light white frost this morning all the streams swollen out of their banks Lots of Cranes seen to day moveing south-ward This country has to me a strange but not unpleasant appearance for the season the grass nearly as forward as June in Illinois and waveing in the wind dotted with cattle and horses feeding on the young grass the mountains to the E however in many places are white with recently fallen snow the alders and other timber that shed the leaf are now nearly bare.

30 Cloudy but not foggy as usual Mount Hood and some other snowy peaks shewed themselves at early Light but ware soon Shrouded again in fleecy clouds the wind from the south with its constant attendant rain in the afternoon.

1844 Sunday Dec. the 1

It continued to rain in showers through the night a thick rainy morning wind S. it continued to rain through out the day in Showers the hills slipery and the vallies muddy our Emigration getting in nearly drownd and suffecated in mud this season said to be the most rainy of any yet seen by the present inhabitants.

2 Several showers of rain fell during the night and the morning thick and cloudy the sun broke through the clouds in the forenoon slight Showers with numerous rain Bows during the day full and Beautifully couloued this is certainly Extraordinary weather for Latitude Forty six and seven.

3 Continued showers of rain.

4 Same I noticed that Horses and cattle do not appear as gentle as in the states owning no dout to the want of being handled sufficiantly but animals have the inclination to go wild in a climate whare there is no winter and are not dependant on their owners for forage but seek their own living at all times & all seasons.

5 It did not rain last night and the morning was clear the Cascade mountains shewed off Handsomely in their white and green drapery it remained clear all day but so moist is the Earth and atmosphere that the dew did not dry off of the green grass even on the Hills The water in the river falling and the low grounds begin to shew themselves greate Quantities of water Fowl still seen on the praries.

6 A rainy Morning Caught what is here called a gopher or Camace rat *[Thomomys]* a Burrowing animal living underground much like a mole. This animal measures 14 Iinches in length exclusive of the tail which is 5 inches long round and without hair coulour a pale purple or mouse colour except the feet which are white and delicately made The Body heavy strong built mouse eared eye small and black hair fine like a mole head large and strong 2 Large strong teeth projecting far forward from both the upper and under Jaws the skin of the head loose and capable of moving forward and forming an extensive pouch around the front teeth the hole to the mouth small and the mouth itself small and far back into the throat whare are a set of fine teeth five to each side 20 in all.

This animal makes its living on roots and is rarely seen above ground excpt when driven out by high wates.

7 Light showers of Rain wind South as usual when wee are sure of rain More or less numerous rain Bows seen to day.

8 Morning fair with as light white frost and extremely heavy dew which hangs in large drops even on dry shrubery.

9 Several Showers of rain fell during the night and a thick foggy morning fleecy clouds of fog asending and Decending all through the day.

10 Bosterous windy rainy night But a fair day.

11 A Rainy night which continued thouout the day Considirable injury was done by the late Freshet heard of 1000 or Twelv Hundred bushel of wheat being lost in the graneries on the low grounds of the Wilhamet Likewise large lots of fencing & in some instances hogs and other stock being drowned or carried away by the water.

12 A light white frost this morning and a pleasant fair day verry still the waves of the paciffic heard distinctly most of our emigration arived at Fort Vancouvre.

13 A thick fog rests on the Earth this morning which continued all day But no rain fell The high water is still abating slowly in the river.

14 Foggy and a thick mist rests on the face of the waters which are under the Firmament of Heaven continued thick and fogy all day But did not rain still without a breeze to tell the course of the wind.

15 The Sun again Broke through the thick mist and removed a slight white frost which shewed itself this morning the fog however soon returned and continued floating around the remainder of the day.

16 Thick and Foggy with a strong appearance of rain.

17 It rained some through the night But most of the day was pleasant several light shower fell in the afternoon and shewed several Beautifull rain Bows.

18 Rained nearly all days moderately untill evening when it slaked up for the present.

19 A rainy night and a rainy day likewise wind.

20 The wind blew a gale from the S. W. all night and there is a slight appearance of clear weather this morning about 11 oclock the fog disperced and the sun broke out fine and clear Noticed young thistles strawberries and a thick groth of other vegitables beginning to start the grass dose not rise up but spread[s] itself over the survace of the ground much like winter grains in the states.

21 A fine clear morning Black birds Snipes and other marsh Birds in greate numbers on the low lands this day was clear and fine throughout and remarkably pleasant.

22 Thick and Foggy and the afternoon rainy.

23 some light showers of rain fell during the night morning dark and cloudy Evening rainy.

24 It rained nearly all night at early light we saw all the higher hills covered in snow but none in the vallies the most of the snow melted off during the day which was fair but not cleare.

25 A blustering windy rainy night succeded our Christmas and the morning was of the same meterial rain hail and snow with the usual accompaniment a strong South west wind the hills whitened again with snow Continued showers of rain and hail and snow throughout the day which melted and disappeared as fast as it fell.

26 A strong south wind all night all the new fallen sno has again disappeared.

27 Considerable rain fell last night this morning however the clouds arose and gave us a view of mountains again which shew some of the recently fallen snow.

Cloudy wind South and Quite warm both day and night.

28 Night Rainy and warm Bats seen flitting about the house seeking their food continued to rain in rapid showers most of the day.

29 Remains Cloudy with rapid showers wind south with an occasional shift to s. W.

30 No alteration but still continues to rain rapidly in showers wind South.

31 Continued the same.

1845 January the 1st

At Early day light it was Raining but slaked up at noon the wind veering to the west the afternoon was pleasant.

2 No rain fell during the night the morning overcast but pleasant the day passed off withou Either wind or rain and the Lowing of cattle and the song of several birds sounded not unlike spring.

3 A fair morning and quite warm and pleasant if it was not for the water that almost covers the Low grounds wind southe I noticed my fine american mare this morning which was bearly able to walk on my arival here in October and is now in good work order without a particle of grain the evening colsed without rain.

4 Cloudy wind South afternoon rainy.

5 (Sunday) A rainy night and the morning ditto the rain slacked up in the afternoon.

6 Morning fair which proved fair throughout the day and pleasant for Oregon in January.

7 Overcast and cloudy.

8 Morning Clear with a stiff white frost remained clear through out the day.

9 Foggy without rain helped to raise a cabbin in the neighbour-hood the sun shone in the evening the melting off of the mountains occasioning a freshet in the river the old settlers say that this is the wettest winter they have yet seen some haveing been in country for 8 and 10 years.

10 Fogy without rain the Earth becomming more firm as the water leaves it the day closed without rain.

11 Verry much the same as yestarday wind South.

12 Clear and Beautifull.

13 Slightly cloudy with light showers of rain or mist passing.

14 It rained som last night But cleared off in the morning with a cool wind from the norgth.

15 Clear and beautifull with a stiff white frost and some ice on Shallow water.

I now witnessed the catching and branding of a lot of wild cattle bout 500 ware drove in to a strong pound and 4 or 5 men well mounted rode in to the pound the animal to be taken being pointed out some one went full speed amongst the herd and threw a rope with a almost dead certainty a round the horns or neck of the animal the cord being made fast to his saddle Bow he stoped his horse and checked the speed of the animal and if his horse was not sufficiently strong 3, 4 or 5 other men threw their cords on the animal then putting spurs to their horses they draged him out of the pound by main force and hampering his legs with cords they threw him then Butchered or branded him as the case might be.

From information I found that in this settlement caled yam Hill their was owned and runing in the hills about Two thousand head of wild cattle and about as many called tame which tameness consists in thir being able to ride amongst them and drive them conveniantly nearly whare you wish the main bulk of these cattle are owned by Five individuals the other settlers being wrthless citizens or late imigrants which have but small stocks of Ten Twenty or thirty head.

16 Cool and chilly light showers of rain and hail.

17 Fogy with light misty showers of rain the [sun] shone the most of the afternoon.

18 A regular days rain.

19 Same.

20 Stormy with wind and rain.

21 Some snow fell on the mountains last night.

22 Continued Showers all night.

23 Regular Showers in continuation.

24 Showers grow lighter & less.

25 Fine and warm and clear.

26 **(Sunday)** Morning pleasant continued fair.

27 Strong winds from the s. s. W. and W. with light showers of rain.

28 Beautifull clear with a light frost we had a view of some of the mountains again during the day which had been closed for the last three weeks with fog and rain.

29 Wet snow & rain.

30 Showers wind variable s. SW and W.

31 Cloudy wind S. W.

Notes on Chapter Ten

Lancaster Clyman, mentioned in the letter Clyman wrote to H. J. Ross following the October 27 journal entry, was a nephew who emigrated to Oregon in 1843 and then to California, where he was a freighter during the Gold Rush. He later gave away land to encourage American settlers; James Clyman may have obtained some of his Oregon holdings in this way. Lancaster was said to have been a "dead shot with a muzzle loader gun," keeping up family traditions.

Chapter 11
The Oregon Territory

[The Oregon Trail; February 1 to July 24, 1845]

In passing thrugh this country on the usual rout no Land is seen that will bear cultivation after pass[ing] the main divideing ridge seperating the waters of the atlantick and the Pacific untill you arive on Bear River whare some small vallies of appearantly cultivateable land are found But here the winters are cold and occasionally deep snows fall Timber is also inconvenient none being found Except in higher and more ruged parts of the mountains there occasional spots of good timber occurs of Pine Firr & Cedar on the lower Hills. However considerable stocks of cattle might be kept on the vallies of Bear River and weebers river on the lower vallies near the greate salt Lake and a resting place might here be made that would verry much assist Emigrants and others passing to and from the states to all parts of the Pacific Country the rout to california would seperate from the rout to oregon at this settlment allso—Aand here should be a military post Established and Perhaps [this] is the cheapest Place to support a Military Post on the Present rout if the head of the Lake dose not fall in to the Mexican Teritory A Low range of mountains divides Bear River from Snake River.

Snake River Issues from the Mountains 80 or 100 miles above Fort Hall and soon passes out in to a wide vally being in many places from 40 to 60 miles wide mostly a dry arid sand plane covered with a Strong groth of wild Sage and prickly pears the lower vally However is well clothed with grass espicially on the moist ground and near the water [is] a thick groth of small willows with an occasional grove of cotton-wood The Hudson bay co. who occupy Fort Hall keep a large Herd of cattl in this vally which do well and Furnish the fort with the fines of Beeff in the fall season These cattle as Likewise a large herd of horses live well through the winter without any food except what they obtain by their own industry on the Praries In the head or Eastern part of this vally stands the three Tetaws which are verry high steep conicle Moun-tains (the) appearantly rising out of an undulated plain and so high that their summits are covered with Eternal snow and frost and may be seen from a great distanc from the S. W. and west The three butes Like-wise stand in this vally nearly opposite or North of Fort Hall and are rounded Detached conicle Hills Likewise But of no greate hight and are formed of roundeded water worn rock Clay Pumice stone and obesian [obsidian] the latter resembling Black glass which is here found in greate abundance and has formerly been the place whar the Natives manufactured great Quantities of arrow points and other instrument of ofence and defense the fragments of which Lay thickly strewn over the surrounding plain continueing down West from the Buetes you come to the most recent appearance of an active volcano that is to be seen in this volcanic region here all the rocks have been in a state of complete fusion and at so late a period that not a particle of vegitation has commenced to grow the Craters appear different from any that I have seen on Record these being holes in the vally all others seem to have arisen above the surrounding country the Scorie of these holes or creaters seem to have been almost intirely composed of compact granite and several of the holes are some hundreds of feet deep mostly of a circular form the edges tops sides and Bottoms formed of a raged Black slag and give a keen sonorous sound when struck togather the slag in many instances being Quite porus.

The extent or number of these holes I cannot tell to any certainty but I should think they extended some 15 or 20 miles in Length in a N. E. and S. W. direction and from 6 to 8 miles cross wise none of which tract can be passed ove[r] with the utmost caution by a man on foot on account of the loose and raged form of the slag and the numerous rents holes pits and chasms which intersept you in all directions In passing over this slag all the small fragmint that become detached drop immediately down and go gingling amongst the opposing rocks below sometimes to an immence depth before they find a resting place in fact I broke loose some pieces and threw them into the fisures which continued to strike and rebound untill they went intirely out of heareing near the western side of this field of Slag rises a ruged steep and high mountain composed of a rough greyish granite nearly Bear of vegitation and in many Places the field of Slag and the mountain approach so near that it was with great difficulty that our pack Horses could find sufficient room to pass and near this western side I observed a greate many large masses of this granite rock s[t]anding in all inclinations between perpendicular and Horizontal and had the appearance of having been affloat in the liquid mass the more weighty parts having sunk and shot up the ligh[t]er end and the Slag cooling left the rocks as they are now seen standing the heat not being Quite entence enough to melt the whole mass on the under side of these masses However the liquidated slag is left hanging in greate Quantities of rounded globules Just in the form that they cooled some nearly Ready to drop off numerous brooks and springs fall from the mountains in the slag and are immediately lost in the loose Slag and most probaby find their way into snake river some 60 or 80 miles S. W. whare a number of spings break out of the most magnificent kind and of the largest dimentions in beautifull gushes and columns of snow white spray some of these fountains throw several tuns of water per minuit cool & pure as crystal on the whole This valy presents many large and Spendid attractions for the Geologist as well as the almost unfathomable depth of the Kenyon that this river fall[s] into immediately below and which falls and cascades commence at the American Falls at the Lower end of the vally From the american Falls to Fort Boise a distance of 300 miles you pass over a dry dusty and in some places sandy as likewise in many places Rocky country bearing but little grass or Timber wild sage Prarie thorn &c making the general vegitation Travelers usually pass through this region as fast as they conveniently can there being no game no grass of consequence Except salmon in their proper season when Quantities are taken and can be had of the Indians for a mere trifle while Fresh.

Fort Boise stands on the North Bank of Snake River a few miles below the mouth of the Boise River the great Woile [Owyhee River] Falling in on the oposite side a short distance above allso the surrounding country dry and parched grass and Timber being verry scarce in the vicinity of the Fort and no cultivatiable land seen in the neighbourhood cnsiderable stocks of cattle and Horses find good grazing in the vicinity as I noticied the cattl in particular ware fine and fat several Butes of considerable hight rais their dark looking summits to the south W. of the fort and a range of bear mountains of considerable length and hight are seen to the S. and S.W. dividing the waters running into snake river and those runing into ogdens Lake and other parts of the vally of the greate sale Lake these mountains no doubt are connected withe the Blue mountains some distance to the west.

Some 50 or 60 miles below Boise snake River takes into the Blue mountains in these mountains is whare Mr Hunt McKenzie and their party suffered so much as related by Mr Ervine [Irving] in his Astoria Nothing is seen in the shape or appearance of cultivatiable Land on the present rout For nearly 200 miles west of Boise when you arive near the (the) head of Powder River a small stream running East ward into snake River and in full view of the Blue mountains you come to several small valies of fair soil and good grazing but no timber of use Except on the mountains. I do not think However that their is any Extent of arable land to be found here Two short camps brings you into the grand round vally a Beautifull green spot in this region of interminable rocks dust and wild sage you are now fairly entered into the Blue mountains which Surround this vally on all sides the vally itself is nearly round and 16 or 18 miles across in either direction and has no doubt once been covered in water numerous small streams falling from the hills in all drictions and winding through the low grounds form a small River which has worn its way through the opposing rocks to a greate depth and takes a Northern course to the columbia as I am informed The winters are here Quite mild and the grass coming up in novembr remains green through the winter The Blue mountains are appearantly not verry high But the Ravines are steep and Rocky and generally covered tops and sides with a thick groth of Pine and other Eevergreen timber and Something the rise of 40 [more than 40 miles] across on the wagon trail which is a rough bad road for teams and scarce of both grass and water.

The asent of these mountains on the western side is generally bear of Timber but thickly set with a nutricious kind of Bunch grass the utilla river running for some distance nearly paralell with the mountains on this stream (which in low water is a fine mill stream) is seen a narrow vally of good cultivateable soil bringing corn wheat & vegitables in good perfection The Skuse Indians cultivate some small spots which poduce well the usual rout passes down the utilla river to the columbia it is generally Believed that a greate number of small valies lie stiuated near the mountains on the South side of the (of the) Columbia but I saw no white man that had ever visited that region but I have no doubt of the correctness of this report Along and near the columbia River nothing can look more discourageing the river running in a deep chasm of nearly pependicular rocks Black and frowning with a scanty supply of grass and not a stick of timbr to relieve the continual monotony of Frowning rock or water with now and then a Field or mountain of sand to pass through Now having arived at the Delles whare you may rest a day or two with Mr Waller who is superintendent of the Methodist Mission at this place and is an accomodating man if he can be well paid but if you are scarce of funds you may hire an Indian to guide you over the cascade mountains or as we did guide yourself These mountains are 70 or 80 miles acoss by the way of the Trail verry thickly timberd. and Extremely steep rocky and rough The columbia on its entrance into the mountains passes through a verry dangerous rapid called the delles whare the river is nearly choked by large masses of sunken rock which raise their black heads in utmost confusion forming Tremendious whirlpools and are nearly impassable in low water and in fact at all times some 50 or 60 miles below is the greate falls which are at all times impassable and whare a portage or two has to be made by all the watercraft passing the river this last fall occurrs 80 or 100 miles above vacouver from this fall the river is clear of obstructions to its mouth for small craft and its navigation would be good for stiam boats Likewise But no cultivateable land of any consequence is seen untill you arive in the vicinity of Fort vancouver whare the mountains recede and the coves and vallies begin to open out all the Best Prairies however are occupied by the H. B. Co. who carry on farming on a Large scale in the viceinity of the fort and in fact continue to extend their agracultural persuits as the Furr and peltries decrease The cascade mountains are one of the greate chain of mountains which strech themselves through nearly the whole length of North america commencing near the gulf of califorrni they keep a northern directon Divideing the Californian vally from the vally of the greate salt lake a chane however diverges from this chane some whare in Lower california and taking an Eastern direction bounds are greate salt Lake vally on the south and dividing that from the vally of Rio colerado and continueing East and N. E. by the head of green & Bear rivers it unites with the greate dividing ridge near the head of snake River.

The Blue mountain chane seperates itself from the Cascades near the head of the clamet and umqua rivers and perhaps for some distance Bound[s] the vally of salt or the greate salt Lake vally on the north to near the head of the Willhamet and river de Shutes whare the Blue Mountain chain inclines to N. and an other chain branches off to the East deviding the Greate salt vally from snake River and continueing E. and N unites with the last mentioned chain near the head of snake River also The Blue chain continueing allmost to the columbia then Turning short to the east snake river bursting through this chain in the curve fall[s] into the Columbia the mountains continueing their eastern Direction dividing the waters of snake and Salmon Rivers unite(s) with the main chain also near the heads of the Southern Branches of the Missouri and North of snake River to These may be added a low chain of mountains linding on and near the coast of the pacific Broken through however by the columbia near the umpquaw the clamet and several other rivers.

Having never traversed any portion of the country north of the columbia I will not attempt to give any discription of the mountains of that part of the country.

The vallies are said by some to be good & are represented as being quite large and finely clothed with grass at one of the H. B. Cos. Establishments I am informed that Thirty thousand sheep are kept and in fact a greate number of Sheep and cattle are kept at all Their Trading posts north of The columbia and more paticularly on Peugetts Sound these sheep are of the spannish breed they yield a large fleece of coars Blankets and other coarse clothes for the supply of their numerous Trading Establishments in all parts of their extensive trade to the north The H. B. Co. Likewise keep a steam Boat running in Peugetts sound to facilatate their (their) trad amongst the numerous bays and Isleands on that coast and carry on a profitable trade with their Neighbours the Russians on Both continents.

The Navigation of the Columbia is not verry good and more particular neare the head of the Bay whare the channel is narrow crooked and interupted by Bars & sand banks.

―――――

Geography, Products, and Government of Oregon

I now come to speak of the Willhamet vally in and near the mouth of this River are several Large Islands thise Islands are good soil and fine grazing but mostly overflow in the winter and spring freshets as Likewise do all the point of land forming the Junction a fine situation is found however immediately below the lower mouth of the Willhamet good water and a good landing but this place is not easily approachable by land and is far from any considerable cultivateable country The Killimook mountains approach nearly to the water on the west or right hand side of the Willhamet as you assend and all the uplands even to the mountains top are covered with a magnificent and lofty groth of

Firr Timber These mountains Extend west to the coast and South nearly to the falls a distance of some 20 miles and are generally verry steep rocky and rugged the Tuallata River takes its rise in these mountains & Running S. E. and E. falls into the Willhamet 2 miles above the Falls on the Branches of this stream & nearly west of the falls lies Quite a large pine Prairi called the Twallata plains this beautifull plain contains upwards of 200 families mostly american.

This Plain is a kind of cove or vally and is bounded on the N.N. W. and west By the Killimook mountains on the East by the Tuallatine Hills and the South by the Jahalem hills the last mentioned Hills are generally Beare of Timber and are excelent pasture lands passing South on the west of the Willhamet Jahalem or Chehalem vally occurs this vally is small compared to The Twalatine but contains some 30 or 40 Farms continueing south over a steep norrow range of Bald Hills an hours ride brings you to the Yam Hill vally or country and From off of the last mentioned you have no mountain or Hill to intercept the view the vally extending south as far as the farthest extent of vision the Mountains However bind you on the East and west that is the Cascades with their snowy peaks on East and the Killimook rang on the west This vally is here not short of Fifty miles wide and perhaps one Hundred and Fifty in length numerous Brooks and rivulets meander their way in various directions through the vally from the neighbouring mountains on either side of the Willhamet and when necessary can easily be converted into the means of driveing all kinds mchineery that be found usefull for a greate manufactureing communety.

I will now take a glance at the willhamet vally on the East side of the river after passing the overflown Lowlands near the Junction of the Rivers an undulating or rather hilly Plain occurs covered with Large Firr and other evergreen Timber interwoven with Hazel Dwarf maple and other underbrush for 20 or 30 miles that is to the Klackimus a rapid rocky stream about 60 yards wide taking its rise from the snowy peaks of (of) the Cascades on this stream are several small Prairies as Likewise a fine Salmon fishery whare greate Quantities are anually taken at the Junction of this stream with willhamet is a Bad shallow rapid Formed by the Rapid wash of the Klackimus as Likewise from the deposits thrown from the Falls of the willhamet (which) only one mile above [which] you Find the Prairies untill you pass The Moleally rivir a Strong Rapid stream draining the snowy peaks of the cascades Likwise and entering willhamet 20 miles above or South of the Falls This stream [is] 60 or 80 yards wide and scarcely ever fordable But haveing passed this streame you immediately enter on the praries as Likewis the oldest and most numerous settlement in the Teritory this settlement composed of mostly French and civilized Indians is organized into a county called Champooick [Champoeg] and contains the catholick and Methodist Missionary station in this vally of which I shall speak Hereafter From the Moleally the Praries Extend south perhaps 200 miles to the Kalapooya mountains this range which I shall speak of again divides the Willhamet vally from the Umpqua vally From the commencement of the Praries the Settlment Extends to the Santaam one of the principle Tributaries of the willhamet a distance of some 50 miles.

South of the Santaam the vally becomes verry Extensive and may be near 100 miles wide E. & W.

I now may speak of the government which is provisional and has only Existed for the year past. The Executive has consisted of three persons one Elected as president the other two as assistants with a Ligislature consisting of nine members all Elected to serve for one year only and untill others are Elected and Qualified The Judiciary [consists] of one Judge and one shirriff who officiate throughout all the organized counties which amount to Five namely Clatsop at the mouth of the columbia Klackimus From the mouth of the willhamet to the Moleally on the E. side of the willhamet Twalata on the west side of the Willhamet shampooik on the E. and yamhill on the west no organization haveing taken place north of the columbia The present Laws However make a considerable change making but [one] govornor or Executive head with an increas in the Legisltive Body of six members and a provision for a Militia organization.

The Laws of Iowa have been adopted and a number of acts or Laws passed by the provisional Legislature of oregon The claim Laws allow every man 640 acres the claiman must build a cabbin on his claim within two months after his haveing taken possession and must be a resident by himself or by a Tenant his claim must be square or oblong the [lines] running North and South and East and West if the nature of the country permit By a Ressolotion of the Legislature last winter the provisional government is Extended over all the country East whose waters flow into the Pacific North to Latitude 54.40 or the line agreed upon Between The United states and the Russian governments and South of Latitude 42 or the line agreed upon between the United states and the Mexican governments Some alterations However will take Effect this season the Legislature will consist of 15 members and one governor in place of the former council of three The other officers cosist of one clerk of the court and one Treasurer Elected For one year Likewis and one Assessor the shirriff being Collector and here let me remark that The Hudson Bay company (have) whare their Intrest or Establishments have fallen into any of the organized counties have entred heartily into the organization themselves with all their influ-ence amongst the French and Half Breeds and (and) their influence and Example has had a remarkable good effct and has assisted much to the Establment of the present Provisional government such as it is.

The commerce of the country has been so far carried on mostly by the H. Bay Company and previous to the arival of the american Emigration of 1843 the country appears to have been well supplied with all the merchandize necesary for the population But since the arival of the last American emigration goods have become scarce and the price nearly doubled.

The closing of the Methodist missionary Establishment has like-wise withdrawn a small but active capital from the trade of the country and at present I see no immediate prspects of the Establishment of capital in the country The Exports of the country consist mostly of wheat and Flour carried to the Pacific Islands and the Russian settle-ment on this contiment this with fish and lumber taken to the pacific Island constitute the present commerce of the country with the white inhabitants the Indian trade in Furrs and peltres is exclusively carried on by the H. B. Co. The present cultivation of the country is confined to the raising of wheat and peas both of which grow to greater perfection here than any place I have heretofore seen and considerable Quantities of wheat is yearly wasted after furnishing all that is required for the Limited commerce of the country and for fatting pork for home consumtion in fact all the domastic stock that is fed at all is fed with wheat and wheat and Flour might and no doubt will in the course of time be Exported to an immence amount when the agriculture Trade and commerce of the country shall be properly opened and Encouraged Corn the western americans main crop dose not succeed well on accout of the coolness of the nights which are never warm even in the middle of summer Fruit apples pears plumbs peaches &c &c yeeld in profusion but are as yet of an ordinary Quality being small and hard Timber the most common timber is the Firr which grows in astonishing quantities and of immence size and Length many trees measureing over 100 feet of clear Timber and producing in good grooves From 20 to Thirty thousand Rails forom one acre and it is quite common for one man to chop & split 300 rails per day Labour is verry high common Labour commanding forom thirty to fifty dollars per month and mechanicle labor commanding from two to three dollars per day owing to the Kind of Work and the Qualifications of the workman The pay however is in Merchandize of the produce of the country The nominal price of wheat is one dollar per bushel and merchandize at forom one to two hundred percent proffit I neglected to finish the article of timber on the oposite page after the Firr which is of two kinds the white and the red pine comes next in importance Thire is of this too speeces Like wise the yallow and the spruce pines Both growing large and plentifull in some districts while cedar grows in small Quantities and is found generally difused Hemlock is also found in the mountains The yew an evergreen Likewis is found in rocky situations a spices of Laurel also resembling the laurel of the states in appearanc grows here to such a size as to make a valuable timber for furniture The oak is rather dwarfish and shrubly as Likewises is the ash but Enough of either is found for the impliments of husbandry and mchanical tools &c &c Two or three Kinds of maple is likewise found here but they do not grow generally large and thrifty.

The Alder of this Tiritory is large compared to that seen in the states The Bark is used for Tanning leather & the wood sawn & used in making furniture for which pupose it is considered verry good several Kinds of [willows] are found some growing Quite large and in fact the willow seems to be more generally defused on all Kinds of soil than any other Timber.

A species of Hazel is also very common and is the only tmbir found Sutable for hoop poles and is also the only Tree or shrub Bearing nutts the nut much resembling a Small Filbert.

Considrable Quantities of Berries are found in their proper season The strawbery & Huckelberry nearly the same as in the States.

A Species of Blackberry and Raspberry. Barberry verry sour. Thimble berry Fine acid. Sallal sweet & one or Two other Kinds of not much importance are occasionally found with goose beries and wild current make up the most of the Berries.

The salmon Fisheries could and no doubt will at future period Be made an object of (and) an Extensive trade carried on in and through the productions of the rivers a small species of oister is found in some places on the coast but I could not learn that they ware plenty no other valuable Fish enters the rivers of This Teritory that I could hear of except salmon some whale are thrown on the coast every winter By the Storms.

The seal is common on the coasts and in the bays and Rivers greate Quantites and greate verieties of waterfowl is found in all parts of The open country during the rainy season such as the Swan the crane goose Brant and innumerable Quantities of Ducks with the wood cock and Snipe The soil is Intirely clay even to the elluvial lowlands on the streams The Bars However in many places is gravel.

The Rock is of The dark rough Bassalt family and appears to have all been in a state of Fusion at some Remote period I did not heare of Lime Being found only at one place, That being near the mouth of the columbia What has been used Heretofore has been brought from the Isleands as ballast on board of vessels.

I did not see or hear of any coal sand stone or any other stratified Rock but various Qualities of clays are found in greate abundance.

The animals are Panthers several kins of wolves The Black the yallow grey and spoted all large and traublesome killing hogs cattle and even in some instances horses and mules The small Prarie wolf is likewise numerous I saw no foxes The Wild [cat?] is not numerous plenty of Elk are found in the mountains and deer in all the Thickets water fowl is plenty Beyond all conception in the rainy season all the Lowlands being litterly covered the[y] all move to the north and east during the months of April and May The Land Fowl are the Firr grous the Pheasant and Quail as kikewise the medow lark which are found in greate abundanc on the open lands a few of the Red brast wood pickers and sparrow are also seen The condor The Buzzard the Raven and crow with several speces of Hawks most of which are Plenty the Hawks feed mostly on mice & moles both of which are numerous.

Several Kinds of squirrels areseen all of which Burrow in the earth and lie torpid in the rainy season some lay up seed to lie on others come out verry lean being nothing but skin and bone.

The Quantity [of water] that pours from the mountains on either side in to the Willhamet vally is truly astonishing every 8 or 10 miles Brings you to a river and brooks innumerable I can give no Idea of (of) the length of This vally as yet but shall probably have a much Better oppertunity in ou rout through and this will be seen in my day Journal.

Feruary the 1st 1845
Several showers of rain and wet snow & several rain bows.

2 The same wind S.

3 Thick and cloudy with a slight drizzilling rain.

4 Fogy with a tremendious heavy dew this morning wind South Afternoon clear and warm.

5 Morning Fogy afternoon clear.

6 White frost cloudy.

7 Fair and warm.

8 Fair Balmy and warm.

9 Same willows Alders & some other early vegetation beginning to Bloom.

10 Rainy.

11 Fair But not clear.

12 Rainy.

13 Heavy showers of Rain.

14 Low grumbling thunder with rain.

15 Rapid Showers.

16 Same the earth covered with water.

17 The rain ceased some what.

18 Fair I noticed several of the Early summer birds ware chirping in the thickets.

19 Cloudy Evening Rainy.

20 Same Showers.

21 Do do.

22 Dame this day fulfills the four months rain and yet no emmediate appearance of clear weather.

23 Strong west winds commenced blowing last night and still continues attended with rapid showers of hail and rain.

24 A stiff frost last night the day Quite pleasant but clou[dy].

25 Cloudy & cool.

26 Same with Showers of rain.

27 Fair.

28 Showers wind west.

Satterday 1845 March the First

Clear and handsome and we enjoyed the fine day after the long rainy season which we hope is now passed away for this season the hills are now fast becomeing dry green and pleasant the grass which spread itself so nicly over the surface of the earth last fall is now beginning to shoot up and lengthen out.

2 Clear and handsome.

3 Do wind West.

4 Rain cold & Blustring.

5 Clear cool N. wind.

6 Clear with a white frost the Eternal snow capt. mountains glittering in bright sun Shine.

7 Clear & Beautifull with a stiff frost.

8 Fair wind west.

9 Fair do N. W.

10 Clear and fine Wind North.

11 Do do W North.

12 Clear & Beautifull I had a Sunset view of the Cascade mountains binding the vally on the East for a great length and in their dark green livery with now and then a high peak shooting his white snow clad [head] far in to the regions of eternal frost while the lower vallies show all the active indications of spring or rather early summer.

13 Unusually Bright and clear the musketoes rather troublesome last night.

Noticed 5 different kins of small vegitables in full Bloom to day the [rain] on the first of this month leaving the low grounds nearly covered in water which has now all disappeared and left us fine smoothe Dry Prarie to pass over and the Plow is now running whare one week since it was covered in water.

14 Clear wind north and verry d[r]ying vegitation comeing rapidly forward.

15 No change Except the vally is some what Enveloped in smoke.

16 Same Quite warm.

17 Same do ditto The water fowl have nearly all left this vally and many of the summer birds Have arived and make the mornings cheerful with their songs.

18 Clear nothing can look more pleasant than clear weather does in this country the hils handsomly rounded smoothe and thickly clothed with green grass the sky intirely clear not a cloud to be seen but one continual bright sunshine from morning untill evening.

19 Slightly Fogy wind west vegetation grows rapidly and a fair appearance of summer.

20 Fair some appearance of rain.

21 Fair I noticed the Maple and white oak bigen to shew the leak [leaf] Strawberries in Bloom and the hills completely covered with small flowers mostly purple & yallow wind West & N.W.

22 Fair and pleasant.

23 A heavy dew last night and a clear Beautifull day a person that has not seen this country can have no Idea of the verieties of Beauties Exhibited here in a clear spring morning.

Attended divine service at a neighbouring house a decent behaved congregation of Gentlemen ware prasent But few Ladies the service was performed by a gentleman of the Mothodist persuasion who gave good advice had some tolerable Ideas but seem to want language to expess them in And I must say that female beauty is not (the) exclusively confined to any particular region or country for here too may be seen the fairy form the fair skin the dark Eye and drk hair so beautifully dscribed by Byron displayed in the person [of] Miss smith who I understood had traversed the interminable plains from the states here from here to Callifornia and from callifornia Back here again and is now Just swelling into womanhood with all the Beauties, if not all the accomplisments Belonging to the sexe.

24 Clear & dry.

25 A Light shower of rain fell last night which gives a deep colour to vegetation this morning the summer birds seem to enjoy the change by their buesy songs and continual chirping The hoarse notes of the firr grouse is heard makeing a Bass for the shrill medow larks trible.

26 Clear.

27 Clear a light shower of rain fell last night Coll light showers of rain fell during the afternoon.

28 Called on Dr. [Elijah] White Indian agent for the Teritory found the Dr. a plasant companionable man makeing out his dispaches for the Express soon departing for the states by the way of canada on my way passed the methodist mission Established by Mr Jason Lee who like many others made an unhappy selection nearly the whole of the mission houses having been overflown by the freshets during the lasts winter and much of their fencing carried away and one thousand Bushel of wheat distroyed Mr [Alanson] Beers occupied the mission hous all the members of the Establishment being scattered and mission opperations all stoped the soil of the mission farmes is [good] but the place wants veriety being an uneven plainworn in gutters by the frishets from the river I did not heare of any advantages of any consequence that had resulted to the Indians from this establishment during its most flurrishing days but it apears that the most of the funds ware aprpopated to individual speculation The day proved disagreeable and severall rapid showers of snow fell during the day which melted as it fell.

29 Morning Fogy cleard about noon made preperations to go by water to the falls of willhamet.

30 Cloudy wind s.W.

31 Rainy arived at the Falls.

Tuesday April the First 1945

The second term of the circuit court opened its session for the county Klackimus and was attended by a small genteel well behaved audience the Judge Mr [James W.] Nesmith charged the gran Jury in a short but appropriate address.

And here might be seen the greate and salatory effects of Temperance the Judge the sheriff and several of the Jurors having left the states their friend[s] society and civilization on the account of the demorilizeing effects of spiritous Liquor here whare no alcahall can be obtained they have become good intelegent industrious citizens accumelating property and filling the highes and most importent offices in the Teritory with honor to themselves and the country they now have become citizens of [Oregon].

2 Continues rainy.

3 Cloudy.

4 Clear & warm Left the falls to assend the willhamet by water our small canoe being only large enough to carry two men and thir Baggage the rocks close in near to the waters edge for about three miles above the falls whare the steep cliffs begin to recede and (and) the vally opens out to a considerable width the Twalatta river enters 2 miles above the falls and tumbles through the rocks in a succession of rapids which renders this river intirely unfit for navigation even for a light canoe about one mile above the mouth of the Tuallata is a considerable rapid in the willhamet whare several boats laden with wheat have been lost during the past winter this rapid however is not dangerous in low water and may be passed by steam boats at common stage 10 miles above the Tuallatta the Molelilla river enters from the east heading in the cascade mountains and is about the same size of the twallatta measuring about 60 yards wide but the latter stream discharges double the water of the former and is scarcely ever fordable the Twalatta being fordable in many places when low made about 20 miles and encamped the whole of the country seen from the river is thickly covered with Firr timbr and impenetrable under brush.

5 Clear and warm about 9 oclock arived at champoeg here a village is laid out but nothing doing in the way of improvement this place is a dry sandy level a few feet above high water and is Twenty five miles above the falls a settlement of about Two Hunded families of Half breeds and canadian French reside in the vicinity stoped with Mr Newel [Robert Newell] the propietor who has been one of the Rocky Mountain trappers and 4 years since gathered his posibles his Flat Head wife and changed his precarious mountain life for a more certain means of subsistance in the Willhamet vally and has had the honor of being one of the members of the provisional Legislature for the past year.

6 Cloudy. I noticed several Beautifull flowering shrubs in thickets now in bloom and a Beautifull species of Humming Bird Hovering around them several showers of rain fell during the day.

7 Fair and warm wind South Doct. McLaughlin arived here from above Few men can out do the venerable Doctor for philanthopy urbanity and Social conversation Too much praise cannot be bestwoed on the venerable superintendant of the H. B. Co for his humanity and fostering care bstowed on the poor and wearied emigrants on their first arival in this country.

8 Attended a convention for the nomination of governor and other Executive officers a Judge and several Military officers all apeared to go off fairly and without Difficulty The day pleasant and warm The Frenchman at whose house the convention was held has a beautifull young bearing apple orchard now casting the Bloom and shewing the young fruit.

9 Clear and warm.

10 Showery the hills which ware purple with flowers lately are now completely covered in yallow.

11 Clear and pleasant.

12 Same a party for the states consisting of about 15 men assemble to day at the falls and will take their final leave in a few days [Camp's 1960 edition indicates that this was Overton Johnson's party of 12 men who left on April 19].

13 Some showers of rain fell during the night the leaves on most of the Trees is now full grown.

14 The morning clear I noticed severable fields of wheat narely knee high and many farmers have not commenced sowing as yet and some have not began to plow.

15 Cool with light showers of rain mingled with hail The court for Yam Hill County met and adjourned without a case (bieing) being filed on docket.

16 Cool and clear.

17 Cool Light Showers.

18 Cloudy most of the day.

19 Clear with a cool Breeze from the N. W. Wholesome Exhilerating and pleasant to the lungs.

20 A stiff white frost this morning cloudy & Quite cool.

21 Another white Frost and cool cloudy day great Qwantities of geese and Brant passing to the N. at so greate a hight as to [be] allmost invisible allso great Qauntities of Firr Grouse on the hills these grouse are fine eating & much resemble a Pheasant in appearance but are nearly double the weight of a Pheasant.

22 Cool and Blustry after a rainy night.

23 Some Frost cool and clear.

24 Rainy.

25 Rainy The [sky] cleared off with a stiff west wind.

26 Clear and fine.

27 Cool and chilly clared off in the afternoon and shewed us the Low mountains covered white in snow a circumstance that hapened But one during the winter.

28 The sun arose clear and splendid the afternoon was not so favourable for in swiming my horse over the Yam Hill river he got tangled in the willows near the shore and after a number of fruitly exertions to clear the brush and assend the nearly perpendicular bank he gave up to drown I swung from the canoe and taking the rope swam ashore one mor exertion with my help brot him out of the Brush and throwing the cord to the men in the canoe they landed safely on the oposite side we then mounted and rode Fifteen miles about 5 miles of which distance it Blew and rained without mercy and extremely cold directly in our faces.

29 Frost this morning yesterday morning Likewise the day proved fair I staid last night with Mr Jacob Reed [Reid] who has a fine farm of 50 acres in wheat allthough he came to the [country] without friends in 1843 he has Likewise one of the most beautifull romantic building places I have yet seen in the country a clear spring of Limpid water breaking out in a grove of low gnarled oaks on a handsome assent surrounded by a high ridge of the same kind of land all smoothe and covered with a fine short grass surrounded by a much higher ridge of firr timber except to the west whare opens a rich level prarie sufficient fo a large farm the view bounded by the Killimook mountains at the distance of a few miles to the west.

30 Without frost pleasant.

Thirsday May the First 1845
Clear and pleasant wind west.

2 Clear and pleasant The mountains have been hid in fog and clouds for some days past but opened handsomely to view again to day and seem to be covered with new fallen snow.

3 Morning clear and cool with a heavy dew spent the day which proved to be verry fine in the novel occupation of dressing a Panther skin for a gun cover The forenoon was warm and sultry the sea breeze came up from the west early in the afternoon coal and pleasant and continued untill after sun set.

4 Another clear day The oak leaves full grown and the oak is the latest of all the timber in this country goose Berries nearly Large Enough for use The Farmers are still sowing wheat and will continue some time yet.

5 Clear and warm to day commences the greate collection of wild

cattle for the purpose of Branding and delivering all that have been solod or Trded for the last six months.

6 Same. A Large dark cloud of smoke seemed to be hovering around the Icy pinicle of mount Hellen for some days past but whether it proceeded forom the crater or not I could not determin the Hills have been for some days completely red with the clover now in full bloom.

7 The wind Shifted to the south & it commenced raining in half an hour.

the afternoon clear and cool went to Mr Jays to see the branding and marking of wild cattle saw a pound full containing some 5 or 600 Head and 10 or 12 men on horse back Lassing and draging out by the saddle.

8 Clear and cool Had a conversation with Mr. [Henry?] Wood who had just returned from a trip to Peugetts sound he informs me that he assended the Cowletts river in a canoe some 25 or 30 miles & found the stream deep with a strong current avarage width about one Hundred yards The Cowlets vally and settlement commences (commences) 25 miles up this stream forom the columbia the river banks high and dry the country back rough and mountainous and thickly covered with timbe[r] the Praries openes out in the vally and are beautiful and rich soil Size of the vally some 40 to 60 miles wide and 60 to 80 Long about one third smoothe Prarie the other two thirds thickly covered with fine timber mostly Firr Two other rivers head in this vally to wit the Jahalis and Black river Both Emtying in to the Pacific North of the columbia and discharging narly the same quantity of water as the Cowletts.

He Likewise passed over the ridge into the vally near Pugetts sound called the Nesqually vally this vally Extends beyond the strech of vision in all directions Except to the East whare it is bounded by the raged peaks of the cascade mountains through these However there is a good easy pass in the direction of Fort walla walla This last mentioned vally is well clothed in grass but timbr is scarce and but little seen excpt neare the mountains or bordering on and neare the streams this latter of a shrubby discription and not generally valuable the former good and valuable but in most places inconvenient.

9 Visited Mr Waldows settlement the day proved showery and disagreeable Mr. Waldow [Daniel Waldo] has made his selection in the Hills devideing the waters of the Moleally and the Santiam rivers and was last season the only person in the colony who cultivated the settlement is now around him extending their farms in all directions over the most beautifull tract of country sinking and swelling in regular rounded forms of all immaginary verieties finely interspersed with groves of oak and Firr Timbr and numerous springs of never failing clear water in many insances bursting out neare the top of the hills.

Mr Waldow has a fine stock of the best blooded cattle I have yet seen in the Teritory.

10 Appearance of Showers and in this we ware not disappointed for a number of rapid Showers fell during the day I rode through the entire upper settlements on the East of the willhamet and was highly pleased with the beautifull veriaty of hill and vally so softly valed and intermingled with hill and dale as Likewis timber and Prarie all luxuriently clothed in a rich and heavy coat of vegetation and litterly clothed in Flowers the upland in yallow and the vallys in purple The Quantity of small flowering vegettiles is verry remarkable & beyond all conception.

11 Clear and Fine some showers passed to the North.

12 A slight Frost and a c[l]eare morning the afternoon cloudy.

13 It rained moderately nearly all night It being the First warm pleasant rain we have had this season.

14 The rain continued all night and all day likewise.

15 Continues to Rain Moderately in the afternoon it ceased to rain.

16 Morning clear and Bright Visited Dr White the [Indian Agent] and in walking over his farm we picked a few handfulls of ripe strawberries which grow here in greate abundance on nearly all the Prarie lands.

18 Clear and Beautifull with fine warm weather My Dog had fine sport catching young Larks All those buisied in preparing for California who intend to make that trip this season the atmosphere verry clear & Bright.

19 Same.

120 Same spent the day in writeing an answer to some Queries propounded by Dr White who leaves for the states on the hopes of obtaining the gubenatorial chair..

———

OREGON

In your Reqest of May the 16 you ask me what I Think of soil I Believe the Soil to be very productive which has been wel proved in all Instances that has come under my observation and I am Free to [say] it has all the appearances of being remarkably durable being formed allmost intirely of clay and decomposed vegitable matter.

The climate is no doubt Beautifull Beyond all conception to an American in the dry season.

The rainy season is verry disagreeable But the temprature is Remarkably even therer being no Intence warm weather nor extreme cold and this Equality of Temprature is no doubt conducive to health.

Health. The American and European population of this country seem To Enjoy remarkable good health in Fact far Beyond all my former observations considering the Hardshps and exposures they yearly undergo.

Scenery in this I know I shall want Language I[n] richness and veriety of Scenery this county cannot be surpassed assend one of your smoothe Handsomely rounded eminences and you have at once glance all the veriety of Scenery that nature ever produced six or eight Heaven towring peaks are visable at once covered in eternal Ice and snow thier ruged time worn sides softned by Distance. your eye desending the region of bear Rocks and Nightly Frosts in a Broad Belt around the Peaks attracts your attention with lower peaks of the same attitude Still desending long ranges of deep green Firr clad elivations of great veriety of shape and apearance Extend themselves to the right and let far beyond the strech of vision.

The Eye still desending you catch the softly rounded grass clad hills with thier shrubby oak groves and Prarie vallies with various shades of green dr.apery untill at last your [eye] rests on the broad vally Striching itself paralell withe mountain

here too you have the veriety of Timber and Prarie with all the meanderings of the large and small streams that wind and intersect the vally in all directions Bring your eye closer and you Distinguish farms and fields still closer and houses and herds appear and last not least of all a few horsemen are seen going like the wind over some smoothe Prarie and disappearing in an oak grove pardon me sir those rapid cousiers ware gentlemen and Ladies out on a ride of plesure.

Timber Nature seems to have Reversed things allmost intirely here you have the noble ash, oak and maple dwindled down in to shrubs and dwarfs while the dwarfish Laurel and alder strech themselves up into valuable Timbrs and the still more dwarfish Hazel and Elder shoot up into usefull sized shrubs But the noble Firr of this country is beyon all conception there being Nothing in the states to bear any comparison But few of the Trees measuring less than 100 feet of clear valuable Timbr and many going Far beyond this length and in many instances yielding from Thirty to Forty thousand rails from an acre [The following is crossed out,—"on the whole I do not know that I can give you a bette discription than to quote of stanza of native Poetry.

Ss to the Rivers streams and water couses of this country they are admirably adapted in many insances for Hydraulic porposes and may be generally verry cheaply used for all the necesary machienery that will eer [be] required for even an extensive manufacturing community.

But for navegation the rivers are generally to rapid and too many and to great obstuctions to ever make the inland navigation cheap easy or safe.

As to natureal advantages so far as Subsistance is concerned such of the Teritory as is cultivatible I have no doubt will yield Bountifullyand many of the dry and arid portions would feed considerable numbers of the several kinds of domestic stock but taking the Teritory as [a] whole seven Eights of it is mere wast land and never can support a civilized population you must consider all my former remarks confined to the west of the cascade mountains.

As to national advantages I concieve they must be but few allowing the settlements of the East to Extend to the Forks of the River Platte then you have Twelve Hundred miles of dry arid mountain Region to pass to arive near the Blue mountain whare Settlements may again possibly exist with a verry few exceptions so that nature [has] thrown insurpassable objections to i[t]s becomeing an intergal part of the United states it may However and no doubt will strengthen the commercial relations with China Russia and the Pacific Islands and coasts.

I am of opinion that a Section of Land ought and will be granted to all those who may be occupents of this Teritory at or before the time of the establishment of the U. S. claim or previous to the organization of a Territorial government on account of their early movement, and unprecedented hard ships as Likewis on account of the encourage-ments By all the movements in Congress in relation to the settlement and occupation of this remote part of the U. S. Teritory.

The appointment of officers I have allways been favourable to the appointment of official agents from the Neighbourhood or country whare their services ware required and I think in this country of all others a selection from her owm citizens would be best Quallified to give general satisfaction Both to the government and the governed.

July 19 1845

19 Morning quite warm the afternoon windy and cool.

20 Morning cool and clear the days begin to [be] verry long.

21 Rain and hail cool & windy & disagreeable the flowers of this region seem to be well filled with honey but the bees are wanting.

22 Continues cool with light showers of rain & hail.

23 Cool and clear with a north wind about this time the farmers begin to think that all their spring wheat should be sown & but a few are still sowing and the crop is never intirely all finished untill the first of June allthough you may commence sowing again by the first of august the rains haveing then intirely ceased the grain will not grow before october or when the winter rains again commence.

24 Cloudy with the appearance of rain Received Letters of Introduction From Doct. McLaughlin and official Documents from Dr White directed to the authorities of California impowering myself to (to) inquire into the cause of the death of one of the Skyeuse chiefs.

Notes on Chapter Eleven

While Clyman was traveling around Oregon in the winter of 1844–45, he apparently recorded some of his observations for the benefit of Elijah White, who was leaving for Washington "in the hopes of obtaining the gubernatorial chair." The section in this journal titled "The Oregon Trail" was part of this work, and was written on notebook pages sewn by hand into Notebook Four of Clyman's journals.

Chapter 12
The Hedding Murder

Clyman's diary entry for May 24 indicates he was carrying "official Documents" directing him to inquire into the death of one of the "Skyeuse" chiefs, Elijah Hedding. The incident was one of those fairly typical of the frontier, and may have had far-reaching consequences. Hedding, an educated son of the Wallawalla chief Peupeumoxmox, was killed by a white man, Grove Cook, at Sutter's Fort in a quarrel over a stolen mule. Camp says Cook was a "notorious killer of Indians, without provocation, or at the slightest provocation."

Dr. Elijah White, "U.S. Sub. Indian Agent" for Oregon Territory, realized the serious implications of the killing, and sent letters to the Secretary of War; to Thomas O. Larkin, the U.S. Consul; to the Governor of the Mexican Territory, Pio Pico; and to Sutter, asking that they investigate the killing. Sutter, in turn, wrote to Larkin, giving him details about the incident. White asked Clyman to carry these various documents to the authorities, and empowered him to investigate personally. Nothing came of the investigation which followed. The unavenged murder, says Camp, was probably one of the causes of the later Whitman massacre (in which one of the children murdered was Joe Meek's daughter by Mountain Lamb, Helen Mar Meek) and the later disastrous Indian wars in the Northwest.

Letter from Sutter to Larkin regarding the Hedding affair:

New Helvetia 21th July 1845
Thomas O. Larkin Esqre. U. S. Consul
Dear Sir!

I received a letter of the U. S. Sub Indian Agent Dr. E. White from
the Oregon Territory from the same Gentleman you will receive letters
concerning the Wallawalla Affaire, likewise he wrote to the Govern-
ment of California about the same. Dr. White writes me that he
reported this affaire to the Secretary of War.

It is not unknown to you what happened here; but now I will give
you every particulars: When this people arrived here, consisting out
the Wallawalla Chief Piopiopio, and his Son Leicer [Elijah] educated
by the Methodists on the Wallamett, the young Chief of the Skyuses,
Capcapelic the Nez-percez Chief, Latazi an other Chief with some
people of the three different tribes amounting to about 36 Men, with
their Women and Children. As I was acquainted formerly with this
Dignitaries when I passed through the Oregon to fort Van Couver, I
received this people well and with great Hospitality, gave them good
Advice how to behalf them self in this country, and gave them in my
Official Capacity Passports and Permission to hunt within the limits
of my Jurisdicion and no further, Knowing very well that the would
have plenty of Difficulty's if the would go in the Settlements.

Leicer the pupil of the Methodists behaved very saucy and
haughty and more independent as the Chiefs, in the first place He
Killed a young Man of his own people when encamped close by the
fort, whose body was eat up by the Hogs, which was the discoverers.
On the road from here to the San Joaquin he would have Killed an
other of his people, if Mr. James Williams had not taken away his
rifle in the Moment he wanted to Kill him, this boy was the terror of
the old Chiefs he had the whole rule over them, and no doubt he
would have become a great tyrant amongs his people. When I
returned from Monterey the last Winter they was encamped again
close by the fort, a good deal of Complains came in, by the people

here, Mr. Grove Cook was among them, he claimed a Mule which they got from the Horse thiefs or the wild Horses. Mr. Cook could prove that the Mule was his property and they would not give her up to him, and Leicer told him to go and take the Mule when he is brave enough, taking his Rifle, and after a few Words leveled the Rifle on Cook. When I called them here to tell them in my Official Capacity to come here with all their Horses in my Corall, to part all the Horses which do not belong to them, out; and that they are entitled to some recompense for their trouble of getting this Horses from the Horsethiefs or from the wild Horses; but the did refuse to give them up, saying that the Rule by them was, to Keep every thing what the can get in this Way.

When I was explaining to them that after the laws of the Country the would have to give up all the Horses which dont belong to them, and that I compell them to give them up.—then I was interrupted and called by Dn. Pedro Kostromitinoff (the Russian Agent) who was on a visit here, I was about ½ an hour with this Gentleman, when we heard a shot, we went to see, and there was Leicer death, shot by Mr. Cook in my house, and in my Office in presence of about 15 foreigners and the Chiefs of these Indians, which fled immediately and I did no more see one of them. Leicer called Cook a Lyar after or in a quarrel which they had together.—It was very disagreeable for me that this happened in my house. I though the Chiefs will come here and deliver the Horses, but the moved Camp and travelled fast the whole Night. The next Morning by day break I did send about 30 armed Men after them, to compell them to give up the Horses; but they could not over-take them and lost their tracks. They was encamped several days near Mr. Lassensfarm about 100 Miles from here above in the Valley, they did not molest him at all, and they told him nothing what has happened here. I though all time that some of them would return here to see me; but they did not, Nearly all of them have a few head of Cattle to receive from me, for Leatherpantalons, Buffalo Robes, Rifle and some Curiosity's etc. for this they have all Orders to receive this Cattle at any time on my farm on feather River.—Doctor White speake of their property which they fled and left here, to give him an

account of it; that is all what they left, and the best would be to sell
their Orders to people of the Wallamett who intends to come here to
buy Cattle, by presenting this Orders the Cattle will be delivered at
anny time.—

Doctor White states also that they are very willing to give up the
Horses which dont belong to them, or as many and as good ones, on
Condition that their property be returned and the Murderer be deliv-
ered up either to him or to the Indians. – The Call the Name of
(Cook) Knight. Dr. White say that Leicer (the pupil of the Missionary)
was by no means viciously inclined, but we believe here all that Leicer
was a great Rascal.

I have the Honnor to remain with entire Respect
Your
Most Obedient Servant
J. A. SUTTER

Elijah White had also written to Thomas Oliver Larkin, recently appointed American Consul for California, sending him a copy of his letter to the Indian Department about the Hedding Affair. (This letter is reproduced in the 1960 edition of Clyman's journals by Camp.) In the letter, White suggests that the Hedding Affair must be quickly resolved, since it is agitating the Indians and thus endangering the small group of Americans in the region. White refers Larkin to Clyman as a source of information on the subject, and says Clyman "has kindly proffered to render us every service in his power in getting the Matter Satisfactorily adjusted."

White further suggests that the quickest and safest matter to resolve the whole problem is to send the murderer to him, but remarks that this may be impracticable, and that he leaves the whole matter "in the hands of Yourself and Mr. Clyman for adjustment and rectification Not doubting but You will do every thing in Your power to bring it as Speedily as possible to the happiest possible issue," thus tossing it into someone else's lap, an action that most of the officials seemed to emulate.

Following is a copy of Larkin's answer to White.
Larkin's answer to White:

Sir,

> *Your letter under date of May 16th 1845. by Mr. Clyman, I received to day.*
>
> *I have heard of the death of the Indian, and Know the murderer, that is, I presume it's the same (you mention no name) I know but little how the murder took place, nor did I Know what tribe the deceased was from.*
>
> *I cannot take up this affair, on your part, your letter does not come to me in an official shape; nor is it accompanied with documents, nor do you even name the murderer; you say Mr. Clyman will assist me, he can do nothing as a single man, nor has he and I right, to do in the case, what we may see proper as you mention.*
>
> *I have no known authority to take up the person you mention, no funds to retain him, nor have I from any person orders to receive him: in fact, from your letter, I can do nothing.*
>
> *In my opinion, if in your letter to the Governor of California (which I shall send to him) you as an Officer of the United States of America, have made a formal demand for the murderer, and have pointed out what you want done; it will be attended to, the Governor, Pio Pico, will not let the affair pass in silence.*
>
> *I shall with your letter send to the Governor, the copy of your letter to the Department in Washington, and request him to act in the case, as he may see fit.*
>
> *You can from me say to the father of the youth who was Killed, that he may, alone go from one end of California to the other in safety; and should he from you or the proper authorities of your part of the country, present themselves to this Government, he will be attended to, and justice done him both in the horrid case in question, and in the property he left here.*
>
> *You can also say to the Father of the deceased and to the Chiefs of the Tribe, that they should by no means act premature in this busi-*

ness; justice may be slow, but it will be sure, untill they, or some
proper person makes a demand on the Government of California,
they cannot expect redress, and whenever they shall make this
demand, they may depend on my attending to the case, to the best of
my Knowledge.

The Chiefs of course are sorry and disappointed from the loss;
should they come to California, to redress themselves, they would
injure a people who not one in a hundred, Know anything about the
affair, and cause trouble to themselves and this Government, who I
am sure will give them justice and satisfaction, when ever they
demand it, should they commence a warfare against our Country-
men, it would end in misiries to hundreds of both parties, and no
satisfaction be obtained.

You will request this Tribe to wait, untill this affair can be
thoughroughly sifted and attended to, tell them through some proper
person, to demand their property of the Government of California,
and justice for the crime commited; and believe that the Californians
will do towards them and all Foreigners, justice and impartiality; as
the distance is great between us, much time will be required to settle
this affair.

I am Sir, with the highest respect,
your most obedient servant
THOMAS O. LARKIN.
E. White, Esqr.
U. S. Sub-
Agent, for In
dian affairs

———

[May 24, 1845 to June 7, 1845]

Heard that a small party of men started for the states about a month
since ware stoped by the snake Indians on account of Two of That

nation being killed by some Stragling americans that came through the latter part of the winter.

This circumstance shews the great necesity of some authority being Established along this rout it being allmost amatter of necessity that people should be able to pass and repass in measureable security from and to the states.

25 It rained all night and the morning looked dark and Disagreeable five of us packed up and started for the California rendavous about noon it commenced raining and rained all the afternoon made 15 miles and encamped in the applegate settlement on the South branches of the yam hill I could not admire the Apple-gate selection all though the soil is good But a portion of the country is a complete mudhole and the settlement is inconvieniently situated The hills as usual as beautiful and picturesque and in many places covered Belly deep to our Horses in clover.

26 A disagreeable rainy night left our incampment passed over a beautifull undulating country near the Killamook mountains made about four miles and encamped on La Creole a handsome clear running stream with fine rich prarie intervales on either side some settlements have commenced to be made on this creek during the past winter and a mill is now in building a few miles above our camp This La Creole or Rockreole is finely adapted for Hydraulic purposes as well as for agracultureal timber is however in many places rather scarce.

27 Cloudy packed up and moved 10 miles to the Lukimute passed over a fine roling country the Lukimute is [a] clear gravelly stream falling out of the Killimook mountains and has some fine rich prarie Bottoms the hills as usual covered with Oak & Firr the white[s] extend this [far] south their being two or three farms commenced here this spring one year ago the nearest house was Thirty miles north so goes the settlments in the willhamet vally.

28 It commenced raining yesterday about noon and still continues to rain we Expect to rimain here about a week waiting for the party [to] collect as we are now in advance of the main camp which are collecting [at] rikreole 12 miles in our rear rode out over the hills and shot severals g[r]ous found the grous quite plenty.

It is remarkable to see the great Quanty of esculent roots that grows in all parts of this vally Ten or Twelve acres of cammace in one marsh is Quite common and in many instances it will yield 20 Bushel to the acre the calapooyas live exclusively on roots but whare hogs are introduced they soon distroy the cammerce fields these extensive fields are allways on wet land and in many places no other vegitable is found to intermix with it Three of our party arived at our camp in the evening.

29 Thick fogy morning continued showery the day thorughout rode out in the evening saw some beautiful small vallis near the mountains one of our party killed a small deer.

30 Had some sunshine during the day a Large party of Klickatat Indians came from the south and encamped near us had a view of the Killamook mountains in the afternoon the rise commencing about four miles west these mountains are low compared with the cascades but are verry ruged and covered with timber to their tops.

Preparation of camas roots

31 The day proved to be verry warm in the low vally The Indians our neigbours ware out early diging roots this operation is performed by sinking a strong hard stick in the ground near the roots to be dug then taking pry on the outer extemity of the stick a portion of earth containing frorm 2 to six roots is taken up the roots being the size of a small onion and much resembling the onion in appearance They are then washed and clensed a hole of suitable size is dug in the earth filled with wood and stones after the earth and stones becomes well heated the fire is taken off and a Layer of green grass laid over the hot stones the roots [are] piled on the grass and a Layer of grass laid over the roots then a thin layer of earth over the whole and a fire outside of all which is kept up some 24 hours when it is allowed to cool down and the rooots are ready for use or for drying and putting away for future use when dry they keep for months or years.

June the First 1845

M. M[oses] Harris visited our encampment Last night and [I] Received lettrs from my Esteemed Friend Dr. White as Likewise from Dr McLaughlin Both wishing me success on my hazardous Journey back to the states the acquaintance I leave in this vally are but few thos few However (are of) are Euqal to any I have ever found in warmth of feeling kindness and generosity with out any of that selfishness so often seen in the States.

2 It rained all day in showers and made camping verry disagreeable.

3 Still continues to rain we moved camp However for the purpose of getting red of our pilfering neighbours the Klickatats crossed over the East Fork of Lickemute River and encamped near the hills this last stream is a deep mudy creek about 20 yards wide and we had to carry our packs over on a drift The Brances of this stream unite a few miles Below our camp forming a large vally of fine rich land the stream uniting with the willhamet about 8 miles below Both Branches of the Lukimute are bold and noble mill streams Timber However is inconvenient to many fine farming tracts the oak which abounds on the hills is shrubby and short Three men arived at camp making our cup [company] 12 men strong.

4 The sun arose nearly clear and we have the prospect of a feew hours sun shine I noticed in many places in the hills that the substrata was a formation of soft shelly rock or (or) indurated clay which washes down by the winter rains and becomes verry soft and impassable for a horse bearing a man.

Rode out over the hills s. E. of our camp had an extensive view of hill vally and mountain far to the North and East passed over some beautiful farming Lands The day proved fair & the grass became dry some showers of rain fell in the afternoon low grumbling thunder heard at a distance and I think this is the third time I have heard thunder in the Teritory as thender and Lightning is verry rare From what cause I cannot tell it may possibly be on account of the lowness of the clouds which rest on the mountains and in fact on the earth even in vallies.

5 The sun arose through a thick fog the forenoon was however pleasant Lighgt showers hovered around all the afternoon to the west and south rode out over some beautifull hills well calculated for pasture land and Exhibiting a beautifull veriety of Scenery the greate veriety however is to be had in many places in this country and had nature given this vally a pleasant climate no country in the known world could compare with it for rural sceenery when the vallies shall become grain fields and the hills covered with flocks and herds of Domestic animals.

6 Drizling rain fell during the night and still continues this morning 5 men and one woman & three children arived at our camp During the day rode out up the vally and mounted an imenence from which we had a large and magnificent view of the vally and lower mountains the uper mountain being covered in clouds and rain returned to camp over beautiful farming and pasture lands observed quantities of wild pigions feeding on the grass seeds several kinds of which are fully ripe.

7 Light showers of rain fell in various directions around us but none on us during the fore noon our party continues collecting and we have a fair prspect of making a regular start Tomorrow on our trip to california.

Tell Everhart to Bring ¼lb Tea and 6 lb sugar.

———————

Oregon Territory March the 21 [1845]

- 2 saddle Blankets
- 5 lb Lead 1 do Powder
- 5 lb Coffee 10 do sugar
- 3 Trail Ropes
- 1 Pair Pants
- Leading Cords
- Cooking utensils
- Linnen for bags & sacks

- Leather for hopples
- Mockasins & soals &c
- Soap Fr John 2 lb rice
- 5 lb sugar
- 1 Hankf Blank Book

POESY BY A NATIVE

The Firrs their length their Extreme hight
As yet remains in doubt
But Tradition throws an obscur light
That many had grown Quite out of sight
Ere Hood Began to Sprout

AN ADDRESS TO MOUNT HOOD

Say mighty peak of tremendious hight
What brot you forth to etherial light
From Earths inmost deepest woomb
Was central earth so Jamd. so pent
That thou arose to give it vent
Or for some other purpose sent
A Monumental Tomb

To shew that once in Licqid heat
The Earth had flowed a burning sheet
Of melted wavering fire
That animation Flaming lay
A molten Mixed wase rocks and clay
When thou a bubble rose to play
Above the funeral pyre

Chapter 13
Notebook Five
On the Oregon-California Trail

William Wolfscale [Wolfskill] in the Town of Purbelo [Pueblo of Los Angeles]
John Warner Same Place
Lemuel J Carpenter

DIRECTIONS BY MR [JOEL P.] WALKER

Be carefull to never camp in the timber if it can be avoided. Be carefull to never Let any Indians come amongt you Never Lit the Indian have any amunition on any account Keep careful watch both day and night Never neglect camp guard on any account

Never Fire a gun after (after) crossing the Umqua mountain untill you cross the siskiew mountain perhaps Five days travel Keep yourselves close as possible in traveling through the Brush

Never scatter after game or [make] any other division

Keep your guns the best firing condition

Sunday June the 8th 1845
Cloudy.
Made a finale start for California our company consisting of 35

men one woman and three children Left four men at camp hunting for a Lost Horse which ran away this morning in a fright.

Passed over a fine undulating country handsomely and thickly clothed with grass some haveing the appeareance of rye and timothy all kinds However covered in seed which [is] rather remarkable for it is well Known to all the western states that but fewe of Prarie grasses ever bears seed.

Here all the grasses are laden down with seed and those grown in the oak Hills the more certain Had a view of mount Jefferson clothed in everlasting winter which has grown into an extensive mountain of considerable length The clouds blew of[f] and the sun shone out as we passed through oak groves In the Evening the 4 men left to Hunt the lost animal came up haveing found the Horse making our paty 39 men strong the day proved pleasant made 10 miles and Encamped on a small Brook about 4 miles from the Willhamet our path lea[d]ing close to the Killamook.

9 Morning Clear the sun arose in splended majisty over the snowy peaks of Mount Jefferson The vally covered in dew like a rain passed through some beautifull country for farming and Likewise some very wet land early in the Day we came to a small river supposed to be the Tom Beoff [Long Tom] found it not fordable but after meandering up the stream some 4 miles when we found a deep ford after some plunging and swiming we all passed safely over but we soon found that we had numerous branches of the same stream yet to pass all of which ware deep and difficult to ford one point on the Killamook mountains shewed considerable of snow on its summit this peak stands near the gorge of the Tom Beoff and near the vally made about 16 miles a large Prarie lies East of our camp and it has a fine appearance at a distance Today we traveled through some fine grass lands which would be good for mowing if hay was necessary the vally on this side of the river dose not exceede 10 miles wide.

10 Clear Left our camp at 8 oclock passed some fine Prarie lands and continued up the south Branch of Tom Beoff a dull muddy stream nearly Bank full and not fordable crossed several deep cammace swamps and several deep muddy Brances of the main stream with difficulty at length we cleared the Tom Beoff intirely and assended the long slope of a ridge had a few miles of pleasant traveling the ridge was thinly clad with oak and pine our rout still lying near the Killimook mountains we not being able to travel in the main vally on account of highness of the waters.

The country we passed to day is deep red clay on the hills the vallys being low and mostly wet The dry vally land however is verry rich Timber shrubby oak and pine and Firr passed severall beautefull round mounds standing in the main vally I cannot conjecture how [they] came to occupy such sittuations unless at some distant period this vally formed a Lake.

Made 20 miles and incamped on a deep dirty small river.

11 The day proved clear and fine and it was all that was pleasant during the day after leaving our low over flown camp we soon passed into a dirty mirey pomd for nearly a mile Belly deep to our hight from which we had a view of nealy all of the upper Willhamet vally and from apearances seven Eights of the level vally was overflown during the winters rains continued up a small river our course a little west of south made an etempt to pass over the creek and gain another trail more easterly with considerable difficulty we succeeded to cross the stream after getting over to our disapountment we foud our selves on a low sunken Island surrounded by Byous and shoughs and ware forced to cross back again through the same miry ford— continued our course up the stream through mud and mire a low pine ridge to our right and large extensive marsh to our left noticed a speces of Black oak to day made 10 miles and encamped on a low pine Bluff near the river.

12 After a full examination of the Primises it was determined to carry all our Baggage over the stream on dift [driftwood] near our camp and take our animals about Four miles up the stream and then swim them over it being the nearest place that could be found whare our horses could get either in or out in a few hours we ware all packed up and on our way from swamp river passed several miles of Pine plain and came to another dirty creek here we again had to unpack and carry on a log the stream being to deep and miry for horses to pass with packs on once more under way we entered the hills to our greate Joy being completely sick of level marshes and overflown vallies. the hills as usual in oregon are covered with fine nutricious grass groves of shrubby oak and fine firr in places made about 15 miles and encamped in the hills a small party of Klickitats going north came to our camp while we ware unpacking our animals hills and mountains have allways been pleasant to me but I think the hills at this time are unusualy pleasant our course to day being a little East of south.

13 From a hill near our camp last night I had a view of Mount Hood Mount Jefferson and five other snowy pinicles south and east of Mount Jefferson as likewise the umpequaw mountains crossing our path to the South Packed up and moved on the trail up the creek after passing a few miles of open hill coumntry we came to a small creek over which we found a (a) good and safe Bridge crossed over and immediately assended the Kalapooya mountain this mountain is thickly covered with Firr and ceader timber and underbrush of hazel dogwood and other Brush.

This ridge is not high but is verry steep in many places and Formed intirely of clay based on a soft rotten Bassalt rock seen in averry few places only the cedar of this country is of a large and verry fine discription made 22 miles and encamped in a narrow vally on one of the branches of the umquaw and near the entrance of the umquaw vally the country so far appears to be much dryer than [the] vally on the north of the mountains.

14 Clear and still the smoke curling around the half bar Hills which seem to be covered in Black taild deer Took the Trail again soon crossed the Elk creek a stream about 30 yards wide clear gravely bottom and sandy Banks the first we have seen since we crossed Rick-reole this stream runs to the S.W. and empties into the Umpquaw Prarie vallies seem to open out immediately below the ford assendid up the stream and up a steep brushy ridge but soon entered a beautifull little vally streching away south Passed on to the head of the vally crossed several ridges all covered more or less in shrubby oak and Firr timber and well grassed.

This vally is quite uneven so far and much more dry than the willhamet vally and equally well timberd. and well stored with game such as deer Elk and Bear during our progress to day we saw anumber of Indians peeping over the hills and viewing us as we passed Made 18 miles and encamped at the Fork of a small creek this appears to be a common encampment for all the travelers to and from California numerous ridges may be seen running in all directions through this part of the vally.

15 A number of Indians came to our camp late last night and remained in camp during the night of the Kalapooya and Umpquaw tribes made an early start soon crossed a considerable creek running westward pased through an uneven vally frequently rising up into mountains at 11 came to the umpquaw river arapid stream about 100 yards wide clear and cool with a solid rock bottom the [banks] rising into mountains in many places from the waters edge Hired an Indian with his canoe to ferry our bagage over this task he performed to our satisfaction all got safely over and encamped on the south side of the stream on the open Prarie as this method of encampment is much the most safe for a Party as large as ours being able to defend ourselves best on the Praries or whare the enemy would be exposed in making an attact mad about 10 miles Two Indians remained in camp last night.

16 Before leaveing the umpquaw I might remark that the Hudson Bay company have a trading house some 20 miles below whare a small profitable trade is carried on From Information this stream bars the same character from Its sources in the snowy butes of the cascades that is going Pitching and Tumbling through the rock untill within some 40 miles of its mouth (its waters being nearly doubled) when it becomes still and moves slowly and Quietly to the ocean through a thick impenetrable forest of lofty timber the Praries tirminating whare the rapids cease in abot one hours travel we reached the south Branch of umpquaw a rapid stream much resembling the main river passed up over some steep Bluffs which raise into mountains the river winding and curving amongst the rocks and Hills the most bear of Timber which are low the higher covered in oak and Firr some Beautifull vallies are found that look allmost like enchantment the rapid little river Tumbling along one side rounded Hills of oak softining down to a vally bounding the others all covered in grass and flowers all wild as natures dream and covered with the light bounding deer Made 16 miles.

17 Lift our camp on the river and proceeded up through a rough ruged country passed several cliffs of rock closing down to the waters edge saw the blackned carcase of a dead Indian lying raped up in his old worn deer skin habliments after considerable winding and turning around hills and pricepces we reached a beautifull level rich but small vally lying on both sides of the river some 4 miles in length and ½ mile wide reaching the head of the vally the mountains closed in so that we had to ford the river three times in less than two miles the first and second fords ware deep the water rapid and the bottom rocky so that nearly all our packs got more or les wet about three oclock we encamped at the foot of the umpquaw mountains having made 16 miles this mountain looks steep and ruged saw a greate veriety of beautifull flowers in passing through this vally if vally it can be fairly called. saw several Beautifull young fawns lying in the grass during the day which did not move by being handled.

18 Arose early we now have to enter the continual war nations of Indians that inhabit the whole extent of country between here and California as son as packed we got on the trail and commenced assending the mountain by the way of following a dim trail up the steep bluffs and winding around decliveties of (of) the mountain after much fatiegue and labour we assended the tumbling mountain torrent untill [it] branched into several smaller streams when we assended the Point of a mountain nearly perpendicular about a mile high traversed its narrow winding summit a short distance and again deceded crossed a small mountain brook and scaled another mountain full as steep as the first but not so high followed around through brush and logs a few miles and again desended to a fine small prarie whare we encamped having traveled 15 miles of unaccontable tiresome difficult road over a high steep mountain covered with brush and logs likewise firr and ceedar timber the streams run through a rocky channel but no rock is found near the summit of the ridges.

19 Clear & warm passed down a handsome Brook with a narrow

Prarie vally running down the north side about 6 miles crossd. the Brook and immediately took [up] the mountain steep ruged and Brushy this ridge has several snowdrifts yit visable on its summit a short distance South of the trail The desent was not Quite so steep crossed a small Brook and assended another mountain not Quite so high as the first but verry difficult on account of the logs and under-grothe some parts of these mountains have Beautifull groves of Pine Firr and cedar but apparantly to remote to be usefull Partially desended the second to a small cove and then mounted a third high ridge at the bottom of which opens a small vally of handsome Prarie whare we encamped haveing made about 17 miles the first six miles being nearly west the latter part S and S.W. deer dose not appear to be abundant.

20 Immedeately after leaving camp we assended a mountain of no greate elevation but verry brushy and steep immediatly on the summit the open country commenced with Pine openings and a lengthy desent of dry hard gravelly soil which continued untill we reached the river on the whole the country is rough poor and fobined [forbidding?] and of little account even the savages that inhabit this region find a scanty subsistanc there being but few roots which are so abundant in the will-hamette vally on our rout to day we saw 4 or 5 squaws hunting after roots which ware much serprised to se us so unexpectedly early in the afternoon we reached the Clamet or Rogues River and a number of the savagers came to our camp but as a matter of safety we would not permit them into camp Made 14 miles severa[l] men went to Examin the river only a short distance ahead several parties came to our camp and made ever effort and divise to come into camp and nothing short of a cocked rifle would prevent them However we succeeded to keep them back without violence and they sung their war songs in hearing of our camp all night.

Made 16 mile.

21 Early we ware on the move the Indians close in the rear we soon unpacked on the bank of Rogues River this stream is about 100 yards wide running Rapid over a generally rocky Bottom the country we passed over was generally poor gravelly hard and dry the vally narrow and uneven the mountains dry parched and covered with shrubby pine and several kinds of evergreen shrubbery some of a beautifull appearance and would grace a walk in any city – we hired two Indians and their canoes who soon forried us over the river while we stood with our guns in our hands for our defence about 2 in the afternoon we passed a narrow point of rocks Juting in neare the Rivir Capt [Green] McMahon and seven or eighht men went ahead and Examined the primises but found no danger lurking there our course to day has been East or nearly so up the South side of the river which came tumbling down impeteously so far the vally of this stream is thinly covered in pine cedar and oak a new speeces of pine is found here haveing sweet turpentin oozeing forom it.

22 Immediately above our camp the [river] passes out from between two high mountains and tumbles down several falls and rapids our trail here left the course of the river and we moved of[f] Easterly up a narro vally which soon brot us in sight of a Beautiful vally in which two branches of the rive[r] seem to form a Junction and Likewise in sight of several snowy peak one nearly east is High round & and sharp with snow a long way down its sides and a Table rock of considerabl Hight the top level and [said] to contain an Indian vilage this is doubtful but it may be a place of safety in seasons of danger Eastwardly up this vally we proceeded and four of us that ware ahead missing the rout rode near the mountain when 4 Natives were discovered to our left we made chase and soon overtook them in the channel of a dry Brook whare they crouched down and gave up to be shot as they expected nothing less they proved to be an old woman two boys and one fine little girl Mr Frazier dismounted and gave the girl a biscuit who took it but as soon as we moved our horses so that they had an open way they took to there heels again and we rode on the vally still widening and ranges of the wildes[t] and most beautiful Hill[s] bounded the North side of the vally these hills rise in a succession of rounded Knolls one above another generally covered in grass but one or two clifs of rock make their appearance traveled about 20 miles and encamped on a small brook haveing several snow drifts in sight toward the south.

The natives of this vally seem to have a hard way of living their being no game and but few roots and when the oak miss to bear they live on clove[r] not unlike the pigs or domistic animal but when the oak bears acorns they are plentifully supplied for the time being in the summer they live on grass and have no clothing Except a deer skin or a short apron of plated grass They are the sworn Enimies of the whites and would be verry dangerous had they the use of fire arms.

23 Under way Early and I could not but admire the varied diversity of the Hills Lying to the North some of the advance came suddenly upon a small party of Indians who all ran but one supposed to be a chief who stood and made signs about a minuet and put out to the brush course still East of south up the vally about 12 we began to climb the Siskiew mountain which is not difficult nor steep compared with some we have passed near the top of this mountain is a bad thicket to pass whare nearly all the parties passing this Trail have been attacted several men with Capt McMahan went in ahead and we drove in our packed animals all came through same & soon had a view of the country south from the summit which was wild and awfully sublime snow was seen in more than 20 places some quite nigh and amongst the timber which goes to shew that an [un] usual Quantity has fallen late in the spring moved on down the mountain which is steep but not difficult made 25 miles.

24 Left our encampment under the Siskiew mountain and proceeded down an uneven mountainous vally [Cottonwood Creek, in Siskiyou County, California] a south Easterly direction the country gravelly dry and Barren passed several old Indian wigwams whar Quantities of acorns had been gathered last fall no game is to be seen in this Region some of our advance pursued a fale [male] and female Native the male made his Escape the female was taken and her horse taken from her (Mr Sears & Mr Owens) Came to the Clamet River a strong swift stream running rapidly over a Rocky bed after some search a ford was found a short distance above when we all crossed over and encamped on the South side This river is about 80 yards wide and is Quite muddy from the thawings of the snow on the Mountains course S.W and appears to fall into a deep Kenyon a short distance below saw the recent marks of a trapping party supposed to [be] Indians Travel to day about 14 miles.

25 Left our camp on Clamet River and immediately left the River the general appearant course of the vally being North of East we going South of East passed a few miles of rough rocky country [Willow Creek] when a fine level vally hove in sight through which we passed steering for a Tripple shaped high round peaked snowcapd Montain known by the name of the Snowy Bute [Mount Shasta] at about 15 miles we came to a clear handsome small stream of water [Little Shasta River] running westward as do all the streams of this region whare we encamped amidtst innumerable swarms of fine large Brown grasshoppers and [so] voraceious ware they that we had to baet them off of our Baggage with sticks and when not allowed to eat baggage the live ate the dead greedily—and five or six living ones fought for the body of one ded one The land of this vally is dry and barren lies very high and is nearly surrounded by snowcapt mountains whose summits do not appeer high above the plain.

26 Again under way we passed through amidst a great number of round conicle peaks of rock standing out in an uneven plain all formed of rock Mostly black rough and porus some nearley as open as a riddle in the forenoooon passed Chesty River a deep clear stream running North of west and probaby falling in to the clammet River some distance below Continued our course East of South over a rough rocky plain and approched near the western base of the mountain came to a clear Brook of water and beautifull small green valley whare we encamped haveing traveled 25 miles the high snowy Butte Lies S. E. of our camp not Exceeding 15 miles from the everlasting snow saw recent marks of a large trapping Party which cannot be far distant from us antelope have been tolerable plenty for 2 days past.

27 Concluded to remain in our present camp to day and rest our animals as we are informed that we have an extremely rough country to pass through on our way down the sacriment a large high rounded rock [Pilot Knob] can be distinctly seen which stands on or near the top of the Siskiew Mountain a few miles East of the pass This vally is no part of it fit for cultivation but is finely clothed in grass in many places but not generally.

Verry little timber is found in the vallies the mountains are covered with pitch pine generally knotty and shrubby game not plenty The two men that went out this morning in search of the trapping party this morning returned again in the evening unsuccessfull a Black conicle Knob [Sugar Loaf] of considerable elivation seems to stand in the center of the pass Between the Bute and the point of a Snowy mountain [Eddy Mountain].

28 Left our camp on Chesty vally proceeded up some small streams Isuing from a snowy mountain Lying to the west of the trail Intered a beautifull pineery consisting of white or sugar and yellow pine Firr and cedar of Large dementions and fine straight stems passed the Black rocky Bute close to the East made 15 miles and encamped on a Limpid Brook [Cold Creek] of cool clear water comeing from the Snowy Bute and Being some of the Extereme Northwestern heads of the sacramento River Land generally timbered gravelly and poor several deer ware seen and some killed on the way the snow on the Bute to the East seems to be Quite nigh and considerable Quantities yet Lying some distance below the point of vegitation but this cannot be a common occurrence or if it is the groth of Pine must be cool as well as rapid.

29 Proceeded down the vally of the Sacramento through some magnificent Timber land some of the finest I Ever beheld after some hours travel we desended into the vally of the main river near whare a Soda spring [Upper Soda Springs] Issues out of the East Bank of the river But this spring is deminutive in comparison to the greate soda springs on Bear River both as to Quality and Quantity not containing but trifling portions of gass still it is a fine pleasant cool dr[a]ught in a warm day as the present has been the river comes tumbling down over the rocks in numerous rapid whirls & is confined all most to its channel between high mountains on either side which rise verry steep and are covered in pine timber and underbrush to their summits generally forded the river at the soda springs and continued down on the west side over steep Bruff and deep ravines traveled 20 miles and encamped on a dry narrow pine plain North west of our camp is an awfull steep craggy cliff of grey granite rock the pinecles of which look as sharp as Icyceles.

30 Early on our saddles and pushing ahead on account of the poorness of the grass and in ½ a mile we assended a steep Bluff of the River which was followed by another and another throughout the day in fact we rode the whole of 20 miles on the steep side of amountain crossin impending ravines desending down one side and assending up the oposite amidst declivities of sharp rock some of which was a whitish grey granite and intermixed with Black slate standing in a perpendicular form pointing at all who ware hardy enough to oppose: the River tumbling and fomeing down a narrow channel at a desperate pitch of rapidity the day proved to be verry warm in the ravine along whose sides we wound our tiresome way not a drop of rain has fallen on us since we left the settlements on the Eighth of the present month but still the mountain Brooks are plenty and well supplied with cool water.

July the First 1845
The sun arose in his strength and looked down upon us in a narrow confined spot near the River the vegitation all dried Brown on the earth our animals striving to pick up a scanty subsistance our selves standing about in groups and you might hear the Question frequently asked or other ways propounded (when will we get out of these moun-tains) Started down the river crossing a rough rocky Brook [perhaps Dog Creek] and turned up the ridge missed the old trail and followed the trail of a recent Trapping party continued to assend the mountain about 4 miles when it was concluded to Retrace our steps so turning around with some difficulty on account of narrowness of the ridge we came to the river again and unpacked our animals to graze packed up and continued down the River some Indians came up with the rear of our party and Mr Sears shot two of them our road this afternoon was some little beter than yesterday and we made about 18 miles over a dry rocky country of a mixture of Slate and granite rock verry keen and

sharp for our horses feet which are verry tender The hills are bald or thinly covered with pine timber intermixed with oak of several kinds grass scarce and vegitation light and starved three Indians came to camp in the evening which ware soon sent away as our camp was not a safe place for savages there being no controle of free americans in this region.

2 The grass was so poor that we packed up from the stake this morning and immediately put to the trail crossed several deep ravines and at length to cap all we commenced assending the side of a nearly perpendicular mountain composed of slate and granite an hours sweating puffing and blowing brought us to the sharp top when we commenced desending on the other side which was worse if possible another hour brot us to the bottom again whare we found a small uneven bottom large enough to graze our animals an hour on a scanty supply of grass and wood enough to prepare our Breakfast 17 [miles].

Immedeately commenced assending another mountain the steepest I ever saw for hoses to climb But we made the summit at last by taking zig zag sheers back and forth over the rough rocks and through the Brush in fact it was almost to steep for brush to grow continued along the ridge which was composed of Slate set edge wise and in many places too narrow for a Rabbit to walk over in such places we had to desend along the perpendicular sides whare a precareous foot hold could be found for a few animals in the decomposed rock that had tumbled from the higher parts at a late hour in the afternoon we dsended on to a small brook running through a Kenyon you could see the water but not taste it some few miles below we campd.

3 Again we saddled at the stake and took down the creek and soon came to [the Sacramento] river which had more than doubled its waters since we left it yestarday but still running through a norrow confined rocky channel onnpacked for Breakfast Before we packed up several Indians ware seen across the river and several guns fired at long shot across the River and eventually one killed.

After packing we again took to the Rocky hills the greate vally in plain view from the hills has occasionally (has) been seen for several days all anxious to leave the Eternal mountain urged our Jaded animals to thier utmost capabilities and about Three in the afternoon we entered the lower vally of the sacramento and threw ourselves under the shad of the wide spreading oak Trees that stand scattered promisquesly over this vally.

The earth seemed to be verry dry for the season and as might be expected the weather we found to be warm our Travel to day 20 Miles.

July the 4th 1845

Again we ware on the march a few miles of midling country broughte [us] to a small River shortly after crossing of which we bore to the right across a range of gravelly hills covered in thorn Bushis and bearing no grass no[r] much vigetation of any [kind] that canbe usefull two or three hours ride brot us to another smal river runing over a gravel and rocky bed on this we encamped having traveled about 20 miles.

5 Took across the ridges again found them gravelly poor and hard course a little west of south about noon we came to the river again Quite Enlarged and the shores lined with willow and Sycamore soil appearantly dry but saw several patches of wild oats now ripe and mostly d[r]oped off the straw has the exact appearance of the culte-vated of the states but the grain or berry is dark brown and covered with a thick fuzzy film snowey mountains can be seen from this vally in all directions except south some Quite large and high others small Travel to day 16 miles and encamped on he River most of the vegita-tion grown and dry and considerable of it rotten the days we found verry warm and the nights ware also.

6 Left our camp on the river and took down the plain some miles from the river the praries [are] hard clay mixed with water worn gravel mostly granite and rough white flint and thinly covered in grass which is (is) generally short passed several chanels of dry Brooks some of considerable width passed one running stream of water deeply sunk in loose gravel Banks some fine grazing lands lying adja-cent but no timbr fit for mechanicle purposess the vegetation to day completely dry and mostly Burned off smokes ware raising in all directions from the grass being on fire Travel to day 28 miles encamped near a hole of stagnent water standing in the channel of a dry Brook the vally here is Quite large and the mountains compartivly Low.

7 Loft our dry camp on dry creek and took down the plain over a hard gravelly surface at a rapid rate of Travelling for Broken down animals the day was cool and cloudy passed some appearantly good soil in the afternoon and several large patches or fields of wild oats the straw still standing but (but) the grain mostly droped out Turned in and encamped on a misserable Slough of Bad water near the river shortly after we unsaddled it commenced raining and [rained] steadily all night a Large village of Natives was in hearing across the pond but as they remained at home themselves we did not visit them Our travel to day being 30 miles near and about our camp is a groth of Large shrubby oak of the white oak spices during the day we crossd a fine small river of running water in a deep gravelly Bed.

8 Continued raining but we saddled and started through the rain passed over beautifull level prarie near the timber and about 10 oclock it Broke away and ceased raining about one oclock the prarie appeared nearly black with Indians to our left but only one approached near us who spoke bad spanish and we still worse so we had but little conversation and continued our rout and shortley turned in to the river and encamped haveing travelled 20 miles of level loose country along our rout Found it verry difficult to water our animals at the river on account of the Loose and soft nature of the banks and bottom the day was cool and pleasant after the rain which Likewise softened the Earth and made it pleasant travelling. the male natives of all this region that I have yet seen go entirely naked.

9 A cool pleasant day after the rain we ware early on our saddles and steered for a gap in the mountain a southwest direction over a level prarie which from appearances is some times covered intirely by water but is dry and firm at present about 2 in the afternoon we reached the channel of a dry creek much disapointed as our selves and animals ware very thirsty and fatigued no alternative was left us but to push forward to a pount of timber about 15 miles ahead so on we urged our Jaded animals and reached a small brook of water about sundown and encamped our guide thought he knew the place and rode out to look for the settlements and in an hour returned with a Mr Sumner [Owen Sumner Jr.] whose father was with us Let our animals run loose for the first time and all lay down and slept Quietly and sound under the spreading oak trees 40 miles.

10 At an Early hour we ware visited by a Mr. [William] Knight who informed us that the country was in a verry unsettled state there haveing been a kind of Revelution or Rebellion during the winter and spring and that the governor had been driven out of the province but was now returning with a strong force to reinstate matters on a more firm Base than heretofore Mr Wolfscale [John Wolfskill] and several other american gentlemen visited our camp during the fore noon could not ditermine what course to pursue in this unsettled state of publick affairs all concluded to remain in our present camp to day and rest ourselves and animals in the afternoon Mr Wolfscale Butchered a Beef and kindly invited all of us to take what we wished without money and without price so that the evening was spent in feasting on the fattest kind of Beef.

11 On account of our animals we remain in our present camp to day to give them rest many of our company are much discouraged at the report of the dullness of all kinds of Buisness as they Expected to find immediate employ at high wages.

Notes on Chapter Thirteen

Apparently Clyman was leading a group of settlers unhappy with the situaton in Oregon into California to look for better conditions. Camp mentions that a Joseph McKay met Clyman's group, and wrote: "The majority of Mr. Clymers [Clyman's] Companions seemed to be thoroughly disgusted with Oregon or Columbia as it was then called, and it was intended to make up a party sufficiently strong to undertake the journey southward, across the mountains into California. The general opinion then was that it was an exceedingly dangerous undertaking on account of the warlike nature of the Indians on the route." (Joseph William McKay, "Recollections of a Chief Trader in the Hudson's Bay Company," Pacific Ms. C-24, Bancroft Library). Clyman doesn't seem to have been especially worried about the dangers of the trip, though travelers from Jedediah Smith's early expedition through the settlers of the 1860s had trouble with these warlike and dangerous Indians.

In Clyman's entry for June 21, the "narrow point of rocks juting in neare the rivir" is identified by Camp as near Grants Pass, Oregon.

Among the snowy peaks Clyman mentions on June 22, the "one nearly east is High round & sharp with snow a long way down its side" is Mount McLoughlin, known to early pioneers as Mt. Pitt; the "Table rock" is one of the table rocks near the junction of Bear Creek and the Rogue River.

Clyman's camp June 24 was on Cottonwood Creek in Siskiyou County, California. The trail crossed the Siskiyou divide where the railroad now runs, according to Camp.

In conversation with Ivan Petroff in 1878, Clyman related more details about the fourth of July celebration. "On this our national holiday a brutal and disgraceful occurrence took place. Some Indians were seen across the river and Mr Sears proposed to kill one of them single-handed if his comrades would keep him covered with their guns. They agreed and he started out armed only with his bowie knife. After swimming across he encountered an Indian who had been firing at him from behind a rock without effect. They grappled and Sears stabbed his man to death and then returned safe and sound across the river. I was so disgusted with this affair at the time that I did not enter it in my notes." (Ivan Petroff's "Abstract of Clyman's Note Book," Ms. Bancroft Library.)

Chapter 14
Notebook Six
Gordon Ranch to Napa Valley

July 12, 1845 to Sept. 8, 1845

July the 12th 1845

Several of our party packed up aand left for Capt Suitors a strong doba or mud walled fort about 40 miles East it is said that Captain Suitor is likewise an alcalda or Justice of the peace and has the right to grant passports for my own part I have come to the conclusion to go down the North side of the Bay of saint Francisco to Sonoma in a few days and see what Buisiness may be found in that direction.

Sutter to Larkin regarding the Oregon Immigration:

New Helvetia 15th July 1845.
Thomas O. Larkin Esqre in Monterey
Dear Sir!

...I send you a News paper from St: Louis send to me over the Rockey Mountains, with a somewhat exagerated description of California. The Company which arrived the 10th instt from the Oregon consists out 39 Men, 1 Widow and 3 Children of which I send you inclosed a list.

All of this people have a descent appearance and some very useful
Men amongs them some of them will remain here, and the Majority
will spred over the whole Country like usual, a good Many will come
to Monterey and present themselves to you, I give them passports, and
give Notice to the Government. I received a letter which informes me
that in about 6 or 8 Weeks an othre Compy. will arrive here direct
from the U. S. a very large Company more as 1000 Souls, familys
from Kentucky and Ohio and a good Many young enterprizing
Gentlemen with some Capital to improve the Country, under lead of
L. W. Hastings Esqre of whom I received some letters which informed
me of this Arrival, I am looking for them in about 8 or 10 weeks from
Now, I am very glad that they meet with some good Pilots at fort Hall,
people who went over there from here, to pilot Emigrants the new
Wagon road which was found right down on Bearcreek on my farm.

I am so much engaged at present that it is impossible to write you
a better letter, and I shall embrace the Opportunity by Mr. Williams
who will leave from here to Monterey in about 5 or 6 days.

I remain very respectfully
Your
Most Obedient Servant
J A SUTTER

P.S.
I send you now the whole History of the last Revolution concerning
the foreigners etc.

July 12 In the afternoon moved about 2 miles up to Mr
[William] Gordons who is the only perminant settler on this (this
Cash) [Cache] creek we found here two other american gentlemen to
[w]it Mr Wolfscale and Mr Knight Mr Wolfscale it appears had lately
been dispossed of a very valuable Ranche or farm some 12 miles south
of this and had his herds here by the pemission of Mr Gordon.

13 Several of us started down the North side of the Bay of St
Fracisco passed over dry level prarie about 12 miles the day being
Extremely warm I took a sun pain in my head which almost prevented

me from being able to ride for several hours passed the nearly dry
channel of a small river [Putah Creek] the water yet remaining being
allmost scalding hot as it came slowly ripling down over a hot gravelly
bed saw Quite a larg stock of cattle and Horses roaming through the
vally of this creek Eight miles further on we came to some handsom
little cornfields without any fenc Except the Indians who watch the
stock (stock) from the grain after leaving this ranch [Berreyessa] the
whole country was thickly set in well grown oats straw the grain
having droped off Toward sundown the Mokotoes made a general and
simultanious attact on ourselves and animals and although I had
fought mosketois through the wabash Illinois and Missisippi vallies yet
I never met with such a Quantity of Blood thirsty animals in any
country as we found here your mouth nose Ears Eyse and every other
assailable point had its thousand Enemies striving which should be
formost in their thirst for Blood we continued to urge our animals on
in hopes to pass the main army and so continued whipping spurring
and cursing across the vally up a rocky steep mountain the musketoes
ware still ahead down the opposite side of the mountain across
another vally and up the steep sides of a higher mountain the enemy
still met us in unnumerable swarms and so continued to the topmost
pinicl of the mountain whare tired exhausted and fatigued we at
length about midnight lay down to sleep in the best way we might a
thick fog hung over the mountain in the morning but the Mosketoes
ware still there and so remained when we left

14 Left our Mosketoe camp on top of the mountain and desended
in to a small handsome vally covered with stocks of cattle and Horses
changed our course to the west passed a low range of hills and arived
at Mr [George C.] younts ranch or farm on a small stream running a
saw and grist mill her we sat down to a Breakfast of good mutton and
coffee having rode 60 miles without food and mostly without water.

15 Remained with our hospitable host Mr Yount who thought we
had better stay to day and rest our animals.

Here I witnessed the Mexican manner of taking in wheat Harvest a
sufficant number of Indians are sent out with a rough kind of sickle
who reap the wheat the squaws and others gather the grain up and

pack it on their backs to a spot of ground ready prepared for threshing whare the grain [is] lain down with the heads up an left to dry a day or two when a lot of wild horses is let in and the grain thrashed out.

16 Left Mr Younts with Mr. Hartgrove [William Hargrave] for the purpose of returning to Mr gordons again by a mountain Rout and Escape the den of muschetoes on our former rout.

Took a northern direction up the vally of the creek on which Mr Younts mills are situated 5 or 6 miles above passed the farm house of Dr. Bales [Edward Turner Bale] this hous looked desolate Enough standing on a dry plane near a dry Black vocanic mountain allmost destitute of (of) vegitation no fields garden or any kind of cultivation to be seen and about 10 or 12 Indians lying naked in the scorching sun finished the scenery of this rural domain.

Continued our rout up the [Napa] vally Early in the afternoon arived at Mr [Benjamin] Kelseys Hunting camp whare we found plenty of fine fat venison here we took up lodgings for the night the whole of this small valey is strewn with obsidian pmmice stone and Black slag and other remains of volcanoes which have existed at some remote period.

17 Left our hospitable hunters camp and proceeded up the vally about 3 miles to another hunters camp found Mrs Kelsey a fine Looking woman at camp with her two little daughters it appears that they had occupied their present camp only over night Mr Kelsey being out with his gun soon returned with his hose laden down with the tallow and fat of two large Buck Elk that he had Slaughtered during the morning the Kettle was hung ower the fire and we soon had a plentifull meal of the fattest Kind of Elk meat bothe roast and stewed in the evening thre of us took our Rifles and walked to the hills in about two hours we returned haveing killed three fine Black tailed Bucks the Evening was spent in telling hunting stories and roasting and packing venison ribs.

18 Left Mr Kelseys camp on my return to Mr Gordons crosse the narrow vally and assended a rough volcanic mountain saw a number of deer that frequently stood gazing at us in easy Rifle shot distance about noon we had crossed the fourth mountain none being more than

2 hours ride across stoped to rest and graze on sooteers [Putah] River now Quite a small stream here we regaled ourselves on the Marrow bones of a deer that we had shot 60 or 80 rods from the water and we might have killed 8 or 10 had we spent the amunition during the fore noon In the afternoon we set forward again soon crossed over a narrow vally and commenced assending a steep high mountain in about 2 hours strugling our animals reached the ruged summit when we immediately commenced the desent which was much longer and rougher than the assent but not so steep I must remark that the mountains are litterly cowered with deer and Bear theer are seen at a great distance winding around the steep precipices and Bear roads are generally passable for a Spanish horse or mule.

19 Encamped last night 6 miles from Mr Gordons and rode in for Breakfast here we Feasted on the ribs of a fat antelope after Breakfast commenced desending the great plain west of the Saccremento which is as level as a pond appearantly and from 10 to 20 miles wid on the west of the river but no water found at this season o the year passed several miles through a pleasant oak grove to near the [Sacramento] river whare we encamped here we found the mosketoes so thick that it was nerely imposible to breathe without being strangled with them There being a large tuly or rush swamp about half a mile from the river these rush swamps are common to this vally large streams of water come tumbling down from the mountains soon loose themselves in the vally and spreading in all directions form extensive lakes of water after the rains cease to fall the lakes begin to dry up and the earth partially dry sends up an immence groth of weeds and rushes so high and strong that a horse is unable to breake thorugh.

20 Left our Musketoe camp on the river proceeded along the narrow strip of land devideing the river from the rush swamp the rushes in many places being 15 feet in hight and thicker than I ever saw hemp grow we continued following this strip of land untill we reached the Landing oposite Suitors fort whare we encamped the sacramento river here is upward of 200 yards wide deep and navigable the tide water ebbing and flowing about three feet.

21 Crossed over the river by swiming our animals and crossing

our baggage in a light whale Boat that was kept here by some of capt Suitors Indians Suitors fort is built of doba or large unburnt brick and has an imposing appearance at a distance standing on an Elevated plain a few miles below the Junction of the American Fork with the Sacreminto and Surrounded by wheat fields which have yielded a good crop of wheat this present season but have born nothing for two crops past but on a nearer inspection it is found that the whole Fort houses and all are built of doba or mud walls and covered in side and out with dust and fleas which grow her to the gratest perfection The Capt keeps 600 or 800 Indians in a complete state of Slavery and as I had the mortification of seeing them dine I may give ashort discription 10 or 15 Troughs 3 or 4 feet long war brought out of the cook room and seated in the Broiling sun all the Lobourers grate and small ran to the troughs like somany pigs and feed thenselves with their hands as long as the troughs contain even a moisture.

22 Left our camp on the creek an proceeded south over a dry level plain without timber or grass about 10 miles when we came to the channel of a dry creek some pools of standing water ware found after pasing our dry creek passed over a shrubby oak plain about 8 miles to a smal river running over sandy bed and nearly swiming deep crossed over with some difficulty and encamped on the South side so far we have seen but little land fit for cultivation of any discription the high lands being poor and liable to anual drougths of a verry severe kind the lowlands are anually over flown to a greate depth during the rainy season.

23 Our not being able to obtain any meat of capt Sutter kept us travilling and hunting being again dependant on our Rifles for a living passed a dry sandy oak plain of about 18 miles across we came to the low marshy lands bordering the head of the St Francisco bay up which we passed to the head of a deep navigable ceek or Slough whare we encamped haveing nothing better than the warm stagnant warm Slough water to use this parte of the country would afford a few ranches for stock but is not inhabited on account of a warlike tribe of Indians that range over it and follow robbing stealing and sometimes murdering all the inhabitants and frequently travellers that pass or remain here any length of time.

24 Remaind in camp to day for the purpose of hunting Elk and antelope in which we succeeded but moderately.

25 Took up the line of march across a dry hard level plain 8 miles a large rush swamp lying to our right appearantly without any tirmination and only bounded by the Bay after passing a few miles of rush swamp we reached the north Bank of the St Waukien [San Joaquin River] over which we passed on rafts made of Rushes this river has a S.E. and N.W. direction Traveled about 6 miles down the South side of the river to a deep navigable Bayau whare we encamped and feasted largely on the fattest kind of Buck Elk flesh which was killed near the camp and was in a manner all tallow.

The St Waukien is over 200 yards wide and deep and navigable running through a large dry level plain litterly covered with Elk and wild horses a Tribe of Indians reside on the river who hold indisputable possession of the country & steal & kill.

26 Crossed the plian about 10 miles wide to the Mountain saw several herds of wild Horses an Elek one herd of Elk had a grand appearance containing more than 2000 Two thousand head and covering the plain for more than a mile in length crossed a low bare range of mountains and soon came to Mr [Robert] Livermores farm or Ranche made 30 miles and encamped at a ranche Belonging to a Mixican [Antonio Maria Sunol] who with his Indian slaves were Slaughtering cattle for the hides and tallow and a more filthy stinking place could not be easily immagined The carcases of 2 or 300 cattle haled 20 rods from the slaughter ground and left to the vultures wolves and Bears several of the latter ware seen feeding or silently moveing off to the mountains at early dawn in the morning The common price of fat cattle is estimated at Eight dollars Two dollars for the hide and six dollars for the tallow all in Trade cash is not Expected and not often demanded.

27 We frequently ride 20 miles without a drop of water and most of the water found is in stagnant pools covered with a thick skum of green vegetable matter now in full Bloom Left our Slaughter yard camp and proceeded down the course of a stagnent pool for some miles when we crossed over the dry channel of a Broad Creek and assended a mountain by a verry good pass had a fair view of Pawblaw Bay [San Francisco Bay] anarm of the Bay of St Francisco on the immediate discent from the mountain we came in sight of the formerly flurishing mission of St Joseph [San Jose] this mission in its best days must have contained several Hundred in mates the whole establishment Houses fences church and all is built of doba.

These Missions ware Established some 70 years since and occupy the choeise sittuations in the country and have fine vinyards and Fruit orchards such as Figs pears peaches &c &c but I do not recollect seeing any apple Trees or apples Tobacco cotton or sweet potatoes it is said do not thrive well in this climate and in fact I do not hear of any grain or vegitables that do well Except wheat Barley or some grains that mature Early in the season before the dough [drought] sets in which usually commences in may or June.

The Mexicans do not labour themselves the native indians perform all the labour and are kept in slavery much like the Negroes of the Southern states but not worked so steady or hard as all depend largely on their cattle stock for support and some fine Blankets are Here manufactured from the wool of their sheep The Mexican Ladies when they ride out alone mount a mans saddle in the same manner their husband would but frequently the husband takes his wife on before him and takes hold of the logerhead of his saddle with his arms around his bride and this method looks Quite loveing and kind and might be relished by the single.

28 Left our camp at purbelow village [pueblo of San Jose] and took up a fine narrow vally [Santa Clara Valley] in a Southern direction this vally has the apearance of being good soil of a lieght yellow complection But no cultivation is seen larger than a good sized vegetable garden This vally is in many places completely covered over with the bones of cattle that have been slaughtered from time to time along the way and has been at some time a regular settlement the old mud walls of cottages are stil seen standing but later seasons seem to have been dryer than formerly & the want of water has driven the inhabitants to a more moist region.

The Indians Likewsise have become more bold and troublesome driveing of[f] their stock continually at least such as happen to range in the mountains and the more unfrequented places and we ware told that a large herd of horses ware driven off from the hills in sight of our camp three days since.

29 The vallies ware wraped in a white fog the sun however arose in greate force and splender and soon disperced the smoke & fog Passed down a vally somewat more fertile crossed some narrow ridges and (and) came in sight of the Mision of St Johns [San Juan Bautista] with its mud walled out buildings and fences of the same meterial. here lay scattered about numerous small corn fields Bean and mellon patches some Indians ware in a wheat or Barly field reaping the straw and grain dry as powder left the church and princeple mission vinyards to the left and assended a high range of hills from the summit of which we caught a glanc through the fog of the Broad Pacific ocean or rather the North side of St Cruz Inlet and a broad plain through which a small river passes along the south side water seems to be the greate dissideratum in this dry arid region and whare ever you find even a stagnant pool of Brackish water you find a small mud walled cottage a Mixican and half a dozen Indians with their stock of cattle and horses they never leave ther horses uless they lay down to sleep.

30 Left our camp on the small [Salinas] River and proceeded over a dry deep sand plain to Monteray Lying on the South East pount of the Santa Cruz inlet The capitol of California has a dingy Black dirty appearanc owing to the Houses being built mostly of Doba or unburt brick and covered with tile the Town contains perhaps 80 or 100 houses and Hovels of all kinds and discriptions no fresh [water] is found but what is obtained from wells and that is Quite brackish the Mexican flag was seen flying near the dwelling of the commandant and the Stars and stripes at the house of Mr Larkins [Thomas O. Larkin] the amirican counsel as Likewise from Two ships in the Harbour The sloop of war warren commanded by Capt [Joseph B.] Hull and the california of Boston capt [James P.] Arthur we rode to Dr Townsends [John Townsend] an amercans who came from the States by land last season whare we put up found the Dr a good feeling man much attached to his own oppinions as likiwise to the climate and country of California his [wife] a pleasant lady does not enter into all of her husbands chimerical speculations Called on Mr Thomas O Larkins the consul and dilivered him all the various letters and documents intrusted to my care but owing to the wrecking of a Brittish merchant vesel on the coast some six miles south Mr Larkins time was completely occupied in endeavouring to save what property might be saved so that I had but little conversation with him.

A low range of hills run south of the town covered thinly [with] pine timber and rising in to steep high mountains toward the East.

I saw but few Ladies in the streets perhaps on account of the greate Quantity of dust and sand that is seen in every direction The English Language is spoken here more or less by most of the inhabitants Indians Excepted There may be some place called the fort intended for the protection of the Town or harbour but I was nt fortunate Enough to find that spot I saw however several small pieces of small cannon mounted in the Prison yard or rather on the commons near the prison The cliffs around the harbour are of redish grey granite in a state of dcomposition some stone however is used in the foundation of some of the houses of a white colour and nearly light Enough to swim.

Monterey to Napa Valley

31 Left Monteray and took back northward to Santa Cruz whare we arivede in the Evening of (of) the First of August Santa Cruz is likewise an old mission establishment and occupies a beautifull situation about 2 miles from the coast and has some fine spring of water from which the fathers draw their water to Erigate their gardens.

This place is likewise dignified by the name of a village scattered along the steep bluffs of a small stream the low grounds have a number of half cultivated gardens as is usual through all Mexican countrys The

Mexicans nor Foreighners never Labour in province Except Mchanicks all the out doors labour is performed by the native Indians who are kept in a state of slaveery and recieve no pay Except what their masters choose to give them they are a Lazy indolent race and nearly and Quite naked those who are house servants excepted which if females ware a long chimise the climate indeed dose not seem to require clothing at this season of the year Except it may be to keep the scorching sun from blistering but in this the natives are proof against any common Heate.

2 & 3 of August Remained with the far famed and redoubtable Capt [Isaac] Graham The hero of Mr. [Thomas J.] Farnhams travels in california and in fact the hero of six or seven revolutions in this province and the chivalrous captain has again during the last winter passed through the ordeal of one more revolution and again been a prisoner in the hands of his old Enimy Colonel Castro the Eex governor and has once more returned to his peacable domicil to his heards and his [saw] mill surrounded by impassable mountains about Eight miles from the Landing of Santa Cruz and if report be correct the hardy vetrian is fast softning down and he is about to cast away the deathly rifle and the unerring tomahawk for the soft smiles of a female companion to nurrish him in his old age and here I must say that the captain has all the Philanthropy and Kindness for his country men that has ever been attrributed to him Inviting me to return and remain with him free of cost as long as I might find it convinient or as long as I wished to remain in california.

4 I Left capt Grahams with many invitations to all again before leaveing caliornia we took a small difficult bridle way that [led] across a verry rugged mountain for Santa Clare and the village Puebla of San Jose] whare we arived in the Evening Two days previous to our arival the mountain Indians had made a desent upon Santa Clare killed one and wounded two of the horse guard and stolen a herd of horses and the inhabitants ware in pusuit of the Murderers in the mountain we had Just passed through we came through however without seeing either party and slept soundly with Mr Weaver [Charles M. Weber] (a german who speaks good English) in the village of Puabla and in the morning of the.

5 We left our kind and hospitable entertainer and bent our course north along that arm of the Bay of St Francisco which communicates with the Mission of Santa Clara in our way down we passed over a beautiful tract of land well stoccked with herds of cattle and a ranche or farm was to be seen in every place whare Living water could be found this tract or vally however is verry dry and water scarce (that is fresh water).

In the Evening of the Sixth we reached Penola [Pinole] or the [Carquinez] Straits or narrows of the Bay of St Francisco whare we encamped for the night a Californian [Ignacio Martinez] who owns the ranche or farm on the South side of the Bay keeps a Boat and with the assistance of his Boat we crossed over in the afternoon of the.

7 In this we had the mots tiresome and Longest swim for our mules that I had so far seen the wind and tide both setting up the bay which is here about a mile wide it carried us up the Bay more than Two miles before we ware able to land and we ware certainly more than 2 hours making the passage These narrows are formed by a range of bare rocky hills or mountains running North across the vally and Bay we found fresh water scarce through all this region But cattle appear to do better and get fatter on brackish water than on good clear spring water on our passage out of the narrows we observed greate and Extensive Bull Rush marches lying to the west of our trail to a greate distance.

8 We arived at Mr Younts again on Napper creek completely satisfied with travelling through California for in 28 days travel mostly through the Spanish settlments we never found one grain of food for our animals and only three places whare we slept in houses and these three owned by foreigners There is no such thing as a tavern in california as I am informed. The settlements being thin and widely scattered you scarcely ever find two farmsers approach nearer than five miles of each other in fact the cultivation of the soil is but verry little attended to by even the americans in this country large herds of cattle seem to be all that a californian desires and those large herds require space to g[r]aze upon so that from six to 12 miles square forms a common ranche or farm some place is then sought then whare living water can be obtaind here a small doba or mud walled cottage is erected covered with grass tile or shingles as the case may be without either floors or windows Tables chairs or any other furniture one or two hundred head of young cattle and fifteen or 20 head of Horses and you are prepared for becomeing rich in process of time and living a true california life.

If However you have a disposition to eat bread with your beef all you have to do is to cut out a suitable branch from some crooked oak and with an axe hew it in to convenient form nail a small piece of Iron on the lower projecting extemity hitch a yoke of cattle to the forward end lay hold of the other end with your hands an you have what is used for a plow this instrument however does not either cut or turn the soil but merely roots a narrow streak whare it is drawn but with this kind of cultivation I am told that the yield is frequently on some of the best spots from 50 to 100 fold of wheat (Barly or peas not so much) corn or other vegitables requiring the whole of the summer season to mature in must be planted near some conviniant brook whare the water can be let on one in Ten days or oftener to supply the want of rain in the latter part of the season and this irigating plan is required throughout the whole of California or nearly so to produce any kind of grain or vegitables that do not mature by the first of July the native grasses and weeds being all dry by that time and the Praries frequently burnt over by that time I immagine that but few americans would like the county or the people or any thing they may find at first sight unless it be the fine fat Beef which is used and wasted here in the greatest profusion and every Callifornian foreighner or native has plenty of fresh beef to his table if he has such apiece of furniture at all times corned Beef is seldom found and salt never as there is no part of the season cool Enough to salt Beef a kind of Jerked or dried Beef is generally used by the Indians but their Laziness and negligence prevents it from being any thing like good and they would rather dig roots for a precarious subsistance for half the year than to take the trouble of making good dried meat to live on and through this nigligent and careless habit hundres of Tuns of the fattest kind of Beef is wasted every season in California alone. and in fact the want of a little cooler season is a greate drawback on the productions of the county there being no time cool Enough to salt Beef so as to save it well at sea allthough nearly every californian will tell you to theat is [it] has not been thouroughly tested and if it is left to them it never will be tested Judging from appearances Beans is one of the regular crops of the californians and beef and beans foms one of their favorite dishes Red pepper is likewise cultivated largely and enters in to all their cookery in greate profusion. I do not believe that Tobacco Cotton or sweet potatoes do well as I have seen niether growing in any part of this region allthough their is Quite a veriety of climate found here.

14 Left Mr Younts and went up the vally of Napper creek to some hunters camps with the intention of haveing some sport arived in the Evening at Mr Kelseys camp which was well supplied with fine fat venison and Elk meat plenty of Bear in the neighbourhood but they are not fat at [this] season of the year and so are not hunted.

15 Got a horse of Mr Kelsey and rode out after Breakfast to see what game might be seen after rideing in the hills some 2 miles and starting several deer whuch ran off I discovered two deer lying under the shade of a Tree dismounted and in approching them one of them discovered me and sprang to his feet I brought my rifle to bear on him and fired he sprang off in greate haste and in a fuw bounds was out of sight reloded and as the other was not alarmed I crawled nigher and rising to my feet I distinctly saw his Eears and one eye taking deliberate aim for his eye I pulld trigger the deer sprang and bounded End wise side ways & in fact in all directions haveing his brains shot out Reloded and walked over the ridge to see what had bcome of the other I heard a desperate screaming and squalling in that direction and on a nerer approach a discovered a large she Bear had got my deer in possession and the squalling proceeded from three others Two cubs and a yearling which ware contending for a portion of the venison the old she snapping and Boxing them whenever they approached she soon turned the vital part of her front to me and the keen crack of my rifle told her the tale of death The others not at all intimidated soon fell to tearing devouring and Quarelling over the carcase of the deer again I soon ramed down another ball and taking aim at the yearling brought her to the earth with many a growl and struggle she died tearing the brush with her teeth and claws I then laid down my rifle as the cubs had become frightned and fled into the brush in walking down to whare the farthest one lay however the cubs raised the yell and came back in Quest of their dam and I had to give way and give them a free passage I thought however I could frighten them and cutting a good cudgel advanced on them in turn but they gave every symtom of fight short of laying hold of me and I had to retreat the second time as soon as an oppertunity occurred I caught my rifle again and promised distruction to the intire family of bears but in my greate hury to load I put down a ball without powder and after several fruitless attempts to kill the cubs I was forced from the field of battle and left the bears in full possession of the venison.

16 Mr Kelsey rode out withe me in to a small cove in the mountains whare we had rare sport shooting deer Bringing in nine skins in the Evening the most of the meat being left on the ground for the wolves and vultures and of the latter the country seems to be remarkbly well stocked Beside the raven and turky Buzzard of the states you see here the royal vulture in greate abundance frequently measureing Fourteen feet from the extremity of one wing to the extemity of the other.

17 Hunted again with poor success killing but Four deer.

18 Five deer came in to camp three of which I brought in myself From the 18 to the.

22 We assisted in building and covering a cabbin as it [is] soon Expected that (it) the early showers of rain will commence falling some fog appeared on the mountains this morning.

23 Continues beautiful weather warm through the day and cool nights the wheat harvest finished.

25 Started for Suitors Fort on the sacramento River we ware interupted considerably last night by two large bear that made several attempts to take our venison laying on a log fifteen or 20 feet from the fire.

26 Crossed several steep ruged mountains these ridges forming the mountains over which we passed seem to have been shot up from the East and stand in greate regularity at an angle of 50 or 60 degrees with the Horizon and are generally dry haveing but few springs of living water in them.

27 At Mr gordons.

28 I was lucky enough to find my horses again that I had left running at large Mr Gordon Recieved a small box of sugar cane from the Sandwich Islands and is about to try the Experiment of growing sugar in this vally but I immagine he will find this country to dry for the cultivation of sugar.

31 Returned yestarday the day being Extremely warm and we rode 60 miles between sun and sun over a verry rough mountainous road but this is not an uncommon dys ride for the inhabitants of [this] country 80, 90 and even 100 miles is sometimes performed on the same horse without food or rest.

[September] the first 1845
Extreme warm weather the parched rocks and Eearth reflect an intense heat the rivers and small streams failling rapidly.

Sunday the 8th of Septembr
Wasq uite warm rode out over the hills taking my rifle withe me had Quite a veriety of shooting Killed 5 Deer one large grissled Bear one wild cat and a Royal vulture this is the largest fowl I have yet seen measuring when full grown full 14 feet from the extemity of one wing to the extemity of the other Like all the vulture tribe this fowl feeds on dead carcases but like the Bald Eagle prefers his meat fresh and unputrefied they seem [to] hover over these mountains in greate numbers are never at the least fault for their prey but move directly and rapidly to the carcase cutting the wind with their wings and creating a Buzzing sound which may [be] heard at a miles distance and making one or two curves they immediately alight and commence glutting.

Larkin to Clyman regarding the Hedding Affair:

San Francisco, October 29, 1845.
Consulate of the United States
Sir,

In answer to your request for information in what I have done in the case of the North West Indian, against Grove Cook, of the United States now living in this Department: I have to say, that from the representation made by Sub Agent, White, to his Department in Washington, I sent a copy to Governor Pico of California, which has been translated, I also offered my services to him in the affair; when I left my Consular House the former month, no answer had been received from Governor Pico.

An account of my proceedings wrote to the Sub-Agent, and sent to Captain Gordon of H. B. M. Ship America, who left here in August, as we supposed for the Columbia River, he refused to receive it under the plea that he was not bound there; I am in expectation to forward the letter next month by some other vessel. James Clyman Esqr.

San Francisco
I am Sir
Your most Obdt. Svt.
THOMAS O. LARKIN
Signed—

Notes on Chapter Fourteen

Clyman's notes for August 16 speak of the "Royal vulture" measuring fourteen feet from the end of one wing to the end of the other. Camp, for once disbelieving, says in a footnote, "This is stretching it considerably, even for the California condor. Condors, now nearing extinction, are not known to exceed ten feet in total spread of wings."

Despite Camp's authority, Clyman was a surveyor, and might be assumed to know fourteen feet if he saw it. Clyman later (September 8) killed a "Royal vulture" so his measurement may have been based on close observation.

The only long gap in the Clyman journals occurs during the months of September, October and November of 1845, when Clyman visited San Francisco. Clyman's first entry for December, 1845, says he was unable to write because he broke his ink stand and lost his pencil. No doubt part of his time was spent investigating—or waiting for authorities to investigate—the Hedding killing, since Camp found this letter from Consul Thomas Larkin in reply to a letter from Clyman about the affair.

Chapter 15
Notebook Seven
California in 1846

Dec. 1, 1845 to Feb. 25, 1846

December the 1st 1845

Owing to my breaking my ink stand and loosing pencil I have not been able to write any since the First of sept since which time I visited San Francisco or Herba Buano and the most of the Bay of San Francisco— The Entrance into this noble bay is fine and Easy of access all vessels passing in and out by the chart with out even a pilot the harbour inside being spacious and completely land locked to the North and west by a high rocky ridge or promontory to the south the land is not so high but is sufficiently high and permanent for good security the achorage is good and secure and good fresh water easily obtained in greate abundance from a spring on the North side of the bay The land However near the entrance of the bay is not fit for cultivation or at least but small portions of it it being generally dry sandy or gravelly soil some fine grazing lands are However found no advantages can be had for Hydraulick purposes whatever which is a great drawback against this noble bay The Sacramento and the St Joachim are the main feeders the former is a beautifull streem and is probably navegable for steam boats 200 miles from its mouth the later is Quite a large

River but when low is not navigablle to any considerable distance two small creeks one from the north and the other from the south is all the fresh water in the dry season that falls into the Bay Both the larger Rivers have their Sources in a Broad high ruged rang of mountains dividing the plains of the Coast from the greate salt Lake valy Lying East of the above mentioned vally and west of the main chain of Rocky mountains seperating the waters of the Atlantic and the Pacific.

Beside these two greate chains of mountains there is still another chain running near and paralell with the coast this like all the others is in many places high and extremely ruged and its perpendicular cliffs in many places stay the Bosterous waves of the Pacific and if report be correct it [is] probably the most ruged Desolate coast yet known for som hundeds of [miles] north [of] the Bay of San Francisco.

These three greate and lengthy chains of mountains are in many places connected by cross chains such as The Umpiqaw dividing th Willhamett from the umpiquaw River the Clamet dividing the waters of the umpiquaw and clamett Rivers the Siskiew dividing the waters of the Clamet and Chesty rivers and the still mor high and rugged range of the Snowy Bute [Mount Shasta] seperating the waters of the Clamet and sacremento with innumerable spurrs of mountains Jutting out in all directions from both and all the main chains and numbers of Isolated and detached hills Knobbs and mountains standing and running in all immaginable directions making the vallies generally small winding and narrow But generally Beautifull and picturesque and well clothed in native grasses.

The—Callifornians are a proud Lazy indolent people doing nothing but ride after herds or from place to place without any appearant object The Indians or aboriginees do all the drudgery and labour and are kept in a state of Slavery haveing no or Receeving no compensation for their labour except a scanty allowence of subsistance during the time they actually imployed and perhaps a cotton Shirt and wool sufficient to make a coarse Blanket which they spin and weave in their own way Their method of manufacturing is simple and curious They beat the wool with two sticks in place of cards and when it is beaten enough they spin it with a stick and lay the warp by driveing a number of small

sticks in the ground it [is] raised by letting a stick run through sufficiently to pass a smal ball through and brought up with the sane stick
of course their fabrick is coarse but they make it verry durable The
californian Plough is a curosity in agraculture being made of a forked
branch of a tree one prong of which answers for a handle the other for
(the other for) a Land side mould Board Coulter & all haveing a small
piece of Iron on the forward part about the size of a mans hand and
half an inch thick Harrow no such thing known.

A small Quantity of wheat a patch of corn and Beans—with some
garden vegetables constitute all the agracultural products of the main
bulk of the californians not half sufficient for a supply and a greate
portion of the inhabitants live exclusively on Beef and mutton both of
which are remarkably fine and fat but want the fine flour and vegetables to make a good meal for an American Several kinds of red peppers
are grown in greate abundance and enter largely in to the californian
cookery so much so as to nearly strangle a Forigner and you find it
necesary to have a good apatite to swallow a meal no such thing as a
good flouring mill is to be found but every family have a small hand
mill on which they mash their grain when they have any to mash and a
coarse sive for a Bolt Their bread is made in thin wafer like cakes and
baked slowly untill they are as hard as a sea buisket Thier sheep are
small and produce a smll Quantity of coarse wool along the back and
belly being entirely bare Their cattle are of a good size and handsomely
built some farms or Ranches have from Five to Twenty thousand head
of neat stock on them with large stocks of horses and sheep no such
thing as a woolen Factory is known nor in fact a manufactory of any
kind or discription and even a coarse woolen hat sells from five to eight
dollars The trade of the country is carried on by some Eight or ten
vessels fitted out from Boston with dry goods which they sell at from
three to five hundred percent advance on prime cost and take Hides
and Tallow in return The tallow is generally sold in the south american
mining districts and the hides salted and carried home it usually takes
about Three year to make a trading trip of this kind.

The govornment of this province has like all the spanish american
govornments gone through several Revolutions and changes But I

believe every change has been for the worse and all though it took a recent change about one year since no change is precieveable except that the revenue has fallen into the hands of other persons The revenue is small and wholey used up by the collectors not a cent going to the central government no such thing as a court of Justice is known higher than an Alcaldas court which is equivolent to a Justice of the peace in the United States and [the] alcalda is bound by no Law but his own oppinions which decides all differences.

In Fact the civil The Military and all parts of the Govenment are weak imbecile and poorly organized and still less respected and in fact but little needed as the inhabitants live so Isolated as to have but little intercourse with each other and therefore few difficulties to settle.

The Forigners which have found their way to this country are mostly a poor discontented set of inhabitants and but little education hunting for a place as they [want] to live easy only a few of them have obtained land and commenced farming and I do not hear of but one man that has gone to the trouble and Expence to get his title confirmed and fixed beyond altiration and dispute.

In speaking of the govornment of California I must say that (that) it is the most free and easy govornment Perhaps on the civilized globe no Taxes are imposed on any individual what ever I saw nor heard of no requrement for Roade labour no Military tax no civil department to support no Judiciary requiring pay and in every respect the people live free you may support Priest or not at your pleasure and if your life and property are not Quite so safe as in some other countries you have the pleasure of using all your earnings And strange as it may seem I never saw a spanish Californian that was a mechanic of any kind or discription and how they formerly made (made) out to cutivate any land is a mistery to me not yet solved nor do I recolect of seeing during my stay in the povince one single instance of a californian having a rail or stone fence all their fencing being made of Brush or willows woven in the form of a Basket and in some few Instances they had taken root and made a living fenc and ware they cut and set in the proper season most of them would live.

Callifornia as a general is scarce of valuable timber the oak predominates and consists of Black oak two or three verieties white oak 5 or 6 kinds Live oak three or 4 varieties but all the oak tribe is short and shrubby and of but little use except for fire wood The Red Firr grow in considerable Quantities in some of the mountains but is likewise hard and gnarled The red wood is generally fine Straight and large but is only found plenty in some of the mountainous districts this is the timber spoken of by travelers as growing to such immence hight and size the appearance [of] this wood much resembles our red cedar it generally splits straight and easy and is certainly a noble tree but is never found on the plains and only on a few of the mountains except those near the coast whare it is found plentifully in places and is fine for building covering and finishing houses and is the only timber fit for making rail fences or in fact to split for any other purpose the mountains are generally all covered with impenetrable thickets of evergreen shrubery which is of no use to the farmer or mechanick it being too small and rough for any usefull purpose in some places neare the coast however it is burned into charcoal and some other Districts a certain kind is Burned for the ashes that it produces containing uncommon Quantities of Potash and perhaps soda or some other mineral which enters freely into the operation of soap making in fact the country produces a root that has all the Qualities of soap and requires nothing but smashing and mixing with the water to have good soap suds as the wash women call it.

2 Started out on a Bear hunt crossed the Napa vally and a high rough high rugged mountain and encamped on the north side of the Kiota vally our company consisting of six and a boy and six Extra pack Horses.

3 A frosty night and a cool morning packed up and troted off north ward over a range of hills covered with Chimisall and other shrubery on the side of a steep bald hill we came to a large natural soda fountain which sparkled up in its own rock formed basin this fountain contains a large portion of soda but a small Quantity of gass saw several Bear at a distance which appered to be mostly poor and not worth the shooting saw a number of recently made tracks four of us parted two to the right and two to the left of our rout.

Heard a fire commenced by (by) those to our left and soon saw two gray bears coming growling in a direction toward us my companion and me dismounted and as soon as they came in good rifle distance we fired and droped both at the first fire the old shee however did not die Quite so easy but at last gave up after recieving four balls through her vitals.

Encamped on the outlet of an Extensive large lake [Clear Lake] Lying noar the summit of a high range of mountains this lake is said to be 80 miles [!] in length from S. E. to N. W. its feeders however must be limited as there is no running water in the outlet only a few miles from the Lake or Lagoona is it is called Feasted Luxuriently on fat Bear ribs and liver— our leaders did not think the Bear plenty Enough to make a full hunt here so we packed up & moved on northward.

4 Crossed a low range of Black chimisal mountains and struck the North fork of cache creek hed consultation whither to go North further or change our course to the East finally took the Eeastern rout down Cache creek and encamped at the head of a verry long Rough Kenyon no Bear seen to day.

5 Took down the Kenyon over immence piles of loose rocks that choked the streaam in its narrow channel our horses however made slow but sure progress down the Kenyon untill at length we found any further passage down the Kenyon impossible so we commenced the assent of a verry steep high mountain on the north side of the creek after greate toil and a profusion of kicks and stripes our animals gained the summit the ridge up which we came being so narrow as to bearly admit of one horse to pass at a time and the sides a nearly perpendicular desent for some thousand feet below The turn of this mountain proved to be a close thicket of Brush through which we forced ourselves to the vally below Encamped on cash creek.

6 Continued down the vally and crossed near the main mountain here we stoped and Examenid the mountain But found no Bear but saw ennumerable Quantities of deer but as we ware not hunting deer we only killed deer Enough to make camp meat no Bear seen.

7 Moved on again down the mountain near the greate Sacramento plain saw greate Quantities of deer but no bear and encamped [on] pooter [Putah] creek close under a Kenyon .

8 Moved up through the Kenyon to near its uppermost verge here we had again to assend a tremendeous high steep mountain almost impracticable for a horse to climb and turn a narrow sharp ridge and desend again on the oposite side whare we reached a fine vally well stocked with cattle and hoses continued up the vally to the head of the same and Encamped on pooter creek again one man went home and Took all our Extra baggage and a heavy horse load of Bears grease.

9 Moved up Pooter creek & through and around several steep rocky Kenyons in the afternoon arivedat an uneven rocky vally which in any other country might be called a mountain saw some indications of Bear and encamped for the purpose of hunting them several ware soon seen and a number of guns ware fired and one large old fat fellow lay dead the others all making their escape.

10 After some considerable hunting and fireing we made out to kill another.

11 Two men with pack horses returned home with the slaughtered animals which proved to be very fat.

12 Killed one more fine fat bear.

13 & 14 Hunted hard without (out) success.

15 A man returned to camp with fresh horses.

16 and 17 Slaughtered two more noble animals and got them safe to camp concluded we had pork Enough to answer our purposes.

18 Slaughtered 17 deer and made preperations for returning home.

19 Returned home heavily (heavily) laden with Bear meat and venison.

————

Remarks on Bear Hunting

All the bear in this country are of grisled or grey species and are extremely dangerous when wounded and in fact frequently attact the hunter or other passenger without any provocation Except being interupted in their lair Therefore the hunter has to be verry cautious in his approach and scarcely ever attempts to drive him out of his fastness Their time of feeding being in the night the hunter watches him late in the Evening or Early in the morning when he is going to or returning from his feeding grounds Taking if possible the advantage of some inexcessable cliff of rocks Bank or Tree or is mounted on a good swift horse off of which he shoots never dismounting untill the bear is dead generally two or three men go in company and when the bear is discovered they all aproach in good rifle distance one firing one at a time in slow succession when if their balls take a good impression it so confuses the animal that he is kept continually fighting the ball holes which he never fails to do so that he has no time to attact the hunters untill it is to late— one which we had the Luck to kill was seen passing to his lair in the morning after sun rise two men attacted him and gave him five shots at a vital part of his body when he made his Escape to an allmost impenatrable thicket in an hour after three of us well mounted followed him more than a mile whare we found him badly wounded and in good disposition for a fight I however had the luck to get a shot at him takeing him close behind the shoulder when he broke back for a desperate thicket several guns ware fired at him on his retreat but he made his Lair and defied all our methods to draw him out again untill one man at the risk of himself and horse ventured in to the thicket cutting open a retreat with his butcher Knife at length the bear charged on him the other man standing on an Eminence shot at him as he passed an open aperture through the brush and had the luck to shoot him in the head on butchering him we found nine balls had taken good effect but owing to the greate thickness of the fat on his sides only one had passed in to his lungs he proved to be a noble animal yeelding more than three Hundred pounds of oil.

The whole of our hunt amounting nine fin fat bear and about 30 Deer.

The whole of the country we passed over during our long hunting Excursion is rough and rocky beyond discription and all the rock and Eearth of a volcanic oregin mostly of a vitrious and red cast large

Quantities of slag and other volcanic rocks standing universally in a nerly prepzendicular direction and Extremely rough and sharp the tops and sides covered with several kinds of hardy Evergreen shrubs nearly as sharp and hard as steel and growing generally from 4 to 10 Feet high and closely interwoven the sides of the mountains covered in addition with immence Quantities of loose rock which have fallen from time to time from the higher regions of the clifs and lay piled in the utmost confusion below.

20 Fine and clear.

21 A hard stiff frosty morning in fact we have had Thirty Two regular successive frosty mornings all though the days have been Quite fine and warm.

22 It rained some during the night and morning.

23 More rain during the night and thick fog all day with several rapid showers of rain.

24 A steady rapid rain fell during the whole of the day the first rain of consequence that has fallen since leaving the Willhamett vally on the Eighth of June last.

25 December 1845

Chistmas it rained all night the morning thick and foggy with several short Rapid showers the grass and wild oats However is Quite green and good pastureage.

26 Cloudy & warm.

27 Excessive rain.

28 Cloudy and warm.

29 Excessive rain all the country covered in water even the mountains send down their torrents of water.

30 A beautifull clear morning after about Thirty hours of the most Tremendous rain storm That perhaps has ever fallen in the present age which awakned all the frogs which had slept during the dry season and are now chirping in every puddle The season for sowing wheat now commences as Likewise for sowing Turnips, parsnips, cabbages, Onions, garden peas, Barley, and several other vegitables which cannot be produced in the dry hot season.

Many of the californians scarcely ever taste Bread but live intirely on fresh Beef Beans and Red pepper which they cook all togather and allways cook their beef verry tender or so that it will scarcely hold togather.

31   Several Light showers or rain during the afternoon yesterday and each producing a Beautifull bow of Promis all though to look at the vallies you might think a second deluge had commenced.

A dull cloudy day in the evening distant thunder was heard which is a rare thing and verry uncommon in this country several showers of rain fell during the night.

January the first 1846

Dull and foggy with a prospect of more rain It did not rain but distant Thunder was heard at intervals during the day a slight Earth Quake was felt in many parts of the Province some days since this is no uncommon circumstance as it is seldom that six months passes without a Quivering and trimbling of the Eearth in some portion of California allthough I have not heard of any that has done any considerable damage for some years past.

2   A dull cloudy day and it commenced raining in the Evening.

3   It rained moderately all night a dull cloudy morning with slight showers of rain—about noon it came on to rain rapidly and so continued most of the night.

4   Dull and Foggy I noticed the manseneto trees in full Bloom— This is an evergreen shrub growing in a thick gnarled clump with a smoothe red coloured bark and a deep green leaf and would make a beautifull shade for a door yard it prefers a dry gravelly soil and grows 10 or 12 feet high and has a sweet small pink white bloom and bears a sour berry of a dark red colour the size of a small plumb.

5   A rainy morning But It cleared up in the afternoon and the sun shone Beautifully onc more.

6   A pleasant day but a cool frosty morning.

7   The same Except the frost a little lighter.

8   Clear and Pleasant.

9   The same.

10   Cloudy and warm in fact a coat has been but little needed this winter except in the rain or for a morning.

11 (Sunday) Warm and cloudy fine growing weather verry much resembling a Missouri April or a Eeastern May The Mansoneta in full bloom—and the wild Oats about acle [ankle] high shewing fine as a wheat field in may of Wisconsin.

Kiled 14 Deer some fine and fat during the last week.

12 Frosty morning.

Heard that Mr Fremont had arived at suitors Fort and still more recently that Mr Hastings and Party had likewise arived Both From the U States. But no information has yet arived of the Politicks of the states in fact information of all Kinds Travels slow and is verry uncertain when it has arived you know nothing certain unless you see it yourself.

1 Showers of rain with a good prospect of another Flood—the rain continued untill night.

14 Morning clear and bright—all hands buisy Plowing and sowing wheat Barly &c or at least all that expect to reape their own grain next harvest.

The recently arived emigration from the U States appear to be Quite industrious in making preperations for living in some civilized form.

15 Cloudy & cool.

16 Showers of rain and Quite warm for the middle of winter.

17 Last night was a night of Excessive rain and this morning all the low grounds are again immerced in water the day however proved clear with a N. W. wind.

17 (Sunday) Lear an fine with a s[t]iff white frost in the morning Kd. 8 Deer.

18 Cloudy and warm the wind seldom blows more than an hour or two and that during the commencement of (of) a rainy spell the mountains are high steep and rocky and the rains rapid so that the water soon collects in the vallies and covers nearly the whole Earth in a few hours The rocks generally stand in nearly a perpendicular direction and what water finds its way down through them goes to an immence depth in the Earth what water continues near the surface soon runs of and leaves large dry tracts of rocky mountainous country without or very scantily supplied with water in the dry seasons.

19 Cloudy with several Light showers of rain.

20 It rained the whole of Last night and still continues to rain with a thick dense fog Had the pleasure of an evinings conversation with Mr [Isaac A.] Flint from Wisconsin Feel a great Disire to see Millwaukie this morning.

21 and 22 Cloudy and warm The Mansoneto Dropping its.

Blows the Alder in full Bloom In fact allthough we have had a number of frosty mornings their has been no day but what has been uncomfortable to walk or exercise in any way without feeling a coat Quite to heavy and warm allthough my wintering ground is in a narrow vally nearly surrounded by high rugged mountains and I find it verry little cooler on (on) the mountains than in the vallys during the hours of sun shine but when the sun is hidden a great differanc is precievable.

23 Cloudy and warm.

24 Clear and warm.

25 Thick Foggy morning and tremendious heavy dew cleared off about noon fine and warm.

Killed during the week 7 Deer.

26 Close and warm and damp.

27 Considerable rain fell during the night and the day proved showery and cool.

28 Showers.

29 Clear & cool.

30 Considerable rain fell.

31 Excessive rains during the night and continued all day the vallies inundated with water again the mountains sending down their Torrents in white form— The climate of oregon and california resemble each other verry much oregon being somewhat cooler .

Sundy the First of February—1846

Killed during the week 8 Deer This day proved clear and pleasant But the country is completely impassable on account of the greate depth of mud and general softness of the earth several thunder showers passed During the last evening and night the Thunder

However was low and grmbling & the Lightning not at all vivid or bright.

2 Warm and moist the dew standing on the green vegitation throughout the day.

3 A cool night and a whit frost this morning the afternoon cloudy.

4 Hazy and cool with a brisk wind from the East.

5 Considerable rain fell during the day Early sown wheat begins to shew green the Peach trees beginning to shew their bloom willow in bloom.

6 Clear and pleasant the grass about ancle high and several kinds of small herbs shewing their Bloom.

7 Rainy dull weather.

8 Continues to rain with a thick dense fog.

9 Cool and Rainy.

10 Snow seen on high peaks of the Napa mountain.

11 The snow that fell yestarday is still visible and the air chilly and cool.

12 Clear with a Keen white frost over all the green vegitation which however did not in the least injure the tenderest herbage.

13 Another frost not quite so Keen as yesterday both days came off fine and pleasant Garden Peas up and growing finely Beets, Cabbages, Onions Radishes and Turnips all up and thriveing wheat Likewise covers the ground fine and green Horses and cattle thriveing the native grasses and wild oats ancle high Clover begins to cover the groud their is five or six species of native clover to be found all coming from the seed annually some Kinds grow large and strong measuring full grown and straight five or six feet in length and setting emmensely thick on the earth.

14 Pleasant & clear.

15 Same.

16 Clear with a strong north wind the Earth becoming some what drained but not dry by any means.

17 Clear the Buck Eye shrubs begining to shew their leaf as some of the Black oaks.

18 Clear with a fair prspect of the rainy season having come to a close.

20 & 22 Continues clear and fine weather The Buck Eye shrubery shews the leaf as Like wise the Black oak the vallies still wet and muddy but the mountains becomeing dry and covered handsomely green with a thick groth of native herbage.

23 Same.

24 Same.

25 Rainy with moderate showers fine growing weather these showers continued Throughout the monthe the season for sowing wheate is over as it is considered a very uncertain prospect for wheat to sow after the first of March all kinds of stock and cattle in particular are now thriveing rapidly on the young pastureage whuch is now green and tender this month is usually considered spring in this region but this season is rather more backward than usual and some kinds of timber scarcely shows the swelling of the bud some considerable talk of prepareing for the states and Oregon for both of which parties are making preperations for and both of which are long tiresome and some what dangerous routs so I close the winter or at least the winer months.

Notes on Chapter Fifteen

Camp also found a petition signed by Clyman and sixteen others, addressed to Consul Larkin urging him to protect the foreign residents of San Francisco against disorders arising after an assault on Capt. Elliot Libbey of the American ship *Tasso*. Cap. Libbey and Nathan Spear had been set upon in the streets of San Francisco by the citizens' patrol and the captain received severe knife wounds. The attackers belonged to native families prominent in the town, and it was feared the guilty persons would not be brought to trial. The petitioners asked that the American sloop of war *Levant* should remain in the bay to prepare to assist. Larkin forwarded this petition to Commander Hugh N. Page of the *Levant*, with the request that his ship remain in the harbor. All this simply contributed to the strong feelings regarding Mexican domination of the area, feelings which were echoed back east, where some politicians called for a war to annex the disputed area, and others counseled peace.

On January 20, Clyman visited with Isaac A. Flint of Wisconsin and felt a great desire to see Milwaukee again. He wrote to Fremont offering him a company of American emigrants as escort, protection, and guides for the return journey. This offer was refused.

Chapter 16
Notebook Eight
In California and across the Sierra

Clyman started east in company with Lansford W. Hastings, James M. Hudspeth, and a party including sixteen other men, three women and two children. Caleb Greenwood had been over the route in 1844 with a party of immigrants by way of Fort Hall, down the Humboldt River and across the Truckee divide.

Hastings had published a book the previous year directing emigrants to take this difficult, but shorter, trail, which thus became known as the "Hastings Cutoff." Incredibly, he had never been over it. Apparently he decided to risk taking his own advice, since he'd have a couple of old frontiersmen along.

Clyman's route probably followed Greenwood's in a general way, though even with his journals it's hard to be precise. Fremont's crossing of the Desert of the Great Salt Lake was one of the earliest, so Clyman's detailed description of the route is important, especially because Clyman and Hastings later argued over its merits. Clyman's meeting with the Donner party (which appears in Notebook Nine), during which he advised them against this route, thus takes on even more importance.

———

Feb. 26 to May 31, 1846

26 Rainy and disagreeable.

27 Same only more so.

28 Cool and cloudy.

1846 March the first

This is one of the climates that makes a fair and beautifull appearance for the commencement of the vernal season to commence with the opening and springing vegitation all of which makes a forward appearanc many of the oak Trees haveing their leaves half thier size and numerous native flowrets are seen in all directions mostly of a yallow and Purple colour and of a small kind The lowlands However are nearly covered in water from the recent excessive rains which have fallen.

An excessive rain fell during last night which overflowed completely the allready half deluged vallies the mountains sending down thier torrents in white sheets of troubled waters in all their ravines—But as the mountains are built of intire rock their is but little except water and gravel to bring down both of which ar.e plenty.

2 Cloudy and warm

3 Clear and warm.

4 Same.

5 Cear and Beautifull the greate flood of water which deluged nearly all of the vallies is begining to subside and leave the earth green and fine to all appearance but desperately miry and I found it verry difficult for my horse to carry me only a few miles.

6 & 7 Still clear and fine.

8 A beautifull day.

9 Same a young Mr [Britton or John] Greenwood came in haveing been out some weeks hunting and Trapping in the mountains north he brought in a beautifull specemin of pure Sulpher and he informs me he saw greate Quantities of this mineral as Likewise a mineral resembling galena Lead ore in great abundance—but as Mr Greenwood had the ill luck to loose his specimens [of] Lead ore I cannot say what kind of mineral it was.

There is greate Quantities of soda found in many places all Through California and Lye made of ashes is never used in the manufacture of soap but a species of earth is found that answers weell for this purpose and in fact in many places there is found sinks or holes in the earth that fills with water in the rainy seasons and which after it has evaporated considerably by the dry weather has all the appearance and Qualities of Lye made from ashes and is collected for soap making.

Mercury or Quecksilver is found in many places and is manufactured in small Quntity [at New Almaden] near the puablau villag [of San Jose] soth of the Bay of St Francisco gold is said to Exist in the same neighbourhood but is not worked silver is Likewise said to have been found near the same place.

Small Quantities of magnetic Iron may be seen in many places But I have not heard of any Iron being manufactured in any part of the country some portions of the countrey is said abound in salt but the salt used in california is brought from the Sandwich Islands and is Quite cheap Salt is an article not much used by the californians.

10 Many of the oak Trees make a fine shade and summer seems to be fast approaching allthough the mountains are still covered white in snow Lettuce and Radishes plenty whare any attention has been paid to gardening.

From the Eighth untill the 15th the weather was fine clear and warm during the hours of sunshine but cool at night and the particular in the mornings which ware chilly and require a coat to feel comfortable.

15 The morning somewhat overcast and cool but the sun soon drove off the Haze and shone warm and pleasant.

16 Cool and somewhat Cloudy wind from the north in the afternoon some light showers of hail or snow fell the first I have seen fall in the vallies sinc I have been in California.

17 The sun arose in his usu[al] bright majesty and splendor. Of all places this is the country for news or false reports there being no report that can be relid on except you have some personal Knowledge of the matter a report is now rife that Capt Fremont has raised the american

flag in Monteray and all good citizens are caled on to appear forthwith
to appear at Sonoma armed and (and) Equiped for service under
General Byaho [Vallejo] to defend the rights and priviledges of
Mexican citizens.

21 From the 17 until the 21st the weather was cool with several
showers of hail and notwithstanding the vegitation has a show of
midsumer yet we had several frosty mornings but I could not precieve
the slightest alteration in the appearance of the tenderest vegitable It
appears from information now recieved that the alarm mentioned a
few days since was created By Mr Freemont having raised an american
Flag at his camp neare the Mision of St Johns, and that he was caled
on to apeare before some of the so caled Legal authorities whice he
declined to do Aand this cercumstance alarmed all of the Californians
and caused General Castro to rais 400 men which report says are now
under arms at Monteray no report However can be relied on as but few
men in this Country can write you may form some Idea of what
reports are carried verbally from one to two hundred Miles by an igno-
rant supersticious people.

It was Charles Camp's belief that Clyman decided on March 21 to
make an offer of assistance to Fremont—a company of armed American immigrants. Clyman's letter was evidently taken to Fremont by
the Mr. Flint mentioned by Clyman in his notes for January 20, but the
original of Fremont's reply has not been found in the Clyman papers.
Ivan Petroff saw Fremont's letter in Clyman's possession in 1871 and
preserved a copy:

Fremont's Answer to Clyman:

To James Clyman, Esq.
at Yount's Mills, California
Dear Sir:

Your favor of the 21st ultimo has been received through the kind-
ness of Mr. Flint, some time since, but as the subject matter is one of
the gravest importance I have taken time to consider before venturing

upon a definite reply. I am placed in a peculiar position. Having
carried out to the best of my ability, my instructions to explore the far
west, I see myself on the eve of my departure for home, confronted by
the most perplexing complications. I have received information to the
effect that a declaration of war between our Government and Mexico
is probable, but so far this news has not been confirmed. The Cali-
fornian authorities object to my presence here and threaten to over-
whelm me. If peace is preserved I have no right or business here; if
war ensues I shall be out numbered ten to one and be compelled to
make good my retreat pressed by a pursuing enemy. It seems that the
only way open to me is to make my way back eastward, and as a
military man you must perceive at once that an increase of my
command would only encumber and not assist my retreat through a
region where wild game is the only thing procurable in the way of
food. Under these curcumstances I must make my way back alone
and gratefully decline your offer of a company of hardy warriors

And remain
Yours Respectfully
JOHN C. FREMONT
Camp on Feather River [?]

December 19th 1845

The date given by Petroff is obviously wrong. If we assume that Clyman wrote on March 21, Fremont would not have answered during the following week and spoken of delay in forwarding his letter. Camp has traced his movements for the latter part of March and early April, and believes that Fremont wrote his reply between April 11 and April 14, addressed to Clyman at Yount's Mills, where Clyman had been on March 31.

Fremont's letter seems to indicate that he was aware that a declaration of war was on the way, and it is probable, according to Camp, that he received this information after April 28. By April 28, Clyman was already on his way back east.

Camp suggests two possible interpretations for this confusion: if Fremont actually wrote to Clyman in March or April, he was refusing Clyman's offer either because the time was not ripe for conquest or, "as is more likely," Camp says, because he had no expectations of military activity. If he wrote to Clyman in May or June, he was concealing his real purpose or hiding his moral support of those who wanted to attach the area to the U.S., the Bear-flaggers.

Camp also indicates that Clyman's offer was definitely one of military assistance to Fremont, in case Fremont was attacked by the Mexican forces, and not simply an offer to join forces for the trip home. Clyman was no doubt aware that he could collect a company of experienced frontiersmen to fight with Fremont if the necessity arose, and he must have been confident of his own ability to raise such a force in order to make the offer to Fremont in the first place.

[March] 22 A stiff white frost.

Report further states that (that) Genl. Castro marche[d] his valerous troops to Capt Fremonts camp whare he found numerous pack saddles and various other Baggage and a considerable Quantity of Specie which capt Freemont had unavoidably left in his rapid retreat.

23 Another Frost.

Heard of a small party Leaving the south part of california For St. A.fee and (and) the United States by the way of Chiwauewa.

24 Still another Frost Active preperations making for the departure of a company or two who are going to Oregon with cattle and Horses this company will consist of 60 or 80 persons mostly of those that came in last season I do not recollect of having mentioned heretofore that the Emigration from the states [during 1845] cosisted of about 150 persons 30 or 40 of which are now going to columbia as oregon is here called.

24–31 Weather fair and cool some slight frosts occasionally Kept packing or rather making pack saddle and other preperations for my intended start for the U. States finaly lift on the 31 the head of Napa vally and proceeded down 18 miles to Mr Yount the vally is far from being dry but is passable—Mr yount is an american that has been in the mexican country for 13 or 14 years and has a Flouring and saw mill in opperation both of which are profitable and as far as I could learn this [is] the only Flouring mill in the province.

1846 April the 1st

Cool with a strong west wind and several light shower of rain.

Left Mr. Younts and proceeded down Nappa vally thorough several sloughs and mud holes passed a farm on our left belonging [to] Signor St Salvador Byaho [Vallejo].

This Ranche of General Byahos contains 33 Leages of land equal to (14600) one hundred and Forty six Thousand acres and allthough he is the largest farmer in Callifornia yet a very small portion of this immence Tract is in cultivation perhaps not more than 4 or 500 acres all the rest being left for the pastureage of his stock haveing 12 to 15,000 head of neat cattle 7 or 8,000 head of Horses 2, or 3,000 head of sheep he has also 300 wrking men with their usual proportion of Females and children all Kept in a nearly naked state and pooly fed and never paid a cent for their labour.

St Salvadors farm as we rode past did not make a very flatering or Tasty appearance being scattered and strung some 4 or 5 miles in length and from 20 to 40 rods wide and whare fenced at all the fence was made of small willows stucke in the earth and wove back and forth into a frail open kind of wicker work the small perishable mete-rials Requiring to be renewed every season and this is a common discription of a california farm there being but few spots of land moist enough for cultivation Except along the meanders of som small streame.

This is the greatest oat field (in) perhaps on the globe containing tow or three hundred thousand acres of land and what is most remark-able scarcely a bunch of grass or a weed to be seen notwithstanding this immence Quantity of native grow[n] oats yet you never see a grain fed to an animal all is suffered to fall off when ripe to seed the earth for another crop or to feed the millions of water fowl that resort here in the winter or rainy season at this season it has a beautiful appearanc the earth being thickly clad in deep green foliage as regular as a well set meadow.

Napa Valley to Johnson's Ranch

2 Clear and quite cool Left the oat Field with its Beautiful smoothe green hills and plains and as we had no place to breakfast we rode to Mr Wolfscales for dinner in Eevening we arived at Mr Gordons whare I found six or Eight young men making preperations for their return to oregon with Horses and Cattle all being completely disgusted with California and Quite willing to return to whare the manners and customs of the inhabitants is more in unison with civilization than can be found in this half Barberous half Indian population which is seen in all parts of Spanish america.

3 Remaind withe Mr Gordon who is a verry friendly man and verry acomodating to his country men whare ever found.

4 The night was clear with slight frost this morning From all that I can Learn I think that our company for the states will be small our Horses took a stampide or fright last night and cannot be seen in any direction this morning most of the men spoken of yestarday are of the party that came from Oregon last season with the Expectation of finding California little short of a Paradse but like most of the pleasure and fortune hunters find themselves awfully disapoiented and are willing to try the long and dangerous road back to Oregon.

Found our Horses without much difficulty I Returned back to Mr Wolfscales for the purpose of drying some beif as Traveling stock.

5 Procured beef of Mr Wolfscale and commenced drying has fine young cattle and they are now fat and Excelent Beef Mr Wolfscale has (has) a Beautifull Ranche of Three Leages of land finely situated on a small River [Putah Creek] whare it bursts through a rough mountain an enters the greate sacramento plain But notwithstanding his fine place and rapid increasing stock his is far from being satisfied and is now making preperations to go to Oregon next season and take with him about 2,000 Head of neat Cattle and a beautifull herd of Horses.

6 Nothing can look more beautifull than this country dose at this season of the year numerous kinds of small herbage being now full grown and som Quite ripe allthough the larger Kinds are now in full Bloom and miles of this greate plain is litterly a bed of Posies and prevailing species being deep Bright gold yellow so bright as to dazzel the eye sight under a clear sun for you see no clouds at this season of any consequence and now is the middle of a Californian Summer and would answer well for June in the middle states fall sown wheat now heading.

7 Clear and bright with a dew like rain finished makeing or drying meat and Returned to Mr. Gordns again the nights continue cool.

In fact this is a common trait of all the country lying near the pacific coast while the interior especially the low vallies are scorched with drough and night and day for 4 months at least every season and some seasons occasionally pass of without any rain such summers become so dry as for to distroy Quantities of stock and human lives likewise if they Exercise much during the day But at such times the inhabitants of the interior remove to the mountains.

Along the coast However no season passes without rain and every morning has its fog and every afternoon its sea Breeze a coat is comfortable every morning the year round and you find woolen clothing necessary during the whole day very frequently.

8 Arived at Mr Gordons last Evening mad a tolerable show for rain and this morning still shews lowering But the time for much rain in this vally is now passed allthough rains are frequent yet on the coast and not unfrequent in the mountains.

9 A slight shower of rain fell last night the day clear and pleasant with a strong west wind.

10 Another light shower of rain fell during the night with a strong cool wind from the N. our company slow collecting and I am waiting for some one to pass as I cannot drive my pack animals alone.

It is imposable to hurry any person in california whare time is no object and every man must have his own time to sleep and move about buissiness as though he was pained to move or even breathe.

11 and 12 Fine cool weather this is the common season for Planting corn Pumpkins beans and Mellons.

13 Packed up and lef Mr Gordons on our way to Suitors Fort on the same Trail that we passed last July vegitation now full grown and the mosketoes proved verry troublesome passed Mr Knights and continued down the sacreemento river along a (a) small horse Trail the only Traveled road that pases through or rather around thies bay of St Francisco.

A short distance above our camp apeared a large colony of Shaggs (a large black duck) whare they ware building and kept up a continual hoarse squaking all night while innumerable Quantities of Brant kept screeming in a large Flag march in an aposite direction assisted by the howling of wolves.

14 Extremely heavy dew.

Left our musical neighbours and proceeded down the Trail a couple of hours which [brought] us to Mr. [Thomas M.] Hardys. at the Junction of the sacremento withe Feather Rivir the latter is one of the principle Tributaries of the sacrimento and is about 200 yards wide at its mouth here we crossed over our baggage in a small Canoe and swam our animal over the main stream being upwards of 400 yards over Mr Hardy gave us his assistance all being safely over we packed and proceeded up Feather about 7 mile and encamped the whole or nearly the whole of the country pased since yestarday noon is over-flown in high water and is now well stocked with moketoes and water fowl The mountains ahead shew a long regular chain all white with snow about 30 or 40 miles distant.

15 Passed Mr Nichols [Nicholaus Altgeier] Early and got directions of a Dutchma[n] [probably Altgeier] how to steer our course to Johnstons & Kizers [William Johnson and Sebastian Keyser] whare those intending to go to the states are asembling traveled all day steadily over a dry arid plain the vegitation not exceding three inches high generaly composed of a small groth of weeds now in bloom and covering the earth in a yellow garment the whole distance we had to travel this morning being 15 mile we encamped in all Probability farther of[f] from our Place of distination than we ware in the morning theere being no such thing as even a path to follow and I advise all

travelers hereafter to be carefull and allways take their own Ideas of
the rout in preferance to follow the directions of a dutchman for he
will confus all the small Ideas you ever had in place of giving you any
new ones.

16 Left our lost camp and (and) changed our course in a contrary
direction that is north Instead of south and in about 4 Hours steady
traveling over the same dry hard soil we came in sigh[t] of civilization
again if cattl Horses and Indians can be so called arived at Mr [Lans-
ford W.] Hastings camp on Bear creek a small river Running into
Feather River about noon Mr Hastings welcomed us to his cam[p] in a
warm and Polite manner and we unpacked under the shade of a
spreading oak tree—Mr Jonston who owns the Ranche is like all of his
california neighbours 15 miles from the nighest inhabitant and not
even a track leading to or from his place at this season of the year
allthough in a dry time all the emigration from the states pass .

17 Purchased a beef and commenced Drying a portion for sea
stock.

18 Continued in camp making preperations—The weather could
not be finer not a cloud to be seen and the beautifull transparency of
Heavens is finely accompanied by a cool northern Breeze.

19 Still Remain in camp makeing preperations.

20 Mr. [Owen] Sumner [Sr.] and his Family arived all prepared for
their Journy Mr Sumner has been in Oregon from thence to California
and still being dissatisfied is now returning to the states again after
haveing [spent] nearly five years in Traveling from place to place as
likewise a small fortune.

21 Cool and windy all the company that we expect are all assembled and consist of nineteen men three women and three children with
a large herd of Horses and mules.

22 Still cool with a strong South wind verry disagreeable several
light showers of rain fell but not enough to lay the dust 18 miles.

23 Left our camp in the valle of Bear creek and commenced
assending the mountains which approach to within a few miles of our
camp our travel to day was over moderate hills cowered with dry
shrubby oaks and pine timber withe various small open glades and

small praries soil (hard whare dry) of a dark red clay mixed in gravel in the after noon we met two indians or rather came upon them who immediately rushed in to the rocks and thickest and immediately disappeared this is the general character of all the natives of the mountains allthough these natives are within a few miles of the greate plains and look down upon thair half civilized neighbours Below yet no inducement can be held out to induce them to come down.

24 A Keen white frost covering all the vegitation made an early move and traviled over a rough uneven range of hills untill late in the afternoon had several views of the snow caped. mountain still Keeping an east course paralel with Bear creek came to deep ravine all most perpendicular over which upwards of 50 wagons had passed last autumn with a greate deal of labour and difficulty came to spots of new fallen snow desended into the Kenyon of Bear creek the snow becomeing more plenty as we passed up this narrow rocky passage the stream roaring and pitching over it[s] narrow rocky bed.

At dusk we came to a small vally surrounded by high rugged mountains mostly covered with snow which to all appearance had lain on the earth since last december made 27 mile and encamped on a small noll which was bear of snow.

25 Spent a cold uncomfortable night for shortly after dark the wind arose and bleww a strong gale all night from the snow capt. mountains which stand in cold and awfull grandure a few miles to the East we ware out Early Examining the vally to see whar our anemall can procure the best grazing moved up the narrow vally about a mile pitched our tents to await the arival of some of our company that is yet behind allthough the night produced ice strong enough to bear a man and the snow reaches down into the vally itself yet the young grass is up in spots sufficient to make tolerable grazeing here we expect to remain several days before we attact the region of all most Eternal snow and ice which is not more than one mile ahead.

26 Remain in camp this is warm and quite comfortable considering our greate elevation and the Quantity of snow that surrounds us Nothing can be more tedious and disagreeable than waiting for dangerous a Journy as that in which we have now embarked our party consisting of six men only we considered our selves two weak to venture to drive our way through and it apears Quite uncertain when the rear of our company will Join us so that we remain here in continual anxiou suspence without any object to relieve anxiety the only animals seen in this vally is a pair of small Prairie wolves which anoy us by eating off the raw hide tugs which we have to tie up our animals and allthough the wolves are scarcely ever out of sight yet they are so watchfull that we cannot come in gunshot of them.

27   Still remain in camp waiting for more company stiff Frost every night in region of snow and Ice.

Walked out to the N. E. of the vally on the point of a Ledge of rock here you have a view or touch of the sublime awfull the first thing that attracts your notice is a high rough ridge of snow capd. mountains proceede a little further the ridge desends in front into an impassable cliff of Black rocks divested of any Kind of covering still further and (and) you behold a river dashing through an awfull chasm of rocks several thousand feet below you your head becomes dizzy and you may change the [view] to [the] right here at the distance you have ridges of snow and ridges of pine timber to the Left you have a distant view of the eternal cliffs of black volcanic rocks that bound the river Eubor.

28   Still Remain in camp allthough all the company that we had Eexpected arived yesterday Evening and it is thought by those best acquainted [with] this rout that it will be impracticable to cross the mountains at this time several of us are However verry anxious to try and asertain that fact several large grey Bear ware seen this morning 25 [miles].

29   Left our camp on bear Creek immediately assended a steep mountain to the south side of the vally and in about one hours ride came to the snow turned and wound around the south side [of] a mountain to avoid the deep drifts of snow that completely filled the small vallies about noon came to the Euba [Yuba] river running N. W. Kept up the stream several miles when we found the snow so deep on the W. side that we could not travel crossed over to the E side of the stream and Kept up near a rough granite mountain through immence drifts of snow and water the day being Quite warm the ravine neare flooded withe water and deep in snow the whole of the way for road we had none at all is covered thickly with a large grothe of pine and Firr a short time before sundown we came to a halt on the steep rough side of a point of rocks whare we found bear ground Enough to bearly camp on and not a spear of grass for our poor animal which had traveled all day in snow and mud so we tied them up immediately after unpacking the Euba roring through its snowy bed.

30 Early under way in hope that the snow would bear us to travel over the crust but as it did not [freeze] much during the night we found our progress but slow all the ravines running full of water under the snow our pack horses ware continually stuck fast and Floundering in the snow to avoid this we assended a steep rocky mountain to the north of our rout but on ariving near the top we found the snow much deeper and (and) as it had not been much thawed during the day privious it would not carry us atall however after an hours plunging and several times repacking we at length desended again to an open Prarie vally that [lies] at the immediate head of Euba and about noon came to an Entire halt for the rest of the day haveing made 3 miles.

May the First 1846

Got under way early the [snow] was hard Enough to bear up handsomely some 2 miles when we arived at the summit of the mountain (the snow being from 3 to 8 feet deep) here we commenced the desent over steep Pricipices rough granite Rock covered in many places through the chasms with snow 15 or 20 feet deep and luckily for us we lost no horses allthough we had to force them down several perpendicular cliffs afer about 3 hours unpacking and repacking we succeeded in clearing the steepest pitches of the whole length of which is not one mile you may imagine that we felt a happy relief to find ourselves on bear ground onc more which we found at the head of truckys [Donner] lake a small sheet of water about two miles in length and half a mile wide the N hill sides being intirely clear of snow but verry little green vegitation made six miles and encamped at the foot of the Lake.

2 Proceeded down the vally of Truckees. River through open pine woods and here we first saw the plains covered with wild sage the chain of mountains we have Just past is the same called the cascade chain in Oregon and is generally covered with several kinds of Pine Firr and other evergreen timber. and here I found out that I had the misfortune to loose my gunlock some whare in the Everlasting snows that we had Just pased. we made a short days travel and encamped on Johns creek [named for John Greenwood; now Prosser Creek] to recriut our half starved animals who had been three days and two nights without a mouthfull of forrage haveing traveled not more than 6 miles this camp is in a large cove in the mountains which are all covered whit in snow now melting rapidly on the lower ranges or hill the vally [Martis Valley] however is barren and no signs of game is to be seen a few naked natives ware seen to day.

3 Proceeded on Early about 4 miles to a fine vally of green grass whare we unpacked again for the day to give our animals a chance to recruit after their long and hard fatiegue several showers of snow fell during the morning and the day was cool and Blustring with the drifts of snow several natives have been about our camp and appear to be friendly they are a poor race and their country is poorly supplied with game and [they] manufacture a kind [of] robe of Rabbit skins which they cut into small stripes and weave them togather with the lint of some kind of weeds from which they Likewis make ropes for snares and fishing tackel in the evening it commenced snowing rapedly and the snofell several inches deep so you may imagin that we spent no verry comfortable night it slaked up toward morning This if vally it may be called is Quite uneven and generally covered in pine timber not of the best Quality Here likewise we saw large camace marshes on which the natives at this season of the [year] Exist mostly in a raw state.

4 As the snow covered all the grass we packed and ware early on the way crossed Quite a large creek [Little Truckee] which has been called wind River a tributary of Truckeys River and proceeded to cross a considerable of a ridge and desended again into a small rich vally 8 miles from our former encampment the natives are still around our encampment nearly naked and do not seem to complain of cold allthough we can hardly get clothes enough on us to keep ourselves comfortable about noon the sun shone out a few minuets which

desolved the most of the new fallen snow in southerm exposures but the evening was verry cold and wind[y] with some few flakes of fine snow but considerable snow fell on the mountains only a few miles from us—The tribe we are now passing through call themselves as well as understood Washee [Washoe].

5 A cool night proceeded S Easteerly about 4 miles and came to the main Truckies River [north of present Verdi] whare it first leaves the timbred mountains and Enters the open Bald hills which would be mountains in any other country The river is about 40 yards wide and falls rapidly over a rough rocky bed the weather cloudy cool and a strong west wind continually blowing to day for the first since we set out no snow is to be seen ahead but any Quantity is to be seen a little to the south of our rout continued down the valy of the River 6 miles and encamped in a fine vally of Excelent grass one aged native followed us from our Last encampment and seems to have greate attatchment for us or for the provisions that he can beg the chasm that Truckies River runs in for it cannot be caled a vally is verry rocky mostly of small sized stones all granite or Baysalt with various mixtures.

6 Proceeded down the river crossing and takeing the South side at about 8 miles we came to a deep muddy Brook [Steamboat Creek, east of Reno] running through a handsome prairie vally went up the Brook about 3 miles before we found a crossing passed down along side of a steep volcanick mountain shewing immence Quantities of rough slagg and other vitrified matter entered the last Kenyon and passed down to a small vally whare stoped for the night the day was extremely rough and windy the wind Blowing from the S. W. so strong that it nearly blew some of the Ladies from their saddles and we could see that the mountains behind us experienced an awfull snow storm while we ware nearly blest with sunshine a feew spits of snow and rain fell on us and we suffered from the cold. our course a little N of E. 12 miles.

7 A little before day it began to snow and snowed rapidly untill about noon haveing a bad camp for our animals we packed up and moved on down the river about 6 miles it continued to snow all the way but finding better pasture we stoped all our progress yesterday and to day the mountains on Either side are bare of timber verry high and ruged mostly composed of Baysalt, Granite and an occasional ridge of rough slate we have seen no game larger than a rabbit and but verry few of them about one oclock the sun broke out and the snow soon disappeared in the [v]allies (afternoon) continued down the south side of the river. verry high rounded bluff and in fact mountains approach so near that we had to assend one of them 1½ miles of steep assent [south of Pond Peak] brought us to the top immediately desended again to the river and continued down encamped at sun set emmidst the most subbime specimens of volcanic mountains all rounded and made up of all colours and hues from brick red to chalk white 13 miles today.

8   After unpacking our horses some one of our party examined a floating Fishing machien that lay a fuw steps from us moored in the river and (and) found an old Indian that had been in managing his fishing spears when we rode up and was so frightened that it was with some difficulty that we coaxed him out after some [delay] however he gained courage and came out and slept with us during the night this morning he made us a present of several beautifull large salmon Trout and we [left] him to persue his fishing again unmolested.

Persued our way doun the river about 6 miles to whare we leave to cross the plains for the sink of Marys river here Truckies river makes a great bend turning nearly N and falls into a lake [Pyramid Lake] at some 12 miles distant the day is Quite cold with a strong N. W. wind vegetation Just begining to spring and many places the willow scarcely shews the bud.

The several parties which have passed through this region have each given this stream a different name Truckies River and Salmon Trout River But as the tribe of natives inhabiting this stream and the ajacent country call themselves the Waushew tribe or nation I think it would [be] crrect to call the stream by the same name viz Waushee River.

9   Struck of to the East leaveing the River to take it course north soon came near the pount of a low range of Black volcanic mountains and observed numerous specimins of rock formed by concreeton from spring that must have existed many years since in fact all the country passed through to day has at some distant period been one immence boiling caldron and is now strewed over with some thousands of upright rocks which have been onc immence projectors of Liquid steam and have discharged immence Quantities of mud which now fills the whole plain over which we passd. and several miles perhaps 8 of this days travel was over a white sheet of salt incrusted passed over and in sight of Large beds of Chalk Likewise which has been involved in Boiling water a low rang of Black slagg lay to our left all day of the moste thirsty sterile appearance near sun set we stoped at some holes of Brackish water haveing traveled 30 miles to day at about 15 miles or half way from Waushee [Truckee] river to the first water near Mays. Lake still exist a cauldron of Boiling water no stream isues from it [at] present but it stands in several pools Boiling and again disappearing some of these pools have beautifull clear water Boiling in them and other emit Quantites of mud into one of these muddy pools my little water spaniel Lucky went poor fellow not knowing that it was Boiling hot he deliberately walked in to the caldron to slake his thirst and cool his limbs when to his sad disappointment and my sorrow he scalded himself allmost insantly to death I felt more for his loss than any other animal I ever lost in my life as he had been my constant companion in all my wandering since I Left Milwawkee and I vainly hoped to see him return to his old master in his native village (But such is nature of all earthy hopes) for several miles back we had been traveling over the bed of a former Lake which to all appearanc has not been dry more than 10 or 15 years and now forms a salt plain and how far to the South it extends I canot tell.

Eastward to Missouri

[May] 10 [1846] Again under way and (on) rather a singular road we had mostly over a bear salt plain which had a few years since been covered in water and costituted Ogdens [Humboldt] Lake which no doubt when Mr Ogden visited this region some 25 [18] years since was Quite a large Lak but shallow now nearly dried up and from appearances will in a few years more intirely disappear and become the most dry thirsty [spot] imaginable as that portion which has now dried off will plainly indicate Nearly the whole of our days travel 20 miles to day and a part of yestarday was evidently under water but a few yares since now at this time Marys [Humboldt] river sinks and disappears intirely some 8 or 10 miles above the small shallow pond know as Ogdens Lake and this whole region is now intirely dried up and has the most thirsty appearance of any place I ever witnessed The whole of several large vallies is covered in a verry fin clay or mud which has vimited from the bowels of the earth mixed with scalding water from the immence cauldrons of heat below.

11 Want of space has prevented me from noting that several Lengthy ranges of mountains are visible and in particular to the East [Humboldt Range] whose tops are covered in snow one Likewise in the S. allso N. E. all appearanty seperatee and distinct. allso that we changed our course from E. to nearly N on our arival at ogdens, Lake.

Continued up the valy of marys river passed over Quantities of concreete rocks of various curious shapes and Sizes the mountains that bound this vally are all of vitrified rock of various hues but mostly of dark red and brown the whole of the vally is composed [of] whiteish volcanic mud and bears no vegitation except a hard thorny shub called by voyagers grease wood and this species seems to thrive without mois-ture at 10 miles we struck the River a small stream not more than 20 yards wide running in a deep channel of fine clay and the water completely saturated with this same mud as thick or thicker than the Misouri in a freshet to day the snow seemed to disappear rapidly on the mountain in front of our camp none of the highlans bear any vegitation.

12 Still up the River over one of the most Steril Barren countrys I ever traversed the hills and mountains producing no kind of vegitation and the more elevated part of the vally bearing nothing but a small shrubby thorn and not even moist enough to poduce the much dispised wild sage from all appearancees their has not fallen any rain or snow since the california emigration passed here last September except a light shower of snow that has fallen a few days since and still remains on the mountain in nearly all directions the grass has made but a feeble start and our animals fare verry poorly the willows have not yet buded and the earth is so parched that we are all day covered in a cloud of dust allmost sufficating to pass through and the water is Likewise poor when obtained as there is none at all Except in the river and the banks are so steep and high that few places can be found to desend to [it] 25 [miles].

13 Early under way continued up the River the sun arose as usual without a speck of cloud or mist for bothe appear to be allmost unknown to this region here the river which hitherto has been coming all most drect from the north makes a bend and comes more East-wardly the vally [contains] the same volcanic mud now become more dry and allmost as loose as ashes at about 6 miles we came to a fine vally of grass [Lassen's Meadows] and umpacked to let our animals graze a Large vally seem[s] to run a great distance north waard The water in the River is much clearer than whare we first struck it below and as earthe is much dryer so also it is much Looser in as much that our animals many timis sink up to their knees in the dry earth our whole company now Togather consists of 19 men and boys 3 women and 2 children and about 150 mules and Horses too many for this rout at so early a season of the year as the grass has Just began to shoot and is yet young and short and we will probably devide our company in a few days.

14 Up the River on an nearly E direction to day 25 miles with a nearly Exact sameness two large vallies seem to spread themselves one to the North and the other to the South passing between two moun-tains composed of Black slag the most Easterly ridge [Sonoma Range] is covered in snow near the tops But allthough their appears to be a considerable depth of snow on several of these mountains now it would seem thawing off rapidly yet so thirsty is the sides and so greate the evaporation that not a drop of water reaches the vally severall Horses gave out to day and from the appearance of many others I begin to conclude that californea Horses are not a hardy race of animals So perfectly Barren and sterile is this region of volcanic matter that scarcely a bird is heard to chirp to the rising Sun and not even the signe of an animal Except Rabbits ever ventures to make a precarious subsistance on these plains a strong South wind is blowing and some thin streaks of clouds are seen gathering around.

15 Still up the River after afeew Hours ride we chnged our course nearly East for some miles and our whole course to day has perhaps nearly N. E. the same appearances as to soil [as] usual However to day we passed several sand drifts no Timber has yet been seen in any part of the high or Lowlans Bordering on this stream except willow and a few other shrebs of verry Stinted groth the same want of moisture still continues and the Travelling is extremely dusty espicially to day as we had an aft wind (as the Sailors say) Travel to day about 22 miles From all appearances this River has overflowed it[s] banks and flooded all the vally as the low ground still indicates by a feeble groth of Bull rushes water flags and other vegitables know[n] to marsh lands as like wise the old stals of large weeds on the plains but at present very little grass and no weeds are seen.

16 Continued up in an E. & S. E. course [Big Bend of the Humboldt] on the South side of the River 30 miles a few miles from our Last camp we passed a groupe Boiling springs [Golconda] near ½ a mile S. of the Trail passed a range of low slate mountains [Osgood Mountains] thorugh which the river passes and makes a Large bend to the South and a large vally extinding bothe sides of the river nearly all of which however is covered in many places several inches thick in a white saline crust nearly strong enough to bear the weight of a man and in most other places shrubby stoots of Prarie thorn know[n] by the tra[v]elers in this region as grease wood passed one Slough of standing water the first I have seen since traveling the stream Large vallies seem to extend in various directions to day bound on either side by mountains of Slag and Scorcia Soil volcanic mud or clay to so dry and loose that our animals sunk in up to their knees observed some willows begining to bud several days have [been] Quite smoky and it seem to increase allthough no fires are to be seen the whole of to day has [been] verry crooked but the earth is so dry that we can not ventur [any] cut off.

17 Passed up the full S E. 26 miles and encamped whare the river breakes between two Black slag hills ["Stony Point" of emigrants at end of Shoshone Mesa] which form nearly regular mountains N. and S. passed over several miles of saline matter in fact the highlands and mountains seem to be formed intirely of slag and scoria and the vallies of volcanic mud salt and soda the vegitation wild Sage and grease wood strong wind blew from the south during the fore noon but shifted to the west in the evening and blew up such a dust that the sun was completely obscured all the afternoon this would seem strang but no stranger than true for the vallies are composed of find mud thrown from the bowels of the earth in greate Quantites mixed with Boiling water and when left exposed to the weather for an unknown time the water being evaporated by the sun leaves this remarkable fine clay which is soft and fine flour whirlwinds and other strong currents of wind carry large Quantitees to a great hight resembling a white smoke which in times of dry weather and strong winds completely obscures the light and resembles thin light fog.

18 Early under way the appearance of the county the same 30 miles First 10 miles East then S. E. The [day] was still and pleasant the valy Large grass short and none except near the water our animals begin to [find] hard travel and poor feed mountains the same Cinder and Slag many of them caped in snow and frost in the vally every night sine we commenced assending the river the rever pretty much the same except clearer and more swift no timber yet seen except willow confined to the margin of the stream the white saline matter not Quite so plenty. a high white snowey mountain [Ruby Dome] seen dead a head at some considerable distance Fresh tracks of Indians seen in the vicinity of camp and as I believe the first seen in passing up this stream they are not however supposed to be dangerous as they are probably shoshones devided our company on the 16 we haveing 8 men and 37 animals. Move ahead.

19 In a few miles above our encampment (we) we the Trail leaves the River [east of Gravelly Ford] and assends a range of hills or mountains of no greate elevation and mostly formed of clay and loose rock about half way across these hills is several springs of cool water crossed over and encamped in tolerable good grass for this season whole distance (16 miles) the rever passes through a Kenyon in these hill and is difficult for Horsemen to follow the stream across the river from our camp is a lot of warm springs [near Carlin] but the water does not run from them about Half a mile above our camp is [a] Beautifull running Brook of clear water [Maggie Creek] the first that the river receives from the [Humboldt] Lake upwards a distance of more than 200 miles which proves the dryness of this country and the xtreme thirstyness of the soil if soil it can be called that produces so stinted a groth of vegitation the river here is more than double as larg as it was whare we first struck it and the water nearly clear.

20 Up the stream once more about 25 miles In about one hours ride we came to whare the river Breaks through a low ruged mountain [Carlin canyon] but as the water is yet low we had no difficulty in passing through by crossing the stream several times this mountain runs nearly N. & S. above it opens out in to a large vally again only a small part of any of the vally is stocked in grass and that neare the Stream all the afternoons travel was nearly N. & N E. a few miles below our camp on the South side of the river as a singular lot of Hot spring which boil and bubble like cauldron[s] and send off a large Quantity of hot water into the river which is only a feew rods from the springs.

Some of the hills and mountains begin to shew a few stinted cedars on thier sides to day passed what I supposed to be the E Branch [South Fork] of Marys River comeing in through a deep Kenyon [Humboldt Canyon] from a range of snow capd mountains [Ruby Range] to the E of us.

———

Fremont's Trail and Hastings Cutoff

21 On the way again as usual N. E. course *1 ½* hours ride brought us to whare the stream came through a Kenyon for a short distance but the trail led over a sandy ridge to the N and after passing another of the same discription we came to a handsome little Brook [North Fork of

Humboldt River] hading to the N. W. On each side of this brook the earth was covered white with a salin incrustation and when broke By the tramping of our mules it nearly strangled them and us causing them to caugh and us to sneeze at 14 miles we encamped this being the point whare Mr Freemant intersected the wagon Trail last fall on his way to California and Mr Hastings our pilot was anxious to try this rout but my beleef is that it [is] verry little nearer and not so good a road as that by fort Hall our encampment is in a large fine looking vally but too cold and dry for any kind of grain the mountains which are no greate elivation above the plain are covered nearly half way down in snow.

22 After long consultation and many arguments for and against the two different routs one leading Northward by fort Hall and the other by the Salt Lake we all finally tooke Fremonts Trail by the way of the Salt Lake Late in thee day the Stream brances again in this vally the Larger [Lamoille Creek] comeing From the S the smaller [the main Humboldt] from the N. up this Northern branch the wagon Trail leads by the way of Fort Hall.

Crosing the N. Branch we struck S. E. for a low gap [Humboldt or Secret Pass] in a range of snow caped mountains [E. Humboldt Range] soon crossed the vally and commenced assending the mountain out of which isues a small Brook [Secret Creek, now called Cottonwood Creek] followed up this brook to neare its source and encamped nearly on the summit of the mountain and within perhaps less than one mile of the snow the air was Quite cool and a few drops of rain fell. on this elevated ridge the grass we found to be nearly full grown while that in the vally was Quite short Here I observed large beds of rock resembling marble 12 mile.

23 Late in the evening last heard rumbling thunder after dark a few drops of rain fell The night was cool and froze a little in fact every night has produced some Ice since we left the plains of California Early this morning the snow fell so as to whiten earth at our camp and laid on the mountains all day another shower fell during the forenoon Continued withe some difficulty to follow Freemonts trail up the brook to a handsome little valy [Secret Valley] and over a ridge to a nother larger vally [Ruby Valley] several small streams fall into this vally and run off to the S & S W and no doubt fall into marys river [actually into Franklin Lake] and the last water seen passing into that stream.

Crossed the vally S. E. and assended a steep narrow mountain [E. Humboldt Range] some remnants of snow drifts ware laying on the summit of this mountain desended the mountain on the South side to a large spring of warm water [Warm Creek] flowing into a large vally [Clover Valley] and spreading into a large swale covered in marsh grass here we encamped at the distanc of 12 miles the day was cloudy and several light showers of snow fell on the mountains.

24 S. E. across the vally of the warm spring and over a ridge of hills [Chase Spring Mountain] covered with shrubby Junts of cedars and into another vally [Independence Valley] of considerable length but not more than 6 or 8 miles wide dis[t]ance to day 14 miles stoped at a lot of small springs [Mound Springs or Chase Springs] on several low mounds but so thirsty is the earth that the water does not run more than 20 or 30 feet before it all disappears to the S. W. of this vally the hills rise in considerable peaks [Spruce Mountain] covered in snow at this time animal life seem all most Extinct in this region and the few natives that try to make a precarious subsistanc here are put to all that ingenuety can invent roots herbs insects and reptiles are sought for in all directions in some parts moles mice and gophers seem to be Quite plenty and in order to precure those that live entirely under the surface of the earth when a suitable place can be found a Brook is damned up a ditch dug and the habitation of the mole inundated when the poor animal has to take to the surface and is caught by his enemy.

25 Again under way E. of S [actually nearly due east] across another dry clay plain [Independence Valley] covered in shrubs of a verry dwarfish character and over as dry a range of low mountains clothed in dwarfish cedars and Pines [Pequop Range at Jasper Pass] Came to a hole of water or rather a cluster of small springs [Flowery Lake] which like the last night disappeared in the parched earth imme-diately here we stoped and watered and nooned on again nearly east [across Gosiute Valley] to a rather rough looking rang of mountains [Toana Range] asended and found several snow drifts about the summit here we lost Fremonts trail and desended a southern ravine to all appearanc dry as a fresh burnt brick Kiln unpacked and prepared ourselves for a night without water I assended one of the dry Cliffs and to my astonishment saw a well of good cool water from the top of this rang [Toana Range] we could have a fair view of one of those greate Salt plains you may give some Idea of its [extent] when I assure you that we stood near the snow drifts and surveyed this plain streching in all directions beyond the reach of vision.

26 Spen.t the whole day in searching for the Trail which I succeeded in finding late in the afternoon

27 Left our camp near the top of the mountain an took a N. E. cours to a high ruged looking bute [Pilot Peak] standing prominent and alone with the tops whitned in snow [Went] along the East side of this bute which stands in the salt plains to near the Eastern point 22 miles and encamped on a fine spring Brook [Pilot Peak Creek] that comes tumbling from the mountain in all its purity This bute affrd's numerous springs and brooks that loose themselves immediately in the salt plain below but the grass is plenty generally and the main bulk of the county produces nothing but a small curly thorn bush winding on the earth To the S. s. E. and East you have a boundless salt plain without vegitatiom except here and there a cliff of bare rocks standing like monumental pillars to commemorate the distinction of this portion of the Earth.

28 Left our camp at the Snowy or more properly the spring Bute for this Bute affords several fine Brooks and took the Trail East and soon entered on the greate salt plain the first plain is 6 or 7 miles wide and covered in many places three inchs deep in pure white salt passed an Island of rocks [Silver Island] in this great plain and entered the great plain over which we went in a bold trot untill dusk when we Bowoiked [bivouacked] for the night without grass or water and not much was said in fact all filt incouraged as we had been enformed that if we could follow Mr Fremonts trail we would not have more than 20 miles without fresh water In fact this is the [most] desolate country perhaps on the whole globe there not being one spear of vegitation and of course no kind of animal can subsist and it is not yet assertaind to what extent this immince salt and sand plain can be south of whare we [are now] our travel to day was 40 miles.

29 As soon as light began to shew in the East we ware again under way crossed one more plain (to cross) and then assended a rough low mountain [Cedar Mountain] still no water and our hopes ware again disapointed Commenced our desent down a ravine made 14 miles and at length found a small spring of Brackish water [in Skull Valley] which did not run more than four rods before it all disappeared in the thirsty earth but mean and poor as the water was we and our animals Quenched our burning thirst and unpacked for the day after our rapid travel of about 20 hours and 30 hours without water.

30 At an Eearly hour we ware on our saddles and bore south 4 miles to another small spring of the same kind of water stoped and drank and continued changing our course to S E passed a small salt plain [Skull Valley] and several large salt springs changed again to E. or N. of E. a ruged mountain [Stansbury Range] to oure right and a salt marsh to our left this mountain is The highist we have seen in these plains allthough 20 peaks are visable at all tines to day 20 miles.

Long before day was visibele a small Bird of the mocking bird kind was heard to cheer us with his many noted Song an this is the only singing Bird that I have heard for the last 10 days in fact this desolaton afords subsistance to nothing but Lizards, and scorpions which move like Ligntning ove[r] the parched Earthe in all directions as we pass along the spring we camp at to night is large and deep sending off a volume of Brackish water to moisten the white parched earth nearly all the rocks seen for .7 days pasd. is Black intersperced with white streaks or clouds and I Judge them to be a mixture of Black Bassalt and Quarts. our spring has greate Quantities of fish in it some of considerable size.

31 N. E. along the mountains to the N. Point whare is an extensive spring of salt water [Big Salt Spring at Timpie Junction] after turning the point of the mountain we changed again to the S. E. along betwen the mountain and the greate Salt Lake Travel to day 20 miles and we passed some 15 or 20 large springs mostly warm and more or less salt some of them verry salt camped at some holes of fresh water [Twenty

Wells in Tooele Valley near Grantsville] in most all drections and two peaks one to the S. W. [Deseret Peak] and the other to the S. E. [Lowe Peak] seem to be highg enough to contain snow all the season. we have had two nights only since we left the Settelments of California without frost and to day is cold enough to ride with a heavy coat on and not feel uncomfortabl.

Journal of a Mountain Man   277

Notes on Chapter Sixteen

Clyman's journal for May 25 and 26 mentions a "well of good cool water" on one of the dry cliffs, and then a long search for a trail. Camp's footnotes reveal a long search for the spring Clyman mentions, which was apparently slightly off Fremont's route.

Chapter 17
Notebook Nine
Great Salt Lake to Independence

June 1, 1846 to July 24, 1846

1846 June the 1st

Proceeded nearly east to the point of a high mountain [Oquirrh Mountains] that Bounds the Southern part of the greate salt lake I observed that this lake like all the rest of this wide spread Sterility has nearly wasted away one half of its surface since 1825 when I floated around it in my Bull Boate and we crossed a large Bay of this Lake with our horses which is now dry and continued up the South side of the Lake to the vally [Salt Lake Valley] near the outlet of the Eutaw Lake and encamped at a fine large spring of Brackish water 20 miles (to) to day.

After unpacking several Indians ware seen around us after considerable signing and exertion we got them to camp and they apeared to be friendly.

In this vally contrary to any thing we had yet seen Lately the grass is full grown and some early Kinds are ripe .(are ripe) and now full grown and still the mountains nearly all around are yet covered in snow

These Ewtaws as well as we could understand informed us that the snakes and whites ware now at war and that the snakes had killed two white men this news was not the most pleasant as we have to pass through a portion of the snake country.

2   acording to promis our Eutaw guide came this morning and conducted us to the ford [near 27th South St., Salt Lake City] on thee Eutaw river which we found Quite full and wetting several packs on our low mules but we all got safely over and out to the rising ground whare we found a fine spring brook and unpacked to dry our wet baggage.

This stream [Jordan River] is about 40 yards wide running in a deep channel of clay banks and through a wide vally in some places well set in an excelent kind of grass But I should think that it would not be moist Enough for grain the mountains that surround this vally are pictureesque and many places beautifull being high and near the base smoothe and well set in a short nutericious grass Especially those to the West.

Afternoon took our course E into the Eutaw [Wasatch] mountains and near night we found we had mistaken the Trail and taken one that bore too much to the South camped in a cove of the mountain making 25 miles the ravines and some of the side hills have groves of oak and sugar maple on them all of a short shrubby discription and many of the hill sides are well clothed in a good bunch grass and would if not too cold bear some cultivation.

3   N. E. up the Brook [Parley's Canyon] into a high ruged mountain [Big Mountain] not verry rocky but awfull brushy with some dificulty we reached the summit and commenced our dissent which was not so steep nor Quite so brushy the Brush on this ridge consists of aspen, oak cherry and white Firr the later of which is Quite like trees this ridge or mountain devides the waters of Eutaw from those [of] Weebers rivers and desended the South branch [East Canyon Creek] of Weebers rivir untill it entered a rough Looking Kenyon when we bore away to the East up a small Brook [Dixie Creek] and encamped at the head springs makeing to day about 18 miles on the top of the mountain we passed several snow drifts that had not yet thawed and the whole range to the S.W. and N. is more or less covered in snow and

many peaks heavily clothed and the air cold and disagreeable some few light Showers of rain fell during the day and one shower of snow fell in the afternoom service berry in bloom as Likewis choke cherries no game seen through this region and it is difficult to determin what the few natives that inhabit this region subsist on 23 miles.

4 North 4 miles down a ravin [Main, or Little East Canyon] to Weabers River we struck this stream a short distance above the Junction of the N. [Lost Creek] and S. Branches and immideately above whare it enters the second Kenyon above its mouth followed up the vally some 3 miles and crossed over found the stream about 50 yards wide muddy from the thawing of snow in the mountains south it has a rapid current over a hard gravelly bottom and it has a considerable Sized intervale through which it pases thickly covored in shrubby cotton wood and willows after crossing we took a deep cut ravin coming direct from the N. E. [Echo Canyon] the Bluffs of this ravin are formed of red rock made of smoothe water washed pebbles and the North side in particular are verry high and perpendicular and in many places hanging over the narow vally is completely Strewn over with the boulder which have fallen from time to time from the cliffs above passed to day several clumps of oak and sugar maple the cliffs however have scattering clumps of cedar on them To day saw one Lonesome looking poor grisly Bear.

This [Weber River] like the Eutaw river heads in the Eutaw [Uinta] mountains and running North some distance Turns to the West and breaks through two ranges of mountain falls into the salt Lake 30 or 40 miles south of the mouth of Bear rivir and has a shallow barr at its mouth stuck over in drift wood. 26 [miles].

5 N. E. Up the Brook on which we encamped [Echo Canyon near Castle Rock] in a few miles it parted into several smaller Brooks and we continued up the most central notwithstanding the frosty morning [along present U.S. route 30 to Evanston] several summer songsters ware warbling their loves or chirping amongst the small willows which skirted the little Brook as we passed along in a few hours ride we arived at the summit of the ridge that devides the waters of Weabers River from those of Bear River this ridge is high and several drifts of winters snow was still Lying a fiw miles to the souths of our rout notwithsanding this summit ridge is smoothe and handsomely clothed in young grass.

Continued down the East side of the ridge and crossed over a small muddy stream [Yellow Creek] running N. into Bear River struck Bear River a rapid stream40 yards wide and running over a smoothe rocky Bed [at Evanston, Wyoming] we found this stream fordable and greate thickets of willows and catton wood growing in the bends Continued our course up a small Brook [Sulphur Spring Creek] a few miles and campd. several times to day we had a sight of the Eutaw [Uinta] mountains completely covered in snow as the weather has been Quite to cool to have much effect upon the peaks of this rang of mountains 30 Miles.

6 Proceeded N. E. through a Barren range of wild sage hill and plains and deep washd. gutters with little alteration Except now and then a grove of shrubby cedars untill late in the afternoon when we struck the wagon trail leading from Bridgers Trading house to Bear River Turned on our course from N. E. to S. E. and took the road Toward Bridger near sun set we came to a small Stream of muddy water and Encamped [at Carter, Wyoming].

7 Packed up before sun rise and Took the road and at 10 A. M arived at the old deserted Trading house Judge of our chagrin and disapointment on finding this spot so long and so anxiously saught for standing solitary and alone without the appearance of a human being having visited it for at least a month and what the caus conjectur was rife but could [not] be certain except that Bridger and his whole company had taken the road N. W. Toward the Lower part of Bear River havin had no grass whare we encamped last nig[h]t and finding plenty here about we unsadled and concluded to remain here to day and consult what was next to be done.

In our weak and deffenceless state it was not easy to fix on any safe plan of procedure some proposed to return to Bear River and risk the hostililty of the snake Indians others proposed to take the trail Travel slowly and risk the Siouxs. which ware supposed to be on our rout to Fort Larrimie so that the day was taken up in discusing what would be the most safe way of disposing ourselves a sufficiant time to await the company from oregon to the states which was generally supposed would be Quite large this season the day was warm and the creek rose rapidly from the thawing of the snow on the Eutaw mountains and this is the season of high water in this region nothing can be more desolate and discouraging than a deserted fort whare you expect relief in a dangerous Indian country and every imaginary Idea was started as to what had been the caus of Bridgers leaving his establishment But nothing satisfactory could possibly be started and we ware still as far in the dark as ever.

8 After greate deliberation and all circunstances brought to bear on the subject it was agreed to part Mr Hastings his man and Indian servant wished to go some 50 or 60 miles N. stop and await the arival of the company from oregon 4 men of us one woman and one boy ware detirmined to go back to Bear River there being two trails from green river to bear rever it was uncertain which the oregon company might take if allready not passed so wa all started togather once more and after comeing to the seperating place we all continued on for the day and encamped in a small vally whare we encamped in Augt 2 yare ago.

And here it is remarkable that the small vally a few years since has been completely covered with Buffalo as their Bones which lay thickly strewed over the Earth plainly indicate and near the same time it has likewis been covered in natives as their camp fires show and for the last 2 years it has at times ben as completely covered with civilization.

9 Again under way and we soon assended the ridge (for in this country it cannot be caled a mountain) and changed our course from W. to N and desended to the Bear river vally this is one of the upper vallies on this stream and is Quite Large being from 30 to 40 miles Long and 6 to 8 miles wide Bounded Both E. and W. by a range of Bald mountains shewing in a peculiar manner their volcanic oragin by their standing in the form of wavse of the ocean at a late hour we came to camp near the N or lower extremity of this vally.

10 A shosne [Shoshone] Indian came to our camp this morning and informed us that no whites had yet arived or passed from the west.

But what was our disappointment on ariving on the Oregon trail to find that a large party of horses and mules had passed appearantly some 5 or 10 days previous so our hopes ware to all appearances Blasted for this season 2d & 6 June.

11 Packed up and concluded to move down Bear River to Bridgers camp and await a few days for more company after Traveling 4 or 5 miles down the wagon trail we met our old companions from california who had come by the way of Fort Hall and as we ware informed that all the company from Oregon had probably passed we turned our course to the East again so accordingly we all Joined once more and took the trail S. E. over high roling mountains diversified with handsome groves of aspen Poplar and Firr of that kind caled the white Balsam Firr we came to camp late at Hamms creek a Beautifull clear running stream about 30 yards wide and running S. E. into Blacks Fork of the Seetskadee or green River.

12 Took the Trail again over the same Kind of high roling country an a number of snow drifs ware seen lying along the hills mostly to our left and we passed as yestarday numerous groves of Aspin and saw a number of antelope coursing over the Hills several of which ware killed and found to Eat well after living so long on dry provision.

———

The Green River valley and LeBarge Creek

Nooned at a fine cool spring which breaks out in a grove of aspin [Traveled] Eastwardly along a verry winding crooked trail and over some rough hilly or rather mountainous country numerous groves of Aspin Firr and willow came in sight of the green River vally and capd. at a small spring this is the third day that thunder showers passed in all directions around us but verry little Has fallen on us.

13 East on the Trail But we soon passed our fine mountain district and desended into the vally of Le Bages. [LeBarge] creek on this stream I met with or rather suffered a Defeat from a war party of Arapahoes [Gros Ventres] in 1824 [1825] and the appearance of the stream brought back some serious reflections as we passed down its

Level vally crossed over the hills and soon came in sight of green River whare we stoped and found the stream 80 or 100 yards wide rapid and Quite too deep to ford The afternoon proved showery and we remained here with the unpleasant Idea of haveing the River to raft if we can find a suitable place.

14 Moved up the River a few miles and made preperations to raft the river and after making the best sort of a craf we could possibly [build] out of such metireal as could be had which was miserably poor we made two attempts to cross over but failed bothe times.

15 Commenced early and after greate labour oweing to the rapidity of the water we ware carried down abut a mile but finally succeeded in landing a small portion of our Baggage on the oposite shore and finding our raft two large we ware unable to take it back so we had to pack timber over a mile and make smaller rafts my mess haveing made a small one we commenced crossing and made land in about Half a mile and with grate exertion ware able to tow it up and recross and so we continued to do some 8 or 10 triips untill we all got safe over this cold rapid river of snow water and encamped on the oposite or East shore.

16 Left the Seetskadee early and mad a push of 30 or 35 miles and Encamped on Big sandy this is a flat Runing stream over a sand bottom and we found it Bank full from the thawing of the snow on the wind river mountain in which it rises but apearantly it had fallen a little.

These wind river mountains are nearly all covered yet in their white winters robes allthough the middle of June most of the snow however goes off by the middle of July.

This is a good vally for grass but scarce of timber their [being] little but willows.

17 Moved up Eastwardly toward the summit of the Rocky mountains the day was cool the country sage plain after crossing little sandy which is not more than 4 miles from our camp The mornings are cold and disagreeable so mouch so that I think we have not had more than 4 or 5 nights without frost since we left the great plains of California and the grass in some places is short.

Campd on a marshy spring [at or near Pacific Springs] plenty of sage but no timber in any reasonable distance I noticed in this neigh-bourhood that there had been a tremendeous hail storm a few days since which in places had beat all the vegetation completely into the Earth.

18   A beutifull clear morning and (and) several of our company commenced prophesying that we should se some persons to day but Quite uncertain wheter white or red in one hours ride we came to the summit [South Pass] of the main rocky mountains which is nearly a level plain with a slight inclination each way and we soon hailed the small river of sweet water and it gave Quite a cheering statisfactory Idea allthough at so greate a distance to think that I was once more on the waters of the Missisippi and its ripling waters sounded in Idea like sweet home.

As we continued down the ridges on the N. side we came in sight of several male Buffaloe feeding on the young tender herbage and our camp at a small grove of Apin was well supplied in Buffaloe meat.

19   The sun set unusually clear and Beautifull Last night behind the everlasting snow covered peaks of the wind River mountains and I had a fine view of this back bone of North America whose crags looked more like a ruined city than a mountain. While Far in the East some large herds of Buffalou ware grazing over their sage clad hills and several antelopes ware frisking and strangely gazing around our camp and animals The morning was cool but as soon as the sun arose it became warm and sultry.

Continued down on the N side of sweet water river saw plenty of Buffaloe in the afternoon made a long days drive and encamped on the open Prarie a short time after dark our animals took a fright and nearly all those that ware tied Broke and away they went with much the same rapidity and nearly the same nois as a great number of rocks would make rolling down a steep mountain you may Judge that some of us at least did not sleep sound under the supposition that a war party of Indians had run them away from us.

20   Early all the environs of our camp was examined but [no] sign of Indians could be found a few of us mounted some of our remaining horses and followed the trail about three miles whare to our greate Joy we found all our animals feeding Quietly.

Saddled and continued East down the stream about noon some of the advance found a horse that [had] been left no doubt by some of the Oregon [train] six or eight days ahead of us.

Saw a few Bufaloe on the hills some miles to the south the day was warm with a south wind.

21 Down the stream and at about one oclock came to the independence rock here our party small as it was split and about half of us concluded to remain over night the others went ahead late in the afternoon we had another stampide last night but our animals did not go far and so soon war collected again.

22 Made an Early start from this morning and here we leave sweet water and take across the hills in a few hours we came in sight of several herds of Buffalo which seemed to be travelling southward an indication observed by old mountaineers that their is some persons Red or White in the direction from which the buffalo come stopd. at the willow spring for some of our party to come in with meat.

23 Near sun set last night two French Trappers came to camp an informed us that the advance party of emigrants war over the North Branch of the Platte Early on our saddles and in about 3 hours we met the advance company of oregon Emigration consisting of Eleven wagons nearly oposite the red Butes when we came in sight of N. Platte we had the Pleasant sight of Beholding the valy to a greate distance dotted with Peopl Horses cattle wagons and Tents their being 30 wagons all Buisily engaged in crossing the River which was found not to be fordable and with the poor material they had to make rafts of it took two trips to carry over one waggon with its lading.

We however ware not long in crossing as we threw our baggage on the returning rafts and swam our animals over and encamped onc more in the Buisy humm of our own Language.

24 Down the N. Platte and during the day we passed three small companies some for Oregon and some for california.

It is remarkable how anxious thes people are to hear from the Pacific country and strange that so many of all kinds and classes of

People should sell out comfortable homes in Missouri and Elsewhare pack up and start across such an emmence Barren waste to settle in some new Place of which they have at most so uncertain information but this is the character of my countrymen.

25 Continued down the River a few miles and Turned south through the Hills on account of the Rocky Kenyons that bind the stream on its passage through the Black hills mountains.

To day we met all most one continual stream of Emigrants wending their long and Tedious march to oregon & california and I found it allmost impossible to pass these honest looking open harted people without giving them some slight discription of what they might Expect in their newly adopted and anxious sought for new home but necessity only could compel us onward.

At our usual hour of camping we came to a small Brook whare a company of them ware Just coming up to camp Likewise and they came to us with Pail fulls of good new milk which to us was a treat of greate rarity after so many long tiresome days travel.

26 South across the hills and to day as yestarday we passed several small Brooks and met 117 teams in six different squads all bound for oregon and california in the evening we again had the pleasur of encamping with a company for california an they kept us in conversation untill near midnight.

27 We met numerous squad of emigrants untill we reached fort Larrimie whare we met Ex govornor [Lilburn W.] Boggs and party from Jackson county Mi[ss]ourie Bound for California and we camped with them several of us continued the conversation untill a late hour.

And here I again obtained a cup of excellent coffee at Judge Morins camp the first I had tasted since in the early part of last winter and I fear that during our long conversation I changed the purposes of Govornor and the Judge for next morning they both told me they inte[n]ded to go to Oregon.

28 Late in the morning we got on the road again and met another party of emigrants cnsisting of 24 Wagons and they told us that so far as they knew they ware the last on the road about noon we passed Bissinetts. Trading house and a few miles further on we met Bissinette himself returning from Missouri with a small supply of goods for the trade and from him we ware informed that thier ware 40 Teams yet on the road and that the Pawnees had killed one man [Trimble] We had previously heard that they had stolen a number of horses and one company had lost 120 head of cattle either Strayed or Stolen.

29 Parted with some of my old acquaintances who ware on thier way (to) some for Oregon and some for california the Ex govornor Boggs and Judge Morin changed their notion to go to Oregon in place of california Passed a small trading house [Capt. Finch's trading post] on the River a few miles Below the old Larrimee establishment and one more company of emigrants most of the Emigrants we have met seemed to be in good health and fine spirits But some are much discouraged and a few have turned back about noon we passed the sumit of Scotts Bluffs and took a drink of good cool spring water in the evening we met a nother party of waggon and with a larger company at night which ware supposed to be the last we should meet on the way.

These last companies have had greate difficulties in passing the Pawnee country and have lost a greate many cattle and some of their horses and one man was killed (was killed) in trying to recover their lost cattle so that we have no favourable reports of our prosspects ahead and it will require all our ingenuity and vigilence for sometine to come for us to travel in any kind of safety.

30 Passed the chimney rock and at noon overtook a party of 12 or 15 men some from oregon and a few that had turned back to Missouri at Larimie in the evening we encamped on the River within about one mile of those a head of us.

July the 1th 1846

A heavy dew last night and a clear cool morning in the afternoon met Mr J. M. Wair [Weir] with a small party of six wagons Mr Wair risidid in Oregon some yares and had went to the states last summer and was now on his return to Oregon again.

This evening shews fair for rain.

2 Rapid Thunder & Lightning last night with a light shower of rain this morning is extremely warm we traveled S of East down the

River untill about noon when we arived at the ash Hallow whare we found a company of Mormon Emigrants Encamped consisting of nineteen wagons these people are on their way to Oregon and informed us that the Pawnees had followed them and stole three horses last night They keeping a strick guard and the animals haveing been Tied to their wagons.

This encampment has the advantage of plenty of fuell and clear spring water and most travelers stop here one day at least there being no timbber East nor West for some distance.

3 South across the ridge deviding the N. and S Branches of the greate Platte River about 20 miles the day was verry warm and the road dusty you think we ware verry thirsty and so we ware But had to Quench our Burning [thirst] with warm water fully half mud for this is the character of all the Platte waters of any size half mud and sand running over a wide shallow bed exposed to the Burning rays of a verticle sun But this is the best that can be had in crossing over this south branch one man and one woman got plunged from their Horses and well drenched in the turbid stream.

4 The sun arose in his usual majestic splendor no firing of canon was heard no flags waving to the early morning Breeze. Nothing no nothing heard but the occasional howl of the wolf or the hoarse croak of the raven nothing seen But the green wide spread Prarie and the shallow wide spread river roling its turbed muddy waters far to the East the only relief is the on rising ground occasionally doted with a few stragling male Buffaloe and one Lonely Junt of a cotton wood Tree some miles down the stream the only occupant of a small low Island (not much veriety) O my country and my Country men the rich smiling surface of on[e] and the gladsome Shouts of the other Here we are 8 men 2 women and one boy this day entering into an enimies country who if posible will Butcher every individual or at least strip us of every means of comfort or convenience and leave us to make our tiresome (som) way to relief and this immediatly on your frontier and under the eye of a strong Militay post The day proved verry still and warm and we overtook a small prarty of Emigrants that ware ahead consisting of seven men 2 young Ladies and one verry sick man some of thier company haveing left them an hour before our arival on account of their slow traveling The eight men that had parted from these in their defenceless state intended to make a rapid Push and travel day and night untill they passed the Pawnee Teritory.

5 The morning verry warm with a dew like rain The sick man seems to grow worse and has a high fever saw greate herds of Buffalo on Both sides of the river We nearly reached the Forks of Platte and late in the evening we had a short rapid showers of rain and in the night our animals took a Fright at an old Buffaloe that approached our camp and we had some difficulty in Keeping our Horses from breaking from the stake.

6 Clear and verry warm Passed the Juction of the N & South Branches of the Platte and came to the Bluffs which are steep and rough with numerous small groves of rid cedar Nooned at ash run the first shade we have found for 10 or 12 days Continued down the River the hills and vallies on this stream are generally well covered in several kinds of grass and some portions of the vally would no doubt bear good grain of several kinds.

7 This morning we had a remarkable heavy dew. the day was warm an Sultry and our animals sweated profusely as well as ourselves saw several Large Herds of Buffalo on the oposite side of the River Probaby the last that will be seen on our direction.

8 A warm night and thee muskeetoes war troublesome all night this fore noon we passed Plumb Creek and nooned a short distance above the head of Grand Isleand we have had a beautifull road for some days being a livel dry Prarie Bottom from 2 to 4 miles wide the Islands and some of the main of the river is generally skirted with willow and small shrubby cottonwood

9 Another warm night with a south wind we are now near the Pawne village and anxiety to pass without interuption at its highest pitch some light showers of rain fell during the day and several horses are failing and will soon have to be left.

Left the Platte in the afternoon and crossed over the ridge and campd. on the waters of Kaw river.

10 A cloudy night without rain a Mr McKizack was left Behind last night being himself nearly Blinde and his horses verry poor his messmate Mr. Stump went back this morning to assist him to come up saw a horse yestarday that had been shot lying by the way side.

Mr stump returned about noon and could find nothing of Mr McKissick we moved on in the afternoon to the west fork of Blue river and encamped early for the purpose of making a more thorough search for the lost man But in a few minuits after stoping the old man hove in sight to the mutual satisfaction of all parties. several thunder showers passed around during the afternoon and a short rapid one but of short duration did not miss us about sun set The west Fork is small here but nearly clear and cool compared with the waters of the Platte the vallies are moderately large and the soil rich but no timber Except cottonwood and willow with here and there a chance Plumb bush now full of green fruit.

11 Down the stream some ash and oak occurred this fore noon with some Elk Likewise The day was cool and Pleasant and the vally fine and green the soil in many places rich.

12 A rremendious heavy dew fell last night and the day proved warm and Sultry heard several familiar noisis such as the whistleing of Quails and the croakings of the Bull frog those sounds are not heard in the far west in the afternoon we left the West Branch of Blue River and crossed the Prarie ridges to the N. E. and encamped on a broad sandy Brook now nearly dry.

13 Continued across the ridges and nooned late at Fosale [Fossil] Brook which detained us 2 days in Passing out [in 1844] now nearly dry some Black walnut and Honey Locust occur here for the first seen S. E. over high rich roling Prarie but without much useful timber and poorly supplied with spring water.

14 Over the same kind of country as yestarday in the fore noon passed rock creek scarcely affording sufficient wate[r] to run from Pool to Pool a rapid shower of rain fell in evening.

15 Continued in the afternoon we crossed greate Blue river and campd. on the East Bank.

This stream affords some fine rich vallies of cultivateable land and the Bluffs are made of a fine lime rock with some good timber and numerous springs of clear cool water here I observed the grave of Mrs Sarak Keys ageaed 70 yares who had departed this life in may [29th] last at her feet stands the stone that gives us this information This stone shews us that all ages and all sects are found to undertake this long tedious and even dangerous Journy for some unknown object never to be realized even by those the most fortunate and why because the human mind can never be satisfied never at rest allways on the strech for something new some strange novelty.

On our Return from California a Mr [Caleb] Greenwood and his two sons made a part of our company this man the Elder is now from his best recolection 80 years of age and has made the trip 4 times in 2 yares in part.

16 Left Blue River and soon passed the Burr oak creek a narrow Rippling stream at this time with wide Extensive Bottoms which in times of greate freshets are completely overflown the land rich and surface roling sub strata white lime Stone of a fine shining appearance.

17 East of South over a roling gravelly Prarie in many Places uneven nooned at cannon Ball Creek which now has but little running water on the ripples.

The afternoon passed over Beautifull rich Prarie but no valuable Timber.

18 In the fore noon crossed the Black vermillion to day the Trail runs nearly East nooned at a small Brook which has a fine small vally of good Burr oak Timber and fine Prarie in the Neighbourhood the water Poor in the afternoon we passed over roling hilly Prarie Country.

19 Started from the stake and came to Knife creek for Breakfast found the muketoes verry troublesome and a goodly number Horse flies met a small party of men going to Fort Larrimie who gave us a more full account of the stat of afairs Between the U. S. and Mexico and further told us that Two Thousand mounted Troops had lately left Misouri for St Afee and that one Thousand more [the Mormon Battalion and Sterling Price's troops] are now Leaveing Early in the afternoon arived at Kaw River and got our Baggage taken over in a canoe and Swam our animals across.

20 Took the Trail down Kaw River passing immediately through a small settlement of Saukie Indians Their small farms had a Thrifty appearance and the corn and vegitables looked well and more like civilization than any thing I had seen lately The flies nearly Eat our horses up campd. on the Waukarusha.

21 Early on our saddles with the intention to cheat the flies But they ware up and out as soon as us in about six miles however we came to a thick settlement of Shawnees and the flies which had anoyed us so much now became Quite Scarce and had it not been for the heat of the weather and the bad Quality of the water traveling would have been comfortable we encamped in the best cultivated part of the Shawnee country this tribe are far advanced in civilization and make their intire subsistance by agraculture and some are begining to learn the more rougher kinds of Mechanism such as hewing of timber making of Shingles and building of common wooden houses Their farms are mostly on the Prarie lands and their crops of grain look tolerable well the corn in Particular.

22 It Thundred and Lightned all night but did not rain in the forenoon we passed through west Porte a small ordinary village one half mile within the state of Missourie and some time before night reached Indipendence the Seat of Justice for Jackson county.

23 It rained the most part of the night last night but the morning was fair and we found ourselves surrounded by civilization and had to answer numerous [questions] about the country we had visited and many more conserning acquaintances that ware in Oregon and California disposed of my mules and mad my appearance at Mr Nolands Tavern and a Rough appearance it was But such things are not atall strange in Independance as it [is] the first place all the Parties r[e]ach from the Mountains from St A Fee California and Oregon.

The [weather] was verry warm and suffocating and in this particular you find a greate difference in the heat of summer in California you find it cool and pleasant in the shade while here you find [it] hot and suffocating in [the] coolest place you can find.

24 A Remarkable warm day But I must say I injoyed the time well in reading the papers that came by last nights mail and in the varied conversation I had with several gentlemen during the day.

On the first day of May

We succeeded in crossing the main summit of the california mountains or the Siera Nevada the snow being from 3 to 8 feet deep on the western slope but on turning down the Eastern side it was perhaps from 8 to 20 or even 30 feet deep owing to the wind being allways from the South West when the snow is falling and carrying larg Quanti[t]ies from the western side which is deposited on the East side near the summit this mountain is generally thickly covered with a large groth of pine firr and other ever green Timber The rock near the summit is a light grey granite lying in large compact masses with a steep irregular rounded surface and none of the usual indication of recent Earth Quakes concrections or volcanic contortions But on desending some 16 or 18 miles thro a rough uneven vally you again arive at the Baysalt region and the stream has broke its way through several hunded feet in depth of Black frowning rock that one would think had onec ben liquidated by intense heat the large timber disappears and the hills are covered with Artimisia or as it is best known by the name of wild sage.

Notes on Chapter Seventeen

On June 1, Clyman refers to his circumnavigation of Great Salt Lake in the spring of 1826, though Clyman says he did it in a "bull boate" and Camp says canoes were used.

Clyman was in Lost Creek Canyon on June 4, where the Donner party later had so much trouble that it made only 40 miles in 30 days.

Camp has retraced Clyman's route in detail in his edition of Clyman's journals. By the time Clyman's group met the "old companions from California" who joined them June 11, the party was dangerously small. Probably Clyman was accompanied only by three other men, one woman and a boy—small numbers for traveling through the West even at this time. The "old companions" were the remainder of the original 19 men and boys and possibly two women and two children, who had taken a different route part of the way. The identities of some in Clyman's party are not known.

In his entry for June 27, Clyman mentions meeting "numerous squads" of emigrants, but reports no conversations with them. Some of the emigrants, in their journals, were discouraged and angry at the stories the people of Clyman's party told them of California. After all, they'd left their homes to emigrate to the newest "land of promise" in American history; they were hardly anxious to hear depressing—or realistic—stories that didn't match their glowing expectations.

Clyman apparently met two important personages at this time, neither of whom rated a very lengthy account in his journals. One was Francis Parkman, who records in his "Journal" various meetings with returning emigrants; but Parkman was more interested in the Indians, and didn't realize he was bypassing one of the explorers of the region that so fascinated him.

As Bernard DeVoto puts it, "Francis Parkman had met a genius of the mountains, perhaps had talked with him, had seen a greatness he was not able to recognize...that was Jim Clyman's party."

Clyman also mentions camping at this time with the Boggs party, and a conversation that continued until "a late hour." Boggs' party included the Donners. Clyman had served in Jacob Early's company in the Black Hawk war with James Frazier Reed, one of the leaders of the Donner subdivision, and later spoke to Montgomery of having a lengthy conversation with him about the route the party was to take.

"I told him," Clyman later said, "to take the regular wagon track [by way of Fort Hall] and never leave it—it is barely possible to get through if you follow it—and it may be impossible if you don't." Reed replied, "there is a nigher route [the Hastings Cutoff], and it is of no use to take so much of a roundabout course."

"I admitted the fact," said Clyman, "but told him about the great desert and the roughness of the Sierras, and that a straight route might turn out to be impracticable."

The Donner party ignored Clyman's advice, took the straighter route and failed to get across the Sierras before the October snows blocked them, with tragic results. Caught in the steep and rocky canyons Clyman describes in his journals, the Donner party fragmented as travelers in some wagons became sick from the hardships of travel and insufficient food. When the early snows caught them, some members of the party built shelters in which they hoped to wait out the winter, while others had no choice but to stay with their wagons further east. As food supplies dwindled, several parties left the encampment and tried to struggle through the snow to the California settlements. By the time some made it through and headed back with food, the survivors in the camps had been reduced to devouring the bodies of members of the group who had already died. (Some were later charged with hastening deaths to provide food.) The area where the party camped has become known as Donner Pass.

Ironically, the Donner party had met with a man eminently suited to give them not only good general advice, but very specific advice about that trail, since he'd just crossed the area they were about to enter.

DeVoto summarizes this encounter well: "But American history in the person of Jim Clyman had told the Donner party not to take the Hastings cutoff from the California trail."

Chapter 18
Overland to California, 1848

Any traveler who returned from California to St. Louis at this turbulent period, with the question of Mexico's claims to California a major issue, was closely questioned. Clyman was no exception. When he returned east in 1846, he encountered a reporter for the *Missouri Republican* who borrowed his diaries long enough to copy sections of interest to readers. News traveled slowly, and was often at least half rumor, with reporters questioning returning travelers like Clyman and receiving a welter of confusing ideas and opinions. Using Clyman's journals, the paper reported the confusion surrounding Lt. Fremont's act in raising the American flag in his own camp. This was interpreted as an act of war, since the Mexicans rightly believed Americans were planning to conquer the territory for themselves, and resulted in Gen. Vallejo's calling upon Mexican citizens to defend their rights. Fremont left the area with some haste, and the war with Mexico was delayed a bit longer.

A gentleman who has passed the two last years in Oregon and California reached this city yesterday. His name is James Clymer, and [he] migrated from Milwaukie, with a view of determining for himself the character of that country. He left California, in company with six other persons, the latter end of April, and has been ninety days on the route.

Mr. Clymer has kindly permitted us to glance at his diary—we could do no more—kept for the whole time of his absence, and to select such facts as may interest our readers. We have, of necessity, to take such incidents as occurred during his return home, passing over many descriptions of country, soil, places, mountains, people and government, in Oregon and California.

On the 16th of March last, Mr. Clymer refers, in his journal, to the extraordinary avidity with which news is manufactured in that country; and says, that Lieut. Fremont had raised the American flag in Monterrey—of course the town of that name on the Pacific—that all good citizens were called upon to appear forthwith, at Sonoma, armed and equipped for service under Gen. Byajo, to defend the rights of Mexican citizens. This report subsequently appeared, was founded on the fact, that Lieut. Fremont had raised the American [flag] at his camp, near the Mission of St. John's and that he declined to call on some of the legal authorities, when ordered to do so. It was said, that in consequence of this state of things, General Castro had raised four hundred men at Monterrey; that he marched to Lieut Fremont's camp on the 22nd of March, from which he had retreated; and that he there found numerous packsaddles, baggage, and a considerable quantity of specie. Lieut. Fremont was last heard of, after Mr. Clymer had left, on the Rio Sacramento; but as he kept his own counsel, no one knew his object in going there, or when he would return to the United States. He had lost one man, who was killed by the Indians, and had discharged others.

Mr. Clymer met, at different times and under different circumstances, parties of Emigrants to Oregon or California, who were roving about discontented, and going back and forth, as whim dictated. On the 22nd of March, he notices having met, in California, a party of one hundred and fifty persons, thirty or forty of whom were then going to the Columbia river, having become tired of *the other paradise.* On the 20th of April, Mr. Sumner and his family arrived at camp, prepared for their journey to the States. Mr. Sumner had been in Oregon; from thence he went to California; and, being still dissatisfied, he was now returning, after having spent five years in traveling and likewise a small fortune.

He met [!], and left Mr. L. P. [L. W.] Hastings, the author of a work on California, at his camp on Bear Creek, a small creek running into Feather River. He was located near the road travelled by the emigrants to California. Mr. Hastings had been looking for some force from the States, with which it was designed to revolutionize California, but in this he had been disappointed. He was then, it seemed, awaiting the action of the American Government, in taking possession of that country—of which he appeared to have some intimation. Mr. Clymer heard, on his return homeward, of the arrival of the several United States vessels of war at Monterrey, but knows nothing more about them....

Ruxton, in writing about his experiences in 1846 near the Colorado-New Mexico border—then part of the territory disputed by the United States and Mexico—reported that he was obliged to watch his animals day and night to prevent them being stolen. Though Ruxton was an Englishman, he was looked upon with suspicion by Mexican settlers of the region because of the ongoing dispute with America.

For the next year and a half Clyman visited friends in Wisconsin and spent the winter with John Bowen, his old Rocky Mountain friend who had dressed his leg after the embarrassing shotgun wound. Some of his friends said long afterward that he tried to interest them in buying land in California. There's no real evidence, but it's a likely explanation for his quick trip east so soon after arriving in California. Or perhaps he was simply making up his mind about the decision to emigrate, and settling his business in the east.

In 1848 Clyman was hired as guide to a company of emigrants, one of the few that crossed to California that year. The great rush of the preceding years had been slowed considerably by problems with Mexico, treaty delays, and the fate of the Donner party. Little is recorded of the immigration of 1848.

Apparently the train Clyman guided belonged primarily to one family, the McCombs of Indiana, well-traveled settlers who had previously pioneered in Ohio and Michigan. The parents were Lambert and Hannah, and the children traveling west, mostly grown and married, included Benjamin Franklin, Jacob Riley, Joseph D., Isaac, Aramintha, Martha, Hannah and Rebecca.

Hannah later became James Clyman's wife. Camp calls her "a forceful and determined woman"; she must have been, to persuade this steadfast bachelor to marry. Camp says she remained physically spry and mentally alert until her death in 1908; by that time Clyman had been dead for 27 years, almost as long as they'd been married.

Clyman kept no diary of this trip, and there are various disputes over the route taken and how quickly the group traveled it, all of which Camp covers in detail. A letter written by Clyman after his arrival in Napa Valley gives some information.

Clyman's Letter to Ross:

Napa Valley, Alta California,
Dec. 25th, 1848.

 Friend Ross: The uncertainty of letters reaching you makes it necessary that I state to you again that we left the west of Missouri on the 1st of May and arrived here on the 5th of September without accident or interruption of any kind worthy of notice. Matters and things here are strangely and curiously altered since I left this country. No business of any kind is carried on except what is in some way connected with the gold mines. You have no doubt seen and heard several descriptions of those mines and supposed them all fabulous, but I am persuaded that nothing has yet reached you that would give you any adequate idea of the extent and immense richness of the mining region. Gold is now found in length from North to South, over a distance of between 400 and 500 miles, and in width from 40 to 60 miles, and nearly every ravine will turn out its thousands. There are at this time not less than 2000 white men and more than double that number of Indians washing gold at the rate of some two ounces per day, making over $300,000 per day, and this great quantity and the ease with which it is produced has caused a tremendous rise in provi-

*sions and all kinds of manufactured goods. Flour in the mines sells at
$1 per lb—dried beef and bacon $2 per lb., &c. I forbear to mention
anything more, for all articles bear the same proportions, as gold is
the most plenty and of course the least valuable.*

*All the inhabitants of this immediate country left their farms to
hunt and wash gold. All of the summer crop and considerable of the
wheat was destroyed by the stock. Oregon has sent us some flour, and
more than half of her male population, all of the foreigners and a
portion of the Natives have arrived from the Sandwich Islands, and
we may expect a large emigration from the States next season. Tell all
of the lovers of gold and sunshine that this is the place to suit them.
But very little else is to be seen or had here. We had a shower of rain
last week for the first time since May, and the grass is beginning is [to]
shoot a little. I shall return to the States again in about one year from
this time. Give my respects to all enquiring friends.*

JAMES CLAYMAN [Clyman]

*P.S. Enclosed you will find a small specimen of gold. It is found in all
shapes and sizes up to twenty pounds weight.*

The letter, though written late in 1848, was postmarked San Francisco March 16, 1849; it took a while to find someone going east to
transport mail in those days.

In 1960, when Camp talked to them, Clyman's descendants still
had some egg-sized gold nuggets he found apparently at this time, but
the party didn't remain near the gold fields long. He and the McCombs
went on to Napa.

The McCombs finally settled on land now within the city. Clyman
lived with them, assisting in the work of laying out the place, and
courting Hannah. Their marriage was the first one in the town, cele-
brated August 22,1849. The groom was 57, the bride 30 years younger.
It is reported that the couple bought all the table crockery to be had in
Napa and San Francisco; also that they spent the winter with the
bride's family and helped put in the next year's crops.

It would be fascinating to have a diary from this period. Clyman had apparently lived and worked alone most of his life. Once he had established his brothers on farms in Illinois, he went on to scout more land, and pursue his own interests, and never mentions his family in his journals. Suddenly he not only guided the McCombs across the plains, but remained with them—farming! His distaste for farming was so intense, even when he was fifteen years old, that he seemed willing to do almost anything—cut wood, harvest, help a surveyor—to avoid it. Either he'd gone through a major change in viewpoint, or his young wife had changed his mind for him.

Once he had married Hannah, he seems truly to have become as "settled down" as any civilized citizen might have wished, and he wasn't alone among the original beaver men in settling on the coast. George Yount, the first white man in the region, had been an old hunter and trapper, as had Peg-Leg Smith, Charlie Hopper, Joel and Joseph R. Walker, Moses Carson, Uncle Billy Gordon, John Wolfskill and Elisha Stephens. Further south, at the Pueblo of Los Angeles, were others, including Nathaniel Pryor and Richard Laughlin, Job Dye and George Nidever. In Oregon were Robert "Doc" Newell, George W. "Squire" Ebberts, Joe Meek and Osborne Russell, who died in the California gold mines.

On March 5, 1850, Clyman bought from William Edgington part of what became his farm at Napa, land which had previously belonged to Salvador Vallejo. Soon afterward the family moved into Sonoma County, between Forestsville and Sebastopol, then back again to Napa. On February 10,1855, Clyman completed the purchase of his ranch by buying part of a tract that belonged to his mother-in-law.

The civilized life soon brought Clyman five children, but it wasn't to last. Before long, four of his children were dead of scarlet fever. Only one daughter survived.

Clyman was seventy-four by that time, but hardly ready for retirement. He kept busy running a fruit and dairy ranch, planting and pruning trees, plowing and harvesting—all the work he'd hated as a youth. He even developed the "Clyman plum," a variety once popular. Mrs. Clyman and their one remaining daughter, Lydia Alcinda, milked the cows; Hannah Clyman always maintained that a man would ruin a good milk cow.

They adopted three foster daughters—Alice Broadhurst, who was Mrs. Clyman's niece, Geneva Gillin, and Edna Wallingford.

During his eightieth year, Clyman wrote his final diary, showing him still living an active life. It contains a short verse in his typical style.

Chapter 19
Final Days—Diary of 1871

And now the mists arise
With slow and graceful motion
And shews like pillow in the skies
Or island in the ocean

Jan. 28, 1871 to Dec. 10, 1871

[Jan] 28, [1871]

A Rainy morning Took my Sheep to pasture....
February the 1 My birthday being the first day of 80 Eightyethe year....
Frosty mornings commenced pruning in the Orchard....
Frost clear and warm afternoon Pruning in the orchard....

[March] 3

Pleasant and warm good growing weather Planted potates Peas & onions beets....
Commenced Breaking fallows yestarday....

Finished pruning....
Finished my fence around the garden

[April] 9

Mr Montgomory [R. T. Montgomery, editor of the *Napa
Reporter]* called on me for information on the early character of
California gave him my Diary of my first trip across the
plains....
Trimed and marked my lambs....
Finished planting corn & potatoes....
Rode out on the mountain....
Commenced sharing sheep
Went to the Odd fellows Picknick Mr Sargent delivered the
adress which was done in oratorical style....

[May]

Finished the cultivation of the home orchard....
Hawled a load of rock for the foundation of Barn....
Comenced framing Barn....
Finished the frame of Barn....

[June]

Went to the picknick at the Boggs ranch heard Mr Ford the
country School Supt make an excellent speech....
Filled all my barn with hay three tuns left....
Brought my sheep down to the home place
Clear sold all our Black Tartaria[n cherries]
Gathered Black Beries....
Took a severe Cold Laid abed half the day....
Still feel seak of a cold....
Hauled one load of wood....

1st July

Warm some wheet being harvested Wind South...Finished
hailing wood due Mr Truebody $3.00....
The 95 Jubille of our countrys Independance as nation Went to
Napa heard the declaration of Indepenance read....
Gathering early apples....
Lent Mrs McCombs $20.00/

[Aug.] 16

The camp Meeting still in Session

[Dec] 10

Sowed our Barley last week....

Though Clyman took little part in public affairs as he grew older, he
didn't spend all his time farming. Early settlers remembered him as a
bent figure taking his rifle to the mountains hunting deer or bear. He
walked with a limp from old wounds, and an accident had cost him the
sight in one eye.

He often sat in the sun and wrote out upon a slate the last part of
his book of reminiscences, resisting to the end whatever temptation he
might have had to include the kind of tall tales and adventures beloved
of mountain men like Joe Meek. He sent his story to Lyman C. Draper,
who published the first part in the *Napa Reporter* in 1871. Later, his
daughter Lydia took up the task of copying what Clyman had written
on his slate, and sending it on to Draper.

In the last ten years of his life Clyman wrote poetry in the style of
the age, dealing with philosophical matters and topics of the time, not
with his past as a mountain man. The poems are interesting as an illus-
tration of Clyman's level of education, and the refinement of his mind,

despite the rough times his body had survived. Mountain men are sometimes pictured as crude ruffians, but perhaps Clyman demonstrates how varied they were. Some of his verses dwelled on the pleasures of home, as the following example shows.

OUR HOME

The winds were in their chamber sleeping
The light from Orient portals peeping
The stars the lesser ones are dimed or gone
The larger ones more brigtly shown
And silver beams of earley daylight
Was breaking through the gloom of night
The little birds in twittering note
Upon the ambient air did float
Again more fervent light behold
The mountain tops in glittering gold
The grass the grain in meadow seen
A gorgeous sight all clothed in green
The dewdrips make a beautious show
In bright translucent globes they glow
All nature now seems to combine
To over flow with bread and wine
And fruit of evrey name and nature
Promise rich returns in the future
The peach the cherry and the pair
In fragrant blooming now appear
And give sweet scent to passing air
The bees then come a perfect swarm
At noon or when the sun shines warm
And sip the necter from the bloom
To fill thier sweetend honey comb
And now we hear the breakfast call
To young to old to friend and all
Now at the table take your seat

A cup of coffee strong and sweet
but first you hear a fervent blessing
To all omnicient power adressing
The mighty source of light
To guide our words and actions right
Through out the day now fast advancing
The glorious sun on nature glancing
Now while hot roles surround your plate
Dont envy either wealth or state
The hour of eight the clock has told
A grumbling first then more Bold
Along the Iron plated way
That runs direct from Napa bay
And if you notice as they pass
A belching forth of steam and gass
They come with raped whirling wheels
The earth blow both quakes and reals
The elements above are riven
By smoke and gas are upward drivn
A heave a blch of scalding gass
Then let the metal monster pass
The hills along the east are seen
Some dark with brush some clothed in green
The sun still shining bold and bright
And not a cloud obscures the sight
The Lilac now in purple bloon
A handsome sight a rich perfume
The Canary in his iron cage
Still chants his love and sings his rage
No answering note no warbling fair
Can touch his melancholy ear,
O give me freedom or a mate
To save me from a lonsome fate.
The sun now strikes meriden line
The laboring men come in to dine

Assembled round the family board
A female blessing now is heard
And then the master carves and sends
The vians round from side to end
Around the yard a playfull noise
This is the prattle of the boys
As up and down the walks they run
With bursting froliich noisy fun
Thier work is play thier play is work
And all is noise from day to day
And infancy is likewise here
A female babe demans our care
Who just begins to crow and smile
And know her mothers voice the while
She fills a space not very small
But she is dear to nurse and all
Our Cottage too is draped anew
And shows in front a handsome vew
As white as bride trips from her room
Steps out to meet her galant groom
The plow for summer crop now turning
The moistned soil in early morning
And soon comes on the planting time
For summer crops of evry kind
As to west the sun inclines
In fervant brightness still it shines
All nature seems to catch the strea[m]
And kiss and drink the glancing beam
And then a slightly southern breese
Comes chanting through the orchard trees
And bends and turns the growing grain
Like tides upon the flowing main
Still lower west the light doth glow
And lengthning shawos [shadows]eastward
Now all the sky in brightest gold

Most beautiful the light unfold
The eastern hills to catch the light
reflected from etherial hight
You see the moons bright cresent form
And silver tips her either horn
The stars now all are brightly shining
And with the moon thier light combining
The galaxy or milky way
Across the zenith makes display
With stars thick studed shining bright
A coronet on brow of night
Is this the hour when lovers meet
Salute each to each in accents sweet
And walk the flowery avanewes
and speak and tell the daily new[s]
Perhaps to taake a walk for life
United in one as man and wife
And call the spangled stars above
As witnesses of mutual love
This natal day now is past
We hope it will not be the last

But even in the midst of such homey reflections, his wit remained sharp and his political sense acute, as in this verse:

The sparrows in convention join
And hold a noisy chirping chime
Like noisy politicians scold
And contradict in axcents bold.

On some topics, Clyman waxed particularly eloquent; the thought of food, for example, made him wax poetic:

Ritch milk rich cream the farmer boast
With butter cakes and swiming toast

And ham and eggs likwise is found
A breackfast rich the table crowns
When at the breackfast take your seat
A cup of coffee is always sweet
And if short biscake grace your plate
You envy not the rich or great
To speak of all you see and find
Cant change the farm for silver mine.

Perhaps it was the good food that changed his mind about farming. He must have sat writing this verse on his slate, thinking of the starving times in the mountains, where ham, eggs, and cream would have been merely dreams. Clyman's journal of June 27, 1846 mentions tasting coffee for the first time in a year, and that was when he was with the emigrants. In the mountains, coffee was mostly a memory.

Clyman had achieved some fame for his exploits, and a number of visitors came to the farm to visit him. They included some small relatives, Mr. and Mrs. Tom Thumb, the midgets.

His daughter, now married to the Rev. Beverly Lamar Tallman, gradually took over management of the farm, and with seven children and elderly parents to look after she simply didn't have time to copy her father's life story at his dictation. She explained rather querulously to Draper. "I can not take time to give fathers life in detail for he has had a long and eventful one. I have a family of seven to look after; three small children doing my own work. We live on a farm and I find my time all occupied. I send a short sketch which is all I promised." If she'd had fewer children, we might have a tale to eclipse that of any other mountain man

On December 27, 1881, Clyman died; he was eighty-nine years old. Burial was at the Tulocay Cemetery in Napa. He had lived through— and helped create—one of the most exciting periods in our nation's history. He was one of the last of the mountain men, and he had completely outlived the times in which he was born and raised. Trails that he followed on foot, starving or gnawing on the remains of a pack horse, knee-deep in snow, held highways and steel rails at the time of his death. Cities had grown up where he and his fur trapping comrades told stories and ate fat buffalo cow. The beaver and buffalo around which so much of his existence was built had become curiosities, preserved in museums and zoos, almost gone from the cold mountain streams and broad prairies. James Clyman lived a life none of us will ever know, but he gave us some of it—bare and without elaboration, but irreducibly authentic—in his journals. Perhaps he was thinking of his own epitaph when he wrote this poem, possibly his last.

DECORATION DAY 1881

Strew flowers oer the heroes head
Who for your country fought & Bled
He fought for eaqul rights for all
Let raining flowers or him fall
He died your countrys life to save
Strew flowers oer the heroes grave

A Look At:
Epic Adventures: Volume One

AN EPIC WESTERN ADVENTURE FULL OF UNFORGETTABLE CHARACTERS AND DEEPLY SPIRITUAL STORIES.

Nominee for the Pulitzer Prize and winner of the Spur Award, *Stone Song* follows the infamous Lakota Sioux mystic warrior, Crazy Horse. Ridiculed as a child for his white man looks, Crazy Horse seeks and receives a powerful vision that guides his destiny. Committed to fighting for his people, he rejects traditional Lakota rewards and personal dreams to fulfill his vision as a mystic warrior. But haunted by his love for a woman and finding peace only in battle, can Crazy Horse harness the eternal wisdom of his people to outmaneuver the U.S. Army at the historic Battle of the Little Bighorn?

RavenShadow follows the journey of Joseph Blue Crow, an American Indian grappling with lost faith and seeking redemption. Chosen before birth to uphold the sacred Sioux traditions, Blue strays onto the white man's path of basketball, alcohol, and despair. Devastated by the loss of his heritage and the suicide of his beloved, Blue's life spirals downward until he faces a life-or-death moment. Heeding his best friend's advice, Blue embarks on a transformative journey. Guided by a shaman and a spirit bird, he confronts the painful history of Wounded Knee, standing with his ancestors as they fall under attack.

Experience the profound journeys of two men whose lives are marked by visions, battles, and the enduring wisdom of their people.

Epic Adventures: Volume One includes *Stone Song* and *RavenShadow*.

AVAILABLE JANUARY 2025

About the Author

Win Blevins was an award-winning author best known for his fiction and non-fiction books of Western lore and Native American leaders, lifestyle, and spirituality. He was the recipient of a lifetime achievement award from the Western Writers of America, and a member of the Western Writers Hall of Fame; a three-time winner of Wordcraft Circle Native Writers and Storytellers Book of the Year; two-time winner of a Spur Award for Best Novel of the West; and was nominated for a Pulitzer for his novel about Crazy Horse, *Stone Song*.

Blevins, whose own origins were a mix of Cherokee, Welsh-Irish, and African American, published his first novel in 1973. That book, *Give Your Heart to the Hawks, a Tribute to the Mountain Man*, is still in print fifty years later and recently returned to the *New York Times* best-seller list.

Over his long career, Blevins wrote nearly forty books, including the historical fiction Rendezvous series, a dozen screenplays, and numerous magazine articles. His *Dictionary of the American West* is held in 750 libraries.

Born in Little Rock, Arkansas, on October 21, 1938, Blevins was an honors graduate of Columbia University—where he earned a master's degree—and the Music Conservatory of the University of Southern California. He began his writing career as a music and drama critic for the *Los Angeles Times* and became the principal entertainment editor for the *The Los Angeles Herald Examiner*. During that time, he hung out with the likes of Sam Peckinpah and Strother Martin, and began diving into the lives of Mountain Men and Native Americans of the West.

He also served as the Gaylord Family Visiting Professor of Professional Writing at the University of Oklahoma. For fifteen years, he was a book editor for Macmillan Publishing and TOR/Forge Books.

Win loved and felt a deep connection with nature. He climbed mountains on four continents and was a boatman-guide on the Snake River. Once caught in a freak blizzard while climbing, he took shelter inside a tree for more than twenty-four hours. His feet were frozen, but he refused to have them amputated. Almost twenty years after that event, he climbed the Himalayas—despite an awkward gait.

Native Spirituality suited him. He was pierced during a Lakota ceremony and was a pipe carrier. He went on twelve vision quests and felt the pull of the red road.

Win spent the last twenty years of his life, living quietly in the Southwest among the Navajo. His passions grew with time. In the center was his wife Meredith, their children, and many grandchildren. Classical music, baseball, roaming red rock mesas, and rafting were great loves, and he considered himself blessed to create new stories about the West. He was also proud to call himself a member of the world's oldest profession—storytelling.

www.ingramcontent.com/pod-product-compliance
Lightning Source LLC
Chambersburg PA
CBHW010856090426
42737CB00020B/3390